THE COMPUTATION AND MODELLING OF ECONOMIC EQUILIBRIA

CONTRIBUTIONS TO ECONOMIC ANALYSIS

167

NORTH-HOLLAND
AMSTERDAM · NEW YORK · OXFORD · TOKYO

THE COMPUTATION AND MODELLING OF ECONOMIC EQUILIBRIA

Edited by:

Dolf TALMAN
Department of Econometrics
Tilburg University
Tilburg, The Netherlands

and

Gerard van der LAAN
Department of Economics and Econometrics
Free University
Amsterdam, The Netherlands

N·H
P C

1987

NORTH-HOLLAND
AMSTERDAM · NEW YORK · OXFORD · TOKYO

ISBN: 0 444 70285 7

Publishers:
ELSEVIER SCIENCE PUBLISHERS B.V.
P.O. Box 1991
1000 BZ Amsterdam
The Netherlands

Sole distributors for the U.S.A. and Canada:
ELSEVIER SCIENCE PUBLISHING COMPANY, INC.,
52 Vanderbilt Avenue
New York, N.Y. 10017
U.S.A.

Library of Congress Cataloging-in-Publication Data

The Computation and modelling of economic equilibria.

(Contributions to economic analysis ; 167)
"Papers delivered at a conference entitled Economic Equilibria: Computation and Modelling, held at Tilburg University in 1985."--Pref.
1. Equilibrium (Economics)--Mathematical models--Congresses. I. Talman, Dolf, 1952- . II. Laan, G. van der. III. Series.
HB145.C64 1987 339'.0724 87-15666
ISBN 0-444-70285-7

PRINTED IN THE NETHERLANDS

Introduction to the series

This series consists of a number of hitherto unpublished studies, which are introduced by the editors in the belief that they represent fresh contributions to economic science.

The term 'economic analysis' as used in the title of the series has been adopted because it covers both the activities of the theoretical economist and the research worker.

Although the analytical methods used by the various contributors are not the same, they are nevertheless conditioned by the common origin of their studies, namely theoretical problems encountered in practical research. Since for this reason, business cycle research and national accounting, research work on behalf of economic policy, and problems of planning are the main sources of the subjects dealt with, they necessarily determine the manner of approach adopted by the authors. Their methods tend to be 'practical' in the sense of not being too far remote from application to actual economic conditions. In addition they are quantitative.

It is the hope of the editors that the publication of these studies will help to stimulate the exchange of scientific information and to reinforce international cooperation in the field of economics.

The Editors

PREFACE

This volume contains the papers delivered at a conference entitled Economic Equilibria: Computation and Modelling, held at Tilburg University in 1985. The papers are original and significant contributions ranging over a variety of issues in equilibrium theory and computational methods.

Algorithms for computing fixed points of continuous mappings emerged over two decades ago; their construction was primarily motivated by a desire to convert general equilibrium theory into a practical tool for the evaluation of economic policy. Prior to the development of these methods, the use of the Walrasian model to estimate the consequences of a specific change in economic policy, or a change in the environment in which the economy was situated, was restricted to those special cases in which an analytic or geometrical solution was available. The earliest algorithms for computing equilibrium prices were quite primitive and had considerable difficulty in solving problems with more than twenty commodities. The progress made in the last two decades has been remarkable; computer codes are now available on a floppy disk which easily calculate the answers to models involving one hundred variables, and numerical methods alone may no longer be a serious constraint on the type of problem that can be solved in practice.

There are substantial theoretical issues that remain in understanding precisely why some of these newer algorithms behave so strikingly well in practice. The paper by Eaves discusses the algorithm initially proposed by Mathiesen, at present the most effective method for the solution of large problems. Mathiesen observes, as have others, that the general equilibrium problem can be converted into a non-linear complementarity problem. Based on an initial estimate of the answer the non-linear problem is approximated by a linear complementarity problem whose solution provides a revised estimate. The cycle is then continued until convergence is obtained. Applications of this Newton-like procedure are also discussed in the paper by Todd. The method performs remarkably well and yet virtually nothing is known, from a mathematical point of view, about global or even local convergence.

A second topic of potential practical importance is discussed in the paper by Forster who is concerned with calculating all solutions to certain systems of non-linear equations. Given that Walrasian models need not have unique equilibria, our confidence in estimating the effects of economic changes - such as increased food production in Bangladesh in the paper by Keyzer - may possibly be weakened if there are solutions which we are unable to find.

The need for sophisticated computational methods was initially motivated by the observation that the most elementary algorithm, in which a price vector is changed by raising the prices of goods in excess demand

and lowering the prices of those in excess supply, need not always converge. Simple examples were produced many years ago for which the Walrasian price adjustment mechanism was globally unstable: when initiated at a vector of prices other than the equilibrium price vector, the process wandered forever and never reached a position of equilibrium. The paper by van der Laan and Talman returns to this theme and discusses a computational method which is globally convergent and which also responds in this intuitively plausible fashion to discrepancies between supply and demand.

The agents of the Walrasian model are passive responders to price. The variables to be determined are the prices for all of the goods and services in the economy. These can conveniently be normalized to lie on the unit simplex, the convex body most frequently used in fixed point computations. If, in contrast, the agents were players in a non-cooperative game, the variables to be calculated are the probability distributions over each player's set of pure strategies. They would lie in a different space: the product of a number of simplices equal to the cardinality of the set of players in the game. The paper by Doup, van den Elzen and Talman is concerned with modifications in computational methods required by such a change in the domain of definition of the problem.

The earliest application of the methods discussed in this volume was to cooperative game theory - in particular to calculating a point in the core of what is known as a balanced n-person game. This application made use of the concept of primitive sets, instead of simplicial subdivisions of the simplex on which current methods are based. But in a similar fashion the numerical procedure moved from a given primitive set to an adjacent one according to a rule based on the labels associated with the elements of the primitive set. These ideas have been given a far reaching generalization in the paper by van Maaren which points to a number of interesting questions for future research. The paper by Van der Heyden replaces the notion of primitive sets by an analogous construction based on the intersection of polyhedra. His argument permits us to calculate a point in the core of a balanced n-person game in which the set of outcomes available to each coalition is given by a convex polyhedron rather than the finite set of points previously assumed.

The concept of the core has been used by previous authors to study a simpler version of the problem presented in this volume by Yamamoto: the existence and computation of an equilibrium in an economic model involving two goods, one of which is available and desired in integer quantities. In his paper, Yamamoto shows, by means of an ingenious argument, that the solution may be found by a standard fixed point computational algorithm. The final paper in the volume, by Ruys and van der Laan, incorporates what the authors term a "semi-public" good in the framework of a general equilibrium model. In contrast to the usual treatment of public goods which enter directly into the preferences of consumers, the level of supply of a semi-public good places upper bounds on the outputs of associated private goods, which are distributed to the consuming units in the economy.

Dolf Talman and Gerard van der Laan are to be congratulated for organizing such an interesting and varied conference and for assembling a series of papers which point in so many productive directions.

Yale University, April 1987 HERBERT SCARF

CONTENTS

ACKNOWLEDGEMENT

The conference on computation and modelling of economic equilibria was held at Tilburg University, Tilburg, The Netherlands, June 19-21, 1985. The Organizing Committee consisted of G. van der Laan (Free University, Amsterdam), P.H.M. Ruys (Tilburg University), H.E. Scarf (Yale University) and A.J.J. Talman (Tilburg University). The conference was attended by 30 participants from 6 different countries and was sponsored by the Netherlands Organization for the advancement of pure research (Z.W.O.) and by the Department of Economics (F.E.W.) of Tilburg University.

A particular measure of gratitude is due to Herbert Scarf for his advice during the planning of the conference and for writing the preface of this volume, to Pieter Ruys for encouraging us to keep on with the idea, to Antoon van den Elzen for his indispensable assistance in the preparation and the conduction of the workshop and these proceedings, to Tim Doup and Lianne Dirven for proofreading the manuscripts, to Jan Pijnenburg for drawing the figures, and finally to Petra Ligtenberg for her invaluable help and patience in the procedure of retyping all the manuscripts.

Dolf Talman
Gerard van der Laan

LECTURES

M.N. BROADIE (Columbia University, New York): Biased average directional densities of subdivisions

T.M. DOUP (Tilburg University): A continuous deformation algorithm on the product space of unit simplices

B.C. EAVES (Stanford University): Finite solution of pure trade markets with Cobb-Douglas utilities

W. FORSTER (University of Southampton): Multiple solutions of systems of nonlinear equations by simplicial pivoting algorithms

V. GINSBURGH (Université Libre, Brussels): General equilibrium with wage rigidities: an application to Belgium

M.A. KEYZER (Centre for World Food Studies, Amsterdam): A general equilibrium model for the third five-year plan of Bangladesh

G. van der LAAN (Free University, Amsterdam): General equilibrium allocations under price rigidities and unemployment compensation

H. van MAAREN (Erasmus University, Rotterdam): On the possibilities and the limitations of general pivoting algorithms

L. MATHIESEN (Norwegian School of Economics and Business Administration, Bergen): Application of the sequential complementarity problem approach to economic equilibrium modelling

P.H.M. RUYS (Tilburg University): A general equilibrium model for an economy with a non-profit sector

A.J.J. TALMAN (Tilburg University): Simplicial algorithms to compute economic equilibria

M.J. TODD (Cornell University, Ithaca): Quasi-Newton methods for computing equilibria

L. VAN DER HEYDEN (Yale University, New Haven): On problems of reflection in higher dimensions

Y. YAMAMOTO (University of Tsukuba): Competitive equilibria in the market with indivisibility

The Computation and Modelling of Economic Equilibria
A.J.J. Talman, G. van der Laan (Editors)
Elsevier Science Publishers B.V. (North-Holland), 1987

THOUGHTS ON COMPUTING MARKET EQUILIBRIUM WITH SLCP

B. Curtis EAVES*

Department of Operations Research, Stanford University, Stanford, CA 94305, USA

1. INTRODUCTION

Over the last several years Mathiesen [13,14,15], Mathiesen and Rutherford [16], and Rutherford [20], have routinely solved, with remarkable robustness and speed various market equilibrium problems with hundreds of variables, also see Preckel [17]. The algorithm employed is an SLCP scheme, that is, it solves a sequence of Linear Complementary Problems; we refer to this algorithm as Mathiesen's SLCP. Our concern is that there is very little theoretical understanding, but not for lack of effort, of this algorithm. We continue the pursuit of an alternative SLCP which appears to lend itself more easily to theoretical analysis; also see Eaves [9] and Stone [23].

Abstract schemes of SLCP are first found in Robinson [18,19] and Eaves [8] where conditions for local convergence are given. SLCP seems to be a natural extension of Newton's method to include linear constraints. Indeed, Mathiesen's SLCP naturally becomes Newton's method in the tail of the sequence. A close cousin of SLCP is SQP, Sequences of Quadratic Programs, which was introduced by Wilson [25] and which has received much attention, see for example, Gill, Murray, Saunders, and Wright [11].

SLCP was first applied to the market equilibrium problem by Mathiesen, where each subproblem LCP is a piecewise linear approximation of the market equilibrium problem and is solved with Lemke's [12] algorithm. However, even in the context of simple economies virtually no theoretical properties are understood, in particular, it is not known when individual

* This research is based on work supported in part by the National Science Foundation under Grant DMS-84-04121 and DMS 86-03232 and by the Department of Energy contract DE-AA03-76SF0000326, PA# De-AS03-76ER72018.

subproblem LCP's have a solution, much less when global convergence occurs. Mathiesen's SCLP scheme applied to Scarf's [21] unstable equilibrium problem is known to generate subproblems without solutions; on the other hand, even here global convergence occurs for most starting points.

Our approach, as that of others, has been to attempt to analyze the SLCP applied to the simplest types of markets, in particular, ones with Cobb-Douglas utilities and linear production. For reasons that will become clear, we refer to such a market as (A,W,P). In an earlier effort, Eaves [9], we dropped all production in (A,W,P), and found a resolution of the resulting pure trade market including a fast finite algorithm for computing equilibria, necessary and sufficient conditions for existence of positive equilibrium prices, and an exact characterization of all positive equilibrium prices. One cannot get simpler production than linear production and yet have production. Moreover, the Cobb-Douglas utilities, at least with positive prices, seem to yield the most convenient demand functions; we note that linear demand is awkward, see Eaves [5]. Thus it seems (A,W,P) is as simple as it can be without losing the features we want to study.

In the SLCP scheme we propose here for computing an equilibrium for the market (A,W,P) the subproblem LCP's always have solutions, there is a mechanism which encourages stable local behavior, and Lemke's method can be used to generate the successive iterates. In addition, using the results we obtained in [9] for the pure trade problem we devise compelling sufficient conditions for existence of an equilibrium for the market (A,W,P). Perhaps these conditions will lead to necessary and sufficient conditions for existence of solutions. Conspicuously absent in our development, as others, are results for local and global convergence.

For additional perspective we remark that the only algorithms with enough power to guarantee convergence to an equilibrium of (A,W,P) under appropriate conditions are of the type discussed in Scarf [22] and their successors. However, these algorithms are currently impractical for a market with, say, fifty or more prices (especially in view of the fact that Mathiesen's SLCP will quickly zip out the solution for one hundred prices, proof or no proof).

2. THE MARKET (A,W,P)

The market (A,W,P), selected for its character yet simplicity, has m goods, n consumers, and ℓ production activities and is completely specified by the three matrices A, W, and P. The $m \times n$ matrices A and W are nonnegative and specify the utility functions and initial endowments respectively. The $m \times \ell$ matrix P is unrestricted in sign and specifies production technology. The utility function of consumers $t = 1,\dots,n$ is defined as

$$U_t(x) = x_1^{A_1^t} x_2^{A_2^t} \cdots x_m^{A_m^t}$$

where $x = (x_1,\dots,x_m) \geq 0$ is the quantity of the m goods to be purchased in the market. So that the utility is continuous in x we define $x_i^{A_i^t} = 1$ for $x_i = 0$ and $A_i^t = 0$. We say that consumer t *desires* commodity i if A_i^t is positive.

Prior to trading and production consumer t owns the quantities $W^t = (W_1^t,\dots,W_m^t)$ of the m goods. If $W_i^t > 0$ we say that consumer t *possesses* commodity i.

Consumers with their utilities U_t and endowments W^t go to market, face nonnegative nonzero prices $\pi = (\pi_1,\dots,\pi_m)$, and sell and buy without expenses exceeding revenues so as to maximize their utilities. Thus each consumer t solves the mathematical program

$$\max_{x \geq 0} U_t(x)$$

$$\text{s.t. } \pi^{\top} x \leq \pi^{\top} W^t.$$

For each consumer $t = 1,\dots,n$, let X^t be an x which solves this program. Consumer t enters the market with quantities W^t and leaves with quantities X^t. The production level is given by Py where $y = (y_1,\dots,y_\ell) \geq 0$ is referred to as the *activity levels*. Positive and negative components of Py indicate net output and net input of the corresponding goods, respectively.

Nonnegative nonzero prices $0 \neq \pi \equiv (\pi_1,\dots,\pi_m) \geq 0$, nonnegative purchases $X \equiv (X^1,\dots,X^n) \geq 0$, and nonnegative activity levels $y \equiv (y_1,\dots, y_\ell) \geq 0$ are defined to be an *equilibrium* if all markets clear and there is no excess profit in production, namely,

$$Xe \leq We + Py$$

$$P^{T}\pi \leq 0$$

$$\pi \geq 0 \quad y \geq 0.$$

We call π an *equilibrium price* if there exist purchases X and activity levels y for which (π,X,y) is an equilibrium, etc. Notice that if (π,X,y) is an equilibrium then so is $(\vartheta\pi,X,y)$ for all positive ϑ, and, in particular, we can confine our search for equilibrium prices to the compact set $S = \{\pi \in R^{m} | e^{T}\pi = 1,\ \pi \geq 0\}$.

For a matrix M, the symbols M^{j}, M_{i}, and M_{i}^{j} are used to denote the j-th column, the i-th row, and the (i,j)-th element, respectively. Similarly for sets of row and column indices α and β, the symbol M_{α}^{β} denotes the corresponding submatrix of M.

3. EXCESS DEMAND FUNCTIONS

If some consumer desires nothing, that is, $A^{t} = 0$, let us motivate him by setting $A^{t} = e$. A moments reflection indicates that an equilibrium (π,X,y) for the new market is also an equilibrium for the original market (A,W,P). Now as each consumer desires something, we can, without loss of generality, assume the normalization $A^{T}e = e$. Assuming positive prices π, it is a simple matter to see that the amount of commodity i purchased by consumer t is, precisely

$$X_{i}^{t} = \frac{A_{i}^{t}(\pi^{T}W^{t})}{\pi_{i}}$$

and that, the net demand for goods beyond endowments by all consumers is

$$\begin{aligned} \xi(\pi) &\equiv Xe - We \\ &= D^{-1}(\pi)E^{T}\pi - Ee \end{aligned}$$

where $E = WA^{T}$ and $D(\pi)$ is the diagonal matrix with diagonal π. We refer to ξ as the demand function. Thus (π,y) is an equilibrium if

$$D^{-1}(\pi)E^T\pi \le Ee + Py$$

$$P^T\pi \le 0 \quad \pi > 0 \quad y \ge 0$$

since, in this case, (π, X, y) is an equilibrium where X is uniquely determined by positive π.

Notice that ξ, being a demand function, has the usual properties of positive homogeneity, $\xi(\vartheta\pi) = \xi(\pi)$ for all $\pi > 0$ and $\vartheta > 0$, and of satisfying Walras' law, that is, $\pi^T\xi(\pi) = 0$ for all $\pi > 0$. If ξ is differentiable and positively homogenous then $\nabla\xi(\pi)\pi = 0$.

4. STATIONARY POINTS

We leave markets for the moment and introduce the notions of a stationary point and an LCP. We return to markets by showing the relationship between stationary points, LCP's, and market equilibria.

Let S be a set in R^n and let $\xi : S \to R^n$ be a function. A point π in S is defined to be a stationary point of (S,ξ) if $\pi^T\xi(\pi) \ge \rho^T\xi(\pi)$ for all ρ in S.

Lemma 4.1. If S is convex then π is a stationary point of (S,ξ) if and only if

$$\text{proj}(\pi + \xi(\pi)) = \pi$$

where proj is the projection to S.

Proof. If π is a stationary point then $\xi(\pi)$ is an outward normal of S at π, or equivalently π is the closest point in S to $\pi + \xi(\pi)$, see [4].

□

Lemma 4.2. If S is convex and compact and ξ is continuous, the pair (S,ξ) has a stationary point.

Proof. $\text{proj}(\pi + \xi(\pi))$ is a continuous map from S to S and, hence, by Brouwer's fixed point theorem, has a fixed point π, thus $\text{proj}(\pi + \xi(\pi)) = \pi$ and by Lemma 4.1, π is a stationary point.

□

Henceforth we direct our attention to the case where S is essentially polyhedral, and in the next lemma we give a Langrangian characterization of a stationary point. Let (A,a) be an ($\ell \times (m+1)$)-matrix and let Q be an open set in R^m.

Lemma 4.3. If S is the set $\{\pi \in Q | A\pi \leq a, \pi \geq 0\}$ where Q is an open set, then π is a stationary point of (S,ξ) if and only if $\pi \in Q$ and there exists ℓ-vectors λ and v and an m-vector s so that

a) $A\pi + v = a$

b) $\xi(\pi) + s = A^T\lambda$

c) $\pi^T s = 0$, $\lambda^T v = 0$

d) $\pi \geq 0$, $s \geq 0$, $v \geq 0$, $\lambda \geq 0$.

Proof. Assuming such (π,λ,v,s) then if $\rho \geq 0$ and $A\rho \leq a$, we have $\rho^T\xi(\pi) = \rho^T A^T\lambda - \rho^T s \leq \lambda^T A\rho \leq \lambda^T a = \lambda^T A\pi + \lambda^T v = \lambda^T A\pi - \pi^T s = \pi^T\xi(\pi)$. On the other hand, if $\pi \in Q$ solves the linear program

$$\max_{\rho} \rho^T\xi(\pi)$$

$$A\rho \leq a \quad \rho \geq 0$$

then by the theory of linear programming such (λ,v,s) exists.

□

Let M be an ($m \times m$)-matrix, I the identity ($m \times m$)-matrix, and q an m-vector. The LCP, linear complementary problem, is that of solving

$$Ix - My = q$$

$$x^T y = 0 \quad x \geq 0 \quad y \geq 0$$

for m-vectors x and y. Henceforth we display the first equation of the LCP as

x	y	
I	-M	q

Lemma 4.4. If S is the set $\{\pi \in Q | A\pi \le a,\ \pi \ge 0\}$ where Q is an open set and ξ defined by $\xi(\pi) = B\pi + b$, then π is a stationary point of (S,ξ), if and only if $\pi \in Q$ and there exists (λ, v, s) solving the following LCP:

s	v	π	λ	
I	0	B	$-A^T$	-b
0	I	A	0	a

$$\pi^T s = 0 \qquad \lambda^T v = 0$$

$$s \ge 0 \qquad v \ge 0 \qquad \pi \ge 0 \qquad \lambda \ge 0.$$

Proof. Specialize Lemma 4.3 to the case $\xi(\pi) = B\pi + b$ and use the definition of LCP.

□

The following theorem from Eaves [6] introduces our avenue for solving the subproblem LCP's, see Eaves [3] and [7] for a second approach.

For the next theorem let $S = \{\pi \ge 0 | A\pi \le a\}$, let ρ be a point in S, and choose (C,c) so that ρ is the unique solution to

$$A\pi \le a \qquad C\pi \le c \qquad \pi \ge 0.$$

For a positive vector p define $\mathbf{S}(\vartheta) = \{\pi \in S | C\pi \le c + \vartheta p\}$ and let $R^m_+ = \{x \in R^m | x \ge 0\}$. Notice $\mathbf{S}(0) = \{\rho\}$.

Theorem 4.5. For the sets $\mathbf{S}(\vartheta)$ and function ξ defined by $\xi(\pi) = B\pi + b$ Lemke's algorithm can be used to compute a (continuous) piecewise linear path $(\Pi, \Theta) : R^1_+ \to R^{m+1}_+$ so that $\Theta(0) = 0$, $\Theta(\tau)$ tends to infinity as τ does, and $\Pi(\tau)$ is a stationary point of $(\mathbf{S}(\Theta(\tau)), \xi)$ for all τ in R^1_+.

Proof. See [6]. □

Notice Θ may not be monotone increasing in τ.

Corollary 4.6. If $S = \{\pi \geq 0 | A\pi \leq a\}$ is bounded and $\xi(\pi) = B\pi + b$, then Lemke's algorithm can be used to compute a stationary point of (S,ξ).

Proof. For sufficiently large ϑ we have $S(\vartheta) = S$, and $\Pi(\vartheta)$ is a stationary point of (S,ξ). Other proofs are found in [3] and [7].

□

Now suppose $S = \{\pi \geq 0 | A\pi \leq a\}$ is bounded and $\xi : S \to R^n$ is merely differentiable. An SLCP scheme for attempting to solve the stationary point problem (S,ξ) is as follows. Given an iterate π^k in S, solve the stationary point problem $(S,\wedge^k)$ for π^{k+1} where $\wedge^k : R^m \to R^n$ is the linear approximation of ξ at π^k, namely,

$$\wedge^k(\pi) \equiv \xi^k + \nabla\xi^k(\pi - \pi^k)$$

where $\xi^k = \xi(\pi^k)$ and $\nabla\xi^k = \nabla\xi(\pi^k)$, and repeat to generate π^{k+2}, etc. We hasten to remark again, that there is, as yet, no theoretical result to justify such an approach. However, local convergence results under conditions stronger than those presently available can be found in Robinson [18,19] and Eaves [8].

We now view the market (A,W,P) as a stationary point problem. Define the set $S_0 = \{\pi > 0 | P^T\pi \leq 0,\ e^T\pi = 1\}$ and define the demand function $\xi : S_0 \to R^m$ as before by $\xi(\pi) = D^{-1}(\pi)E^T\pi - Ee$ where $E = WA^T$ and $A^Te = e$.

Lemma 4.7. The pair (S_0,ξ) has π as a stationary point, if and only if π is a positive equilibrium price for the market (A,W,P) and $e^T\pi = 1$.

Proof. The positive price π with $e^T\pi = 1$ and the activity level y is an equilibrium if and only if

$$D^{-1}(\pi)E^T\pi \leq Ee + Py$$

$$e^T\pi = 1 \qquad P^T\pi \leq 0$$

$$\pi > 0 \qquad y \geq 0.$$

By Lemma 4.3, π is a stationary point if and only if there is a solution to

$$D^{-1}(\pi)E^T\pi - Ee = Py - e\mu$$

$$e^T\pi = 1 \qquad P^T\pi \le 0 \qquad \pi^T Py = 0$$

$$\pi > 0 \qquad y \ge 0.$$

Now from the first system we have $0 \le \pi^T Py$ and $y^T P^T \pi \le 0$ so $\pi^T Py = 0$. From the second system we have $0 = \pi^T Py - \pi^T e\mu$ so $\mu = 0$ and the result follows.

□

As the set S_0 in Lemma 4.7 is not compact we cannot directly apply Corollary 4.6 to prove existence of equilibria. We use instead the sets $S(k) = \{\pi | P^T\pi \le 0,\ e^T\pi = 1,\ \pi \ge e/k\}$ as k tends to $+\infty$.

5. ASSUMPTIONS

Our market as it stands may or may not have an equilibrium, see [9]. But, of course, to analyze the proposed algorithms, or any algorithm, it is necessary to clarify the matter of existence of equilibria. Here we introduce assumptions which are sufficient for such existence. We assume full access among goods and that production requires input. We proceed to explain these notions.

By a set of goods α, that is, by goods α, we mean a subset α of $\{1,...,m\}$, the set of all goods. We say that goods α and β partition the goods, if they are nonempty, disjoint and their union is all goods, that is $\alpha \ne \emptyset$, $\beta \ne \emptyset$, $\alpha \cap \beta = \emptyset$ and $\alpha \cup \beta = \{1,...,m\}$.

Given goods α and β we say that α has trading access to β if some consumer both possesses some commodity in α and desires some commodity in β, that is, $E_i^j > 0$ for some i in α and j in β.

We say that α has production access to β if there is a activity level which produces the goods α at a nonzero nonnegative level, that is, $0 \ne (Py)_\alpha \ge 0$ for some $y \ge 0$.

We say that goods α access goods β if α has trading or production access to β. We say that there is full access among the goods if for any partition α and β of the goods, the goods α access the goods β.

We say production requires input if the system

$$0 \ne Py \ge 0,\ y \ge 0$$

has no solution, or in other words all goods do not have production access to the empty set of goods.

Lemma 5.1. The system $0 \neq Py \geq 0$ with $y \geq 0$ has no solution, if and only if there is a solution π to the system $P^T\pi \leq 0$ with $\pi > 0$.

Proof. This is merely a matrix alternative theorem.

□

Our economic interpretation of the notion that α accesses β is that there is economic linkage whereby demand for goods α can generate demand for goods β. If $E_i^j > 0$ for some i in α and j in β the linkage is through trading, whereas if $0 \neq (Py)_\alpha \geq 0$ and $y \geq 0$ the linkage is through production.

In the next section we see that full access and production requires input are sufficient for an equilibrium. Our notion of trading access here can be shown to be equivalent to access as used in [9]. Full access as used in [9] implies resource relatedness as in Arrow and Hahn [1]. However, full access as used here does not imply resource relatedness. Nevertheless it should be interesting to explore the relationship.

6. EXISTENCE OF EQUILIBRIA

We can now state and prove existence of equilibria with positive prices for the market (A,W,P) under the assumptions of full access and production requires input. Also of interest is the computational avenue indicated in the proof.

Theorem 6.1. The market (A,W,P) has an equilibrium with positive prices, if there is full access among goods and if production requires input.

Proof. We have already argued that it is sufficient to show that the system

$$D^{-1}(\pi)E^T\pi \leq Ee + Py$$

$$e^T\pi = 1 \qquad P^T\pi \leq 0$$

$$\pi > 0 \qquad y \geq 0$$

has a solution where $E = WA^T$ and $A^T e = e$.

In view of Lemma 5.1 and the fact that $0 \neq Py \geq 0$ with $y \geq 0$ has no solution, the set $\mathbf{S}(k) = \{\pi \geq e/k \mid P^T\pi \leq 0, \ e^T\pi = 1\}$ is nonempty for sufficiently large k. Thus for sufficiently large k there is a stationary point π^k to $(\mathbf{S}(k),\xi)$, see Lemma 4.2.

Using Lemma 4.3 there is a solution (y^k,λ^k,μ^k) to the system

$$D^{-1}(\pi^k)E^T\pi^k = Ee + Py^k - I\lambda^k + e\mu^k$$

$$P^T\pi^k \leq 0 \qquad e^T\pi^k = 1 \qquad \pi^k \geq e/k$$

$$(y^k)^T P^T\pi^k = 0 \qquad (\lambda^k)^T(\pi^k - e/k) = 0$$

$$y^k \geq 0 \qquad \lambda^k \geq 0.$$

Premultiplying the first equation of this system, hereafter the first system, by π^k we obtain

$$\mu^k = (\pi^k)^T\lambda^k \geq 0.$$

The theorem is proved once we show $\mu^k = 0$. Select a subsequence K of k's so that π^k converges to, say π^∞, and so that coordinates of y^k and λ^k which are nonzero remain nonzero and which are zero remain zero, for all k in K.

Let α index the goods with $\lambda_i^k > 0$, let β index the goods with $\lambda_i^k = 0$ and $\pi_i^k \to 0$, and let γ index the remaining goods, namely, those with $\lambda_i^k = 0$ and $\pi_i^k \to \pi_i^\infty > 0$. Let ζ and η index the production activities which are positive and zero, that is,

$$y_\zeta^k > 0, \ y_\eta^k = 0, \text{ and } \zeta \cup \eta = \{1,\ldots,\ell\}.$$

By rearranging the order of our goods according to (α,β,γ) and the activities according to (ζ,η) we obtain a solution $(\pi^k,y^k,\lambda^k,\mu^k)$ to the second system:

$$\begin{bmatrix} D^{-1}(\pi_\alpha^k) & 0 & 0 \\ 0 & D^{-1}(\pi_\beta^k) & 0 \\ 0 & 0 & D^{-1}(\pi_\gamma^k) \end{bmatrix} \begin{bmatrix} E_\alpha^{\top\alpha} & E_\alpha^{\top\beta} & E_\alpha^{\top\gamma} \\ E_\beta^{\top\alpha} & E_\beta^{\top\beta} & E_\beta^{\top\gamma} \\ E_\gamma^{\top\alpha} & E_\gamma^{\top\beta} & E_\gamma^{\top\gamma} \end{bmatrix} \begin{bmatrix} \pi_\alpha^k \\ \pi_\beta^k \\ \pi_\gamma^k \end{bmatrix}$$

$$= \begin{bmatrix} E_\alpha e \\ E_\beta e \\ E_\gamma e \end{bmatrix} + \begin{bmatrix} P_\alpha^\zeta & -I & e \\ P_\beta^\zeta & 0 & e \\ P_\gamma^\zeta & 0 & e \end{bmatrix} \begin{bmatrix} y_\zeta^k \\ \lambda_\alpha^k \\ \mu^k \end{bmatrix}$$

$$(\pi_\alpha^k)^\top P_\alpha^\zeta + (\pi_\beta^k)^\top P_\beta^\zeta + (\pi_\gamma^k)^\top P_\gamma^\zeta = 0$$

$$(\pi_\alpha^k)^\top P_\alpha^\eta + (\pi_\beta^k)^\top P_\beta^\eta + (\pi_\gamma^k)^\top P_\gamma^\eta \le 0$$

$$e^\top \pi_\alpha^k + e^\top \pi_\beta^k + e^\top \pi_\gamma^k = 1$$

$$\pi_\alpha^k = e/k \qquad \pi_\beta^k \ge e/k \qquad \pi_\gamma^k > e/k$$

$$\lambda_\alpha^k > 0 \qquad \lambda_\beta^k = 0 \qquad \lambda_\gamma^k = 0$$

$$y_\zeta^k > 0 \qquad y_\eta^k = 0 \qquad \mu^k \ge 0.$$

As $(\pi^k)^\top P^\zeta = 0$ and $(\pi_\alpha^\infty, \pi_\beta^\infty) = 0$ we have $(\pi_\gamma^\infty)^\top P_\gamma^\zeta = 0$. As $\pi_\gamma^\infty > 0$ and $D^{-1}(\pi_\gamma^k)E_\gamma^\top \pi^k$ is bounded, upon examining the second system and using $\mu^k \ge 0$ we see there is no i in γ with $P_i^\zeta y_\zeta^k \to +\infty$. If for some $i \in \gamma$ we have $P_i^\zeta y_\zeta^k \to -\infty$, then since $(\pi_\gamma^\infty)^\top P_\gamma^\zeta = 0$ and $\pi_\gamma^\infty > 0$, there is a $j \in \gamma$ with $P_j^\zeta y_\zeta^k \to +\infty$ which we have just argued cannot happen. Therefore $P_\gamma^\zeta y_\zeta^k$ and the μ^k are bounded. As $D^{-1}(\pi_\alpha^k)E_\alpha^\top \pi^k$ and $D^{-1}(\pi_\beta^k)E_\beta^\top \pi^k$ are nonnegative and as μ^k is bounded there is no i in $\alpha \cup \beta$ with $P_i^\zeta y_\zeta^k \to -\infty$. Suppose there is an i in $\alpha \cup \beta$ with $P_i^\zeta y_\zeta^k \to +\infty$. As $(\pi^h)^\top P^\zeta = 0$ and $\pi^h > 0$ there is some j with $P_j^\zeta y_\zeta^k \to -\infty$ which again cannot happen as we have just argued. Thus all of $P^\zeta y_\zeta^k$, λ^k, and μ^k are bounded. Multiplying the first two equations of the second system by $D(\pi_\alpha^k)$ and $D(\pi_\beta^k)$, respectively, taking the limit and using $(\pi_\alpha^k, \pi_\beta^k) \to 0$ we see that $E_\alpha^{\top\gamma} = 0$ and $E_\beta^{\top\gamma} = 0$ so that $E_\gamma^{\alpha\cup\beta} = 0$. Thus no consumer owns a commodity in γ and desires a commodity in $\alpha \cup \beta$. As $e^\top \pi^\infty =$

1 clearly γ is not empty. If $\alpha \cup \beta$ is not empty, then as goods γ access goods $\alpha \cup \beta$ there is an activity level $y \geq 0$ with $0 \neq P_\gamma y \geq 0$. Thus, $\pi^\infty_\gamma > 0$, and $(\pi^\infty)^T P \leq 0$ yields $0 \geq (\pi^\infty)^T Py = (\pi^\infty_\gamma)^T P_\gamma y > 0$ which is a contradiction. Thus $\alpha \cup \beta$ must be empty. Thus for all sufficiently large k, in K or not, we have $\lambda^k = 0$ and $\alpha \cup \beta = \emptyset$, and as $\mu^k = (\pi^k)^T \lambda^k$ we see that $\mu^k = 0$. Thus for sufficiently large k, the pair (π^k, y^k) is an equilibrium of the market (A,W,P) with positive prices.

□

The next lemma shows that all equilibrium prices are positive under full access.

Lemma 6.2. If the market (A,W,P) has full access, then any equilibrium price is positive.

Proof. Let π be an equilibrium price and let α and β partition the goods with $\pi_\alpha > 0$ and $\pi_\beta = 0$. If the goods α have trader access to the goods β some consumer owns a commodity $i \in \alpha$ and desires a commodity $j \in \beta$. Thus the consumer i has positive funds and desires the commodity j. He could then drive his utility to $+\infty$ by buying a little bit of each commodity he desires and infinite amounts of commodity j. The commodity j would not clear and we have a contradiction. If goods α have production access to goods β, there is an activity level $y \geq 0$ with $0 \neq (Py)_\alpha \geq 0$ and as $\pi^T P \leq 0$ we have $0 \geq \pi^T Py = \pi^T_\alpha (Py)_\alpha > 0$ which is a contradiction. Thus β is empty and the price π is positive.

□

Future studies will include an attempt to find necessary and sufficient conditions for existence of an equilibrium with or without positive prices. Henceforth we concern ourselves with positive prices, in particular, we impose our conditions to guarantee positive prices. Admitting zero prices complicates matters as we are then denied the convenient form of the demand function.

7. PROPOSED SLCP

Motivated by the succes reported in Mathiesen [13,14,15] and Mathiesen and Rutherford [16], the fact that they have discovered subproblem LCP's without solutions, the belief that SLCP is a natural generalization of Newton's method to include linear constraints, Theorem 4.5, and the proof of Theorem 6.1, we propose an alternative SLCP where subproblems do have solutions, and where there is a mechanism which, perhaps, keeps successive iterates in control. We view this SLCP as having the best available theoretical properties and as a prototype, but not as having the best or even good computational features. The main point is, under the SLCP we propose, hopefully the theoretical investigations can be revived and turned to the matter of local and global convergence. Computational efficiency can be improved considerably but we delay these considerations until the convergence, or lack of it, is better understood.

For π^k in $S_0 = \{\pi > 0 | P^\top \pi \le 0,\ e^\top \pi = 1\}$ and $\xi(\pi) = D^{-1}(\pi)E^\top\pi - Ee$ define the linear approximations $\Lambda^k : R^m \to R^m$ of ξ at π^k by

$$\Lambda^k(\pi) = \xi^k + \nabla\xi^k(\pi - \pi^k)$$

where $\xi^k = \xi(\pi^k)$ and $\nabla\xi^k = \nabla\xi(\pi^k) = D^{-1}(\pi^k)E^\top - D^{-2}(\pi^k)D(E^\top\pi^k)$. Also let $S^k(\vartheta)$ be the set

$$\{\pi \ge (1-\vartheta)\pi^k | P^\top\pi \le 0,\ e^\top\pi = 1\}$$

for $0 \le \vartheta \le 1$.

For π^k in S_0 use Lemke's algorithm as in Theorem 4.5 to compute a (continuous) piecewise linear path of stationary points $(\Pi^{k+1}, \Theta^{k+1})$ to $(S^k(\Theta^{k+1}), \Lambda^k)$ beginning with the stationary point $\Pi^{k+1}(0) = \pi^k$ of $(S^k(0), \Lambda^k)$ where $\Theta^{k+1}(0) = 0$, ending with the stationary point $\Pi^{k+1}(1)$ of $(S^k(1), \Lambda^k)$ where $\Theta^{k+1}(1) = 1$, and $\Pi^{k+1}(\tau)$ is a positive stationary point of $(S^k(\Theta^{k+1}(\tau)), \Lambda^k)$ for $0 \le \tau < 1$ where $0 \le \Theta^{k+1}(\tau) < 1$. The next step is to select π^{k+1} from the set $\{\Pi^{k+1}(\tau) | 0 \le \tau \le 1\}$. Following Mathiesen's suggestion one could set $\pi^{k+1} = \Pi^{k+1}(1)$ if $\Pi^{k+1}(1)$ is positive and set π^{k+1} equal to some point near the "middle" of the set $\{\Pi^{k+1}(\tau) | 0 \le \tau \le 1\}$ otherwise. Once π^{k+1} is selected the process is repeated for the next value of k.

The details for computing the path $(\Pi^{k+1}, \Theta^{k+1})$ of stationary points of $(S^k(\Theta^{k+1}), \Lambda^k)$ is given in [6], we recapitulate. First notice we want a path in $(\lambda, s, \pi, v, y, \mu, \vartheta)$ from $\vartheta = 0$ to $\vartheta = 1$ of the system below

λ	s	π	y	μ	
I	0	$\nabla\xi^k$	$-P$	$-e$	$-\xi^k$
0	I	P^T	0	0	0
0	0	e^T	0	0	1

$$\lambda^T v = 0 \quad s^T y = 0 \quad \pi - v = (1-\vartheta)\pi^k$$
$$\lambda \geq 0 \quad s \geq 0 \quad y \geq 0 \quad v \geq 0.$$

Use the change of variable $\pi = v + (1-\vartheta)\pi^k$ to obtain the second system

λ	s	v	y	μ	ϑ	
I	0	$\nabla\xi^k$	$-P$	$-e$	0	$-\xi^k$
0	I	P^T	0	0	$-P^T\pi^k$	$-P^T\pi^k$
0	0	e^T	0	0	-1	0

$$\lambda^T v = 0 \qquad s^T y = 0$$
$$\lambda \geq 0 \quad s \geq 0 \quad v \geq 0 \quad y \geq 0 \quad \vartheta \geq 0.$$

It is this system which we complementary pivot on to generate the path. The following scheme always works, but usually more efficient steps can be taken, see [6] for example. Using perturbations if necessary, the initial solution is with $s > 0$, $\mu > 0$, $\vartheta > 0$, all components of λ are positive but one which is zero, say $\lambda_i = 0$, and all other variables are zero. Now complementary pivot with respect to $(\lambda, s)^T(v, y) = 0$, that is, first, pivot in the complement of $\lambda_i = 0$, that is, v_i, and continue until $\vartheta = 1$. Notice that μ is unrestrained in sign. The path traced out by $\pi = v + (1-\vartheta)\pi^k$ and ϑ, parameterized properly, is the desired $(\Pi^{k+1}, \Theta^{k+1})$.

There are a multitude of unanswered questions. Towards verifying our SLCP has worthwhile properties, the next step is the matter of local convergence. If one begins close enough to an equilibrium, when does the scheme converge to that equilibrium?

We have spent considerable effort attempting to analyze Mathiesen's algorithm and our best thoughts on the matter, at the present, weak as they are, are encompassed in [9] and herein.

ACKNOWLEDGEMENT

The author would like to express appreciation to Ken Krenzin and Tom Rutherford for a number of clarifying conversations.

REFERENCES

[1] K.J. Arrow and F.H. Hahn, *General competitive analysis*, Holden-Day, San Francisco, 1971.

[2] G.B. Dantzig, B.C. Eaves, and D. Gale, "An algorithm for a piecewise linear model of trade and production with negative prices and bankruptcy", *Mathematical Programming* 16 (1979) 190-209.

[3] B.C. Eaves, "The linear complementarity problem", *Management Science* 17 (1971) 612-634.

[4] B.C. Eaves, "On the basic theorem of complementarity", *Mathematical Programming* 1 (1971) 68-75.

[5] B.C. Eaves, "A finite algorithm for the linear exchange model", *Journal of Mathematical Economics* 3 (1976) 197-203.

[6] B.C. Eaves, "Computing stationary points", *Mathematical Programming Study* 7 (1978) 1-14.

[7] B.C. Eaves, "Computing stationary points, again", in: *Nonlinear programming*, O.L. Mangasarian, R.R. Meyer, and S.M. Robinson, eds., Academic Press, New York, 1978, pp. 391-405.

[8] B.C. Eaves, "Where solving for stationary points by LCP's is mixing Newton iterates", in: *Homotopy methods and global convergence*, B.C. Eaves, F.J. Gould, H.-O. Peitgen and M.J. Todd, eds., Plenum Press, New York and London, 1983, pp. 63-77.

[9] B.C. Eaves, "Finite solution of pure trade markets with Cobb-Douglas utilities", *Mathematical Programming Study* 23 (1985) 226-239.

[10] C. Engles, "Economic equilibrium under deformation of the economy", in: *Analysis and computation of fixed points*, S.M. Robinson, ed., Academic Press, New York, 1980, pp. 213-410.

[11] P.E. Gill, W. Murray, M.A. Saunders, and M.H. Wright, "Model building and practical aspects of nonlinear programming", SOL 85-2, Department of Operations Research, Stanford University, Stanford, CA, USA, 1985.

[12] C.E. Lemke, "Bimatrix equilibrium points and mathematical programming", *Management Science* 11 (1965) 681-689.

[13] L. Mathiesen, "Computational experience in solving equilibrium models by a sequence of linear complementarity problems", *Operations Research* 33 (1985) 1225-1250.

[14] L. Mathiesen, "Computation of economic equilibria by a sequence of linear complementarity problems, *Mathematical Programming Study* 23 (1985) 144-162.

[15] L. Mathiesen, "An algorithm based on a sequence of linear complementarity problems applied to a Walrasian equilibrium model: an example", *Mathematical Programming* 37 (1987) 1-18.
[16] L. Mathiesen, and T. Rutherford, "Testing the robustness of an iterative LCP algorithm for solving Walrasian equilibrium models, Discussion Paper 0883, Norwegian School of Economics and Business Administration, Bergen, Norway, 1983.
[17] P.V. Preckel, "Intertemporal equilibrium models: development and results", Ph.D. Thesis, Stanford University, Stanford, CA, USA, 1983.
[18] S.M. Robinson, "Generalized equations and their solutions, part I: basic theory", *Mathematical Programming Study* 10 (1979) 128-141.
[19] S.M. Robinson, "Generalized equations and their solutions, part II: applications to nonlinear programming", *Mathematical Programming Study* 19 (1982) 200-221.
[20] T. Rutherford, "MPS/GE user's guide", Department of Operations Research, Stanford University, Stanford, CA, USA.
[21] H. Scarf, "Some examples of global instability of the competitive equilibrium", *International Economic Review* 1 (1960) 157-172.
[22] H. Scarf, *The computation of economic equilibria*, Yale University Press, New Haven, 1973.
[23] J.C. Stone, "Sequential optimization and complementarity techniques for computing economic equilibrium", SOL 84-9, Department of Operations Research, Stanford University, Stanford, CA, USA, 1984.
[24] M.J. Todd, "A note on computing equilibria in economies with activity analysis models of production", *Journal of Mathematical Economics* 6 (1979) 135-144.
[25] R.B. Wilson, "A simplicial algorithm for concave programming", D.B.A. Thesis, Harvard University, Cambridge, MA, USA, 1963 (revised 1964).

The Computation and Modelling of Economic Equilibria
A.J.J. Talman, G. van der Laan (Editors)

REFORMULATIONS OF ECONOMIC EQUILIBRIUM PROBLEMS FOR SOLUTION BY QUASI-NEWTON AND SIMPLICIAL ALGORITHMS

Michael J. TODD*

School of Operations Research and Industrial Engineering, College of Engineering, Upson Hall, Cornell University, Ithaca, New York 14853, USA

We discuss various aspects of economic equilibrium problems which suggest certain reformulations before applying solution procedures. Many of the ideas are motivated by quasi-Newton algorithms but they are also useful for piecewise-linear homotopy methods. We also propose a new quasi-Newton update formula for a subclass of equilibrium problems. Limited computational experiments are presented.

1. INTRODUCTION

A number of computational procedures can be applied to approximate equilibria in economic models. These methods generate a sequence of price vectors or a sequence of utility weights using either successive linearizations, a sequence of mathematical programming problems, or a homotopy algorithm; see for example other papers in this volume and those in Scarf and Shoven [13]. In general the homotopy algorithms are guaranteed to converge, but on large problems they usually require more computation than the other approaches. One particular method that appears to be very efficient is the successive linear complementarity problem technique of Mathiesen [10], see also Eaves' paper in this volume.

Here we are concerned with reformulations of equilibrium problems that may render them more amenable to solution approaches that generate sequences of price vectors. These ideas were motivated by quasi-Newton algorithms but are also useful for (piecewise-linear) homotopy methods, for which global convergence can be maintained while employing reformulations

* Research supported in part by NSF grant ECS-8215361 and the Sloan Foundation.

for efficiency. We also propose a new quasi-Newton update formula for certain equilibrium problems.

In Section 2 we describe the three problems with which we are concerned and obtain an explicit form for the nonlinear functions involved in one case. Section 3 presents the Newton and quasi-Newton philosophies, while in Section 4 we discuss various formulations of economic equilibrium problems. Section 5 describes the new update formula and why it may be of interest. Finally, Section 6 contains the results of some limited computational experimentation.

2. PROBLEMS

In all cases there are n goods indexed by i and m consumers indexed by j. Lower-case roman letters generally denote n-vectors, while lower-case greek letters are reserved for scalars. Upper-case roman letters denote matrices, except that diagonal matrices are denoted by upper-case greek letters. We use nonnegative superscripts for indexing, so that possibly nonnegative powers are indicated by enclosing their arguments in parentheses.

A. Partial Equilibrium, Pure Trade

The economy is described by the following for each consumer j: his initial endowment ω^j of money, his consumption set $\mathbb{R}^n_+$, and a utility function $u^j : \mathbb{R}^n_+ \to \mathbb{R}$. There is also an initial endowment $w \in \mathbb{R}^n$ of goods. We assume $w > 0$ (i.e., each component of w is positive).

For given prices $p \geq 0$, consumer j maximizes u^j over his or her budget set

$$\{x^j \in \mathbb{R}^n_+ | p^\top x^j \leq \omega^j\}.$$

We assume that the maximizing vector exists and is a continuous function d^j of the price vector p. The excess demand vector is then

$$g(p) := \Sigma_j \, d^j(p) - w.$$

We seek a price vector p with

$$p \geq 0, \; g(p) \leq 0, \; p^\top g(p) = 0. \tag{2.1}$$

The fact that the demand functions d^j arise from utility maximization, even with several regularity assumptions on the u^j's, imposes very little structure besides continuity on the aggregate excess demand function g (Debreu [4]). However, we will be interested in instances of (2.1) in which -g is strictly monotone, i.e.

$$(p-q)^T(g(p)-g(q)) < 0 \qquad (2.2)$$

for all distinct $p,q \geq 0$. Such a property can be deduced under certain hypotheses with a continuum of consumers (Hildenbrand [8]). If g is continuously differentiable with derative g', (2.2) follows if g' is negative definite everywhere. It may also be true that g' is negative definite in a neighborhood of a solution to (2.1). This may occur if the income effects are (locally) dominated by the substitution effects.

B. General Equilibrium, Pure Trade

Here the consumers have an income determined by the sale of their initial endowment vectors $w^j \in \mathbb{R}^n_+$, and the total initial endowment is $w = \Sigma_j w^j$, which we assume to be strictly positive. Hence consumer j maximizes u^j over

$$\{x^j \geq 0 | p^T x^j \leq p^T w^j\},$$

yielding his demand $d^j(p)$. Again we set $g(p) = \Sigma_j d^j(p) - w$, and assume that g is defined and continuous at all $p \geq 0$, $p \neq 0$, and moreover satisfies Walras' law $p^T g(p) = 0$. We seek a price vector p with

$$p \geq 0,\ p \neq 0,\ \text{and } g(p) \leq 0. \qquad (2.3)$$

Because of the homogeneity of g we can normalize p, for example by requiring $e^T p = 1$ where e is a vector of ones of appropriate dimension. Then the problem reduces to one on the price simplex $S^{n-1} = \{p \in \mathbb{R}^n | p \geq 0, e^T p = 1\}$ of dimension n-1. As we shall see, however, this is not a particularly natural normalization.

Example. Suppose the utility functions are of constant elasticity of substitution (C.E.S.) so that for appropriate $a_{ij} \geq 0$ and $\sigma^j > 0$ we have

$$u^j(x^j) := \begin{cases} \sum_i (a_{ij})^{\sigma^j}(x_i^j)^{1-\sigma^j} & \text{if } \sigma^j \neq 1 \\ \sum_i a_{ij} \log x_i^j & \text{if } \sigma^j = 1. \end{cases}$$

Then the economy is described by the n×m matrices $A = (a_{ij}) \geq 0$ and $W = [w^1,\ldots,w^m] \geq 0$ and the vector $(\sigma^1,\ldots,\sigma^m) > 0$. Here $We = w > 0$; we also assume $e^TA > 0$, so that each consumer desires something, and by rescaling the utility functions we can then suppose that $e^TA = e^T$. Let us write

$$\Omega := \text{diag}(w) \text{ and } \Pi := \text{diag}(p), \tag{2.4}$$

then for $p > 0$ we find

$$g(p) = \Pi^{-1}(\bar{A}(p)W^T - \Omega)p \tag{2.5}$$

where

$$\bar{A}(p) := [\bar{a}^1(p),\ldots,\bar{a}^m(p)]$$

and

$$\bar{a}^j(p) := (\Pi)^{(1-1/\sigma^j)} a^j / e^T(\Pi)^{(1-1/\sigma^j)} a^j \tag{2.6}$$

and where a^j denotes the j-th column of the matrix A. Note that if all the σ^j's are equal to one (i.e., we have Cobb-Douglas utility functions), then $\bar{A}(p) = A$ is constant. For further results on Cobb-Douglas economies see Eaves [7]. Let us make a simple observation that follows immediately from (2.5): for any Cobb-Douglas economy given by m, A, W there is another given by m', A', W' with $w = We = w' = W'e$, the same excess demand function g, and $m' = n$. This follows by taking $W' = \Omega$ and $A' = (AW^T)\Omega^{-1}$. This is a concrete illustration of the fact that any continuous function g on S^{n-1} satisfying Walras' law is essentially the excess demand function of an economy with n consumers (see Debreu [4]).

Most utility functions used in economic modelling are of C.E.S. type (sometimes nested) and thus the form of the excess demand function in (2.5) can be a useful guide for devising algorithms to compute equilibria.

C. General Equilibrium, Activity Analysis Production

The consumption side of this economy is described as in case B, but we add a production side. There are ℓ producers indexed by k; the k-th has a production set $\{b^k \zeta^k | \zeta^k \geq 0\}$ for some vector b^k of inputs and outputs. Let

$$B := [b^1, \ldots, b^\ell]$$

and assume that free disposal is allowed, so that $B = [-I, B']$. We seek a price vector p and a vector of activity levels z with

$$p \neq 0, \; g(p) = Bz, \; B^T p \leq 0 \text{ and } z \geq 0. \tag{2.7}$$

Note that $B^T p \leq 0$ implies $p \geq 0$, and again we can renormalize by requiring $p \in S^{n-1}$.

Observe that the price p_i of the i-th commodity is measured in a unit that is the reciprocal of the unit of measurement of commodity i while $g_i(p)$ and w_i are measured in this unit, and that $p_i g_i(p)$ and $p_i w_i$ are dimensionless. (We suppose "money" is dimensionless.) In particular, this implies that normalizations such as $e^T p = \Sigma_i p_i = 1$ are somewhat meaningless. It may be useful to view p and g(p) as lying in dual abstract vector spaces; a choice of particular units for the goods specifies particular dual bases for these spaces, and then p_i denotes the component of p corresponding to the i-th basis element.

3. NEWTON AND QUASI-NEWTON PHILOSOPHIES

In this section we discuss the basic concepts of Newton and quasi-Newton approaches to the solution of hard nonlinear problems. These concepts are used in the next section to motivate certain "natural" reformulations of equilibrium problems.

The general form of a finite-dimensional nonlinear problem is: find $x \in \mathbb{R}^n$ such that P(x) holds, where P is some property involving nonlinear functions. The main idea of a Newton-like approach is the following algorithm schema:

Iteration k: Given a current trial point $x^k \in \mathbb{R}^n$:

Test x^k for convergence;

Approximate the functions appearing in P by simpler (usually linear) functions to get P^k;

Solve the model problem: find x^+ such that $P^k(x^+)$ holds;
Update: Use x^+ to get the new trial point x^{k+1} (usually $x^{k+1} := x^+$) and proceed to iteration k+1.

The difference between Newton and quasi-Newton approaches is that the former approximate functions by first- or second-order Taylor approximations, while the latter employ information obtained about the nonlinear functions by evaluations at x^k and x^{k+1} to update the approximations used at iteration k to those for iteration k+1.

This general schema includes Newton's method for nonlinear equations (using linear approximations) and for unconstrained minimization (using quadratic approximations), and also embraces naturally the approach to solving nonlinear complementarity problems (for example (2.1)) by solving successive linear complementarity problems. (Eaves [6] has shown that the latter technique enjoys some of the desirable properties of Newton's method for nonlinear equations.)

Let us illustrate two applications of the quasi-Newton approach.

Nonlinear equations. Find x such that $f(x) = 0$, where $f : \mathbb{R}^n \to \mathbb{R}^n$. Thus $P(x)$ corresponds to $f(x) = 0$ and we let $P^k(x)$ correspond to $f^k(x) = 0$, where

$$f^k(x) := f(x^k) + J^k(x-x^k). \tag{3.1}$$

We let $x^{k+1} = x^+$ (this is the simplest choice) and

$$J^{k+1} := J^k + \frac{(y-J^k s)s^T}{s^T s}, \tag{3.2}$$

where $s = x^{k+1} - x^k$, $y = f(x^{k+1}) - f(x^k)$. Note that J^{k+1} satisfies the secant condition $J^{k+1}s = y$, thus incorporating new information about the function f. This is the algorithm of Broyden [3]. In particular, (3.2) is known as Broyden's (first or good) update. Given that we have either a factorization of J^k or its inverse explicitly, x^+ is easy to obtain from (3.1). Since J^{k+1} in (3.2) is a rank-one update of J^k, a factorization of J^{k+1} or its explicit inverse is easy to derive from one for J^k.

Unconstrained minimization. Find a local minimizer of a C^2 function $\varphi : \mathbb{R}^n \to \mathbb{R}$. Then $P(x)$ corresponds to x being a local minimizer of φ and $P^k(x)$ to x being a local minimizer of φ^k, with

$$\varphi^k(x) := \varphi(x^k) + f(x^k)^T(x-x^k) + \tfrac{1}{2}(x-x^k)^T H^k (x-x^k)$$

where $f \equiv \nabla\varphi$ (we assume that the gradient of φ can be evaluated) and $H^k \approx \nabla^2\varphi(x^k)$. If we insist that H^k be symmetric and positive definite then φ^k has a unique global minimizer x^+, and the direction $x^+ - x^k$ is a descent direction for φ. Thus we choose $x^{k+1} = x^k + \lambda(x^+ - x^k)$, with $\lambda \geq 0$ selected to give "sufficient decrease" in φ, and to assure that $y^T s > 0$ with y and s as above. Finally we set

$$H^{k+1} := H^k - \frac{H^k s s^T H^k}{s^T H^k s} + \frac{y y^T}{y^T s}. \tag{3.3}$$

This update is independently due to Broyden, Fletcher, Goldfarb, and Shanno (see Dennis and Schnabel [5]) and is guaranteed to be symmetric and positive definite if H^k is and if $y^T s > 0$.

These two examples are to illustrate that (i) there is no need to take $x^{k+1} = x^+$, and (ii) there is no need to make linear approximations, only to obtain tractable subproblems (i.e. model problems that can be solved easily).

4. NATURAL FORMULATIONS OF ECONOMIC EQUILIBRIUM PROBLEMS

In the partial equilibrium situation, case A, we are trying to solve the nonlinear complementarity problem (2.1). According to our discussion in the previous section, it is natural to solve a sequence of linear complementarity problems of the form:

$$\text{find } p \geq 0 \text{ with } g^k(p) \leq 0 \text{ and } p^T g^k(p) = 0 \tag{4.1}$$

where

$$g^k(p) := g(p^k) + J^k(p-p^k). \tag{4.2}$$

This approach has been suggested by Eaves [6], Hogan [9] and Mathiesen [10]. However, it is worth noting that under several reasonable assumptions we know that an equilibrium price vector will have all components positive; in this case we are equivalently searching for a (positive) solution to $g(p) = 0$, and then nonlinear scalings can be applied to g, as we shall see later.

In the general equilibrium pure trade case B, we might similarly consider linearizing g. However, here the problem is just (n-1)-dimensional; p can be restricted to S^{n-1} and g(p) satisfies $p^T g(p) = 0$. We can convert the problem to one in $\mathbb{R}^{n-1}$ by choosing an $n\times(n-1)$ matrix Z whose columns are orthonormal and orthogonal to $e \in \mathbb{R}^n$ (see for example Section 6 of Awoniyi and Todd [2]). Also let $p^0 = e/n \in S^{n-1}$. Then the problem is equivalent to:

$$\text{find } x \in \mathbb{R}^{n-1} \text{ with } p^0 + Zx \geq 0,\ g(p^0+Zx) \leq 0,$$

or, if we know that all prices will be positive, to

$$\text{find } x \in \mathbb{R}^{n-1} \text{ with } \bar{g}(x) := Z^T g(p^0+Zx) = 0 \tag{4.3}$$

$$(\text{and } p^0 + Zx \geq 0).$$

Note that $-\bar{g}$ is strictly monotone if $-g$ is.

Finally, in the general equilibrium with production case C, we similarly arrive at an equivalent problem:

$$\begin{aligned} -\bar{g}(x) + Z^T Bz &= 0 \\ B^T Zx + s &= -B^T p^0 \\ s \geq 0,\ z \geq 0,\ s^T z &= 0 \end{aligned} \tag{4.4}$$

with $\bar{g}$ as above. Thus in these two cases, we obtain a system of linear equations or a linear complementarity problem by replacing $\bar{g}$ by a linear approximation

$$\bar{g}^k(x) := \bar{g}(x^k) + J^k(x-x^k). \tag{4.5}$$

Natural questions that arise concern existence and uniqueness of solutions to the model problems, and how J^k should be updated. In particular is the Broyden update (3.2) appropriate? We adress this last point first.

Note that the Broyden update includes the term $s^T s$ in the denominator. This implies that the euclidean norm is taken to be a reasonable measure of the distance between two price vectors (or the vectors in $\mathbb{R}^{n-1}$ corresponding to the price vectors in the general equilibrium cases). However, our discussion of the arbitrariness of units suggests that the euclidean norm is not a reasonable measure. The presence of the $s^T s$ term shows that this arbitrariness affects the algorithm. More precisely, Broyden's update is not invariant under scalings of the domain. To fix this problem we use a natural scaling of the problem: let

$$q := \Omega p = (w_i p_i)$$

be the new independent variable. This reformulation is equivalent to scaling the units of the goods so that the total amount available of each commodity is one, and is possible if $w > 0$, as in case A and B. In case C, with production, it can happen that there is no endowment of some goods. In this case, we can scale so that the maximum possible amount of each commodity that can be produced from the initial endowment is one, by solving the linear programming problems

$$\begin{aligned} w_j' = \text{maximize } & (Bz)_j + w_j \\ & Bz \leq -w \\ & z \geq 0 \end{aligned}$$

for each j. Standard assumptions imply that all these problems have optimal solutions, and the optimal values provide scaling factors to be used in place of the components of w.

The discussion above suggests that we perform a similar rescaling in the range, that is, replace g by $\Omega^{-1}g$. Strictly speaking, this is unnecessary, since Broyden's update is invariant under arbitrary (linear) scalings of the range, if the initial matrix J^0 is appropriately changed. We prefer to simply set J^0 to be a multiple of $-I$, and thus to rescale both domain and range corresponding to the same change of units. Thus in (2.1) we may substitute

$$\tilde{g}(q) := \Omega^{-1} g(\Omega^{-1} q) \tag{4.6}$$

for g, and in (4.3) and (4.4)

$$\hat{g}(x) := Z^T\Omega^{-1}g(\Omega^{-1}(q^0+Zx)) \tag{4.7}$$

for $\bar{g}$ where $q^0 = e/n$. The notation used is to stress that $q = q^0 + Zx$ is dimensionless while the argument of g is $p = \Omega^{-1}q$. If production is allowed, $\Omega' := \text{diag}(w')$ can be used instead of Ω and $(\Omega')^{-1}B$ should replace B. Thus $q_i = w_i p_i$ represents the (dimensionless) value of the total endowment of the i-th commodity, and is dimensionless. Similarly, x in (4.7) represents an othogonal transformation of these dimensionless values. In either case, the euclidean norm is reasonable to measure changes in q or x. We might therefore prefer to apply Broyden's method (or a successive linear complementarity problem approach) to the reformulated problem.

However, when it is known that all prices will be strictly positive a nonlinear scaling of the range may be even better. Recall that Newton-like approaches typically make linear approximations to the nonlinear functions, and note the form of the excess demand function g of (2.5). If the elasticities σ^j are all equal or close to 1 (so that the utility functions are close to Cobb-Douglas), then Πg is linear or close to linear while g is not. Also zeroes of g and of Πg that are strictly positive coincide. (However, note that Πg may have many other zeroes that are not zeroes of g.) Thus it may be suitable to make linear approximations to

$$\mathring{g}(p) := \Pi g(p) \tag{4.8}$$

or to

$$\mathring{\bar{g}}(x) := Z^T \Pi g(p), \quad \text{where } p = p^0 + Zx, \tag{4.9}$$

instead of to g or $\bar{g}$ themselves. We can also combine this idea with that of scaling to get

$$\mathring{\tilde{g}}(q) := \Pi g(p), \quad \text{where } p = \Omega^{-1}q, \tag{4.10}$$

and

$$\mathring{\hat{g}}(x) := Z^T \Pi g(p), \quad \text{where } p = \Omega^{-1}(q^0+Zx). \tag{4.11}$$

Another way to view this process is that we are making approximations of the form $\Pi^{-1}(Jp+k)$ to g. When we are seeking zeroes in the model problem, this is tractable. However, when production is present the model problem becomes difficult and we suggest the use of (4.7). It is also worth remarking that, if $J^T e = 0$, the function $\Pi^{-1}Jp$ is homogeneous of degree zero and satisfies Walras' law. Thus such a function appears a much better model for an excess demand function than any linear function could be.

Approximating g(p) by $\Pi^{-1}Jp$, when $J^T e = 0$ and J has negative diagonal entries and nonnegative off-diagonal entries, corresponds to approximating the economy by one in which all consumers have Cobb-Douglas utility functions. However, the updates we propose for J (or more accurately, for an approximation to the Jacobian of $\hat{g}$ or of $\mathring{\hat{g}}$) do not preserve this sign structure, and we do not see how it can be preserved for any reasonable update.

Both Broyden's update (3.2) and the update (5.1) to be proposed in the next section are based on least-change principles (see Dennis and Schnabel [5]). Note that the use of a matrix Z with orthonormal columns in (4.7) and (4.9) implies that least-change principles in $\mathbb{R}^{n-1}$ and in S^{n-1} lead to the same updates.

To conclude this section we consider the extent to which our reformulations can be combined with piecewise-linear homotopy algorithms, which (at least for cases B and C) guarantee global convergence to a solution. First, it is clear that $\tilde{g}$ and $\hat{g}$ can be used instead of g and $\bar{g}$ in such methods with no penalty, since they merely correspond to a rescaling of the problem. Indeed, these reformulations are likely to be advantageous, since piecewise-linear methods employ regular triangulations, which are most suited to well-scaled problems. Our computational results in Section 6 bear this out. We can use $\hat{g}$ instead of $\bar{g}$ to create a fixed-point problem to which simplicial algorithms can be applied.

More precisely, we consider two functions from S^{n-1} to itself whose fixed points give equilibria. Define

$$f^1(p) := \frac{(p+\mu g(p))_+}{e^T(p+\mu g(p))_+} \tag{4.12}$$

where μ is positive and for a vector $u = (u_i)$, u_+ denotes the vector with components $(\max\{0,u_i\})$. Alternatively,

$$f^1(p) = p + \lambda(p)h^1(p), \text{ where}$$

$$\lambda(p) := \mu/e^T(p+\mu g(p))_+ \text{ and} \tag{4.13}$$

$$h^1(p) := \max\{g(p),-p/\mu\} - e^T\max\{g(p),-p/\mu\}p,$$

where $\max\{u,v\}$ denotes the vector with components $\max\{u_i,v_i\}$. The other function we use is

$$f^2(p) = p + \mu h^2(p), \text{ where}$$

$$h^2(p) := \max\{g(p) + \lambda e, -p/\mu\} \text{ and} \tag{4.14}$$

$$\lambda = \lambda(p) \text{ is chosen so that } e^T h^2(p) = 0.$$

It is easy to see that fixed points of f^1 and f^2 (or zeroes of h^1 and h^2) are equilibria, and that $\lambda(p)$ is unique and continuous. The function f^1 appears in Arrow and Hahn [1] while f^2 was motivated by a suggestion of Eaves. We can then apply a piecewise-linear homotopy algorithm to find a zero of $\bar{k}^j : \mathbb{R}^{n-1} \rightarrow \mathbb{R}^{n-1}$, with

$$\bar{k}^j(x) := Z^T h^j(p^0+Zx). \tag{4.15}$$

Note that, when $g(p) + \lambda e \geq -p/\mu$ (we choose $\mu = 10^{-5}$ in our computational tests to encourage this), then $\bar{k}^2(x) = \bar{g}(x)$. However, $\bar{k}^j$ is related to a fixed-point problem so that convergence is assured. We similarly define

$$\hat{k}^j(x) := Z^T\hat{h}^j(q^0+Zx), \tag{4.16}$$

where $\hat{h}^j$ uses $\Omega^{-1}g(\Omega^{-1}p)$ in place of $g(p)$, in analogy with (4.7).

Next we ask whether the nonlinear scaling of (4.8) - (4.11) can be used while maintaining convergence. For this, let

$$p' = p'(p) := \max\{p,\nu e\} \tag{4.17}$$

for some $\nu > 0$. Then, with $\Pi' := \text{diag}(p')$, set

$$\tilde{f}^1(p) := \frac{(p+\mu\Pi'g(p))_+}{e^T(p+\mu\Pi'g(p))_+}.$$

There is an alternative representation:

$$\tilde{f}^1(p) = p + \lambda(p)\tilde{h}^1(p), \text{ where}$$

$$\lambda(p) = \mu/e^T(p+\mu\Pi'g(p))_+ \text{ and} \tag{4.18}$$

$$\tilde{h}^1(p) := \max\{\Pi'g(p), -p/\mu\} - e^T\max\{\Pi'g(p), -p/\mu\}p.$$

Note that, if $\nu = 1$, then $p' = e$ and $\tilde{f}^1$ reduces to f^1. However, for small ν and μ (we choose $\nu = 10^{-3}$ in our computational tests), if $p \geq \nu e$ and $p \geq -\mu\Pi g(p)$ (which follows if $\mu \leq 1/w_i$, all i), then $\tilde{h}^1(p) = \Pi g(p)$. Thus, except close to the boundary of S^{n-1}, $\tilde{h}^1$ coincides with $\mathring{g}$. Further, $\tilde{f}^1$ clearly maps S^{n-1} continuously into itself and the proof of Theorem 2.2 in Arrow and Hahn [1] shows that its fixed points are equilibria. Of course, we can also rescale the problem by replacing $g(p)$ by $\Omega^{-1}g(\Omega^{-1}p)$ everywhere. Then $\tilde{h}^1$ will coincide with $\mathring{\tilde{g}}$ except close to the boundary of S^{n-1}.

In our computational tests in Section 6, we use slightly modified mappings, since in our examples g is not defined for price vectors with nonpositive components. Following Arrow and Hahn [1], we replace $g(p)$ in (4.12) - (4.13) and $\Pi'g(p)$ in (4.17) - (4.18) by

$$(1-\alpha)g(p) + \alpha\rho e$$

and

$$(1-\alpha)\Pi'g(p) + \alpha\rho e$$

respectively, and by ρe if $g(p)$ is undefined, where $\alpha = \alpha(e^Tg(p))$ and $\alpha(\lambda) := \max\{0, \min\{1,(\lambda-\rho)/\rho\}\}$ increases from 0 for $\lambda \leq \rho$ to 1 for $\lambda \geq 2\rho$. We choose $\rho = 100n$ in our tests. The resulting functions are somewhat different from those suggested by Arrow and Hahn, but are smooth in larger neighborhoods of equilibria. It is straightforward to show that the functions obtained are continuous (mapping $\{p|\ e^Tp = 1\}$ into S^{n-1}) and that their fixed points are equilibria. However, this is no longer true for the corresponding modification of f^2 in (4.14), since any price vector in the boundary of S^{n-1} is then a fixed point. Hence we replace $f^2(p)$ by $f^2(p'')$, where $p'' := \max\{p,\mu e\}/e^T\max\{p,\mu e\}$ for $\mu = 10^{-5}$. Again, rescaling can be performed with these modifications (and makes sense, since α depends on $e^T g(p)$, which is only natural when scaling renders g(p) dimensionless).

5. MAINTAINING MONOTONICITY

We have pointed out in Section 2 that under certain conditions the excess supply function -g is globally strictly monotone. This is a strong condition which implies for instance the uniqueness of equilibria. Indeed, the axiom of revealed preference holds. For completeness we give a short proof.

Proposition 5.1. If -g ($-\bar{g}$) is strictly monotone, there is at most one solution to (2.1) ((4.4)).

Proof. Suppose p and q both solve (2.1). Then

$$(p-q)^T(g(p) - g(q)) = -q^T g(p) - p^T g(q) \geq 0.$$

Since -g is strictly monotone, p = q. Next suppose x and x' solve (4.4), with associated (z,s) and (z',s'). Then

$$\begin{aligned}(x-x')^T(\bar{g}(x) - \bar{g}(x')) &= (x-x')^T(Z^T B(z-z')) \\ &= (B^T Z(x-x'))^T(z-z') \\ &= (s'-s)^T(z-z') \\ &= (s')^T z + s^T z' \geq 0.\end{aligned}$$

Again, strict monotonicity implies that x = x'. Note that we cannot claim that z = z', although this will follow under a nondegeneracy assumption.

□

Even if -g is not globally strictly monotone, it may well be strictly monotone in a neighborhood of an equilibrium. For instance, if substitution effects dominate income effects near p, then -g'(p) should be negative definite (although not necessarily symmetric). In this case there are cogent reasons for approximating -g or $-\bar{g}$ by a strictly monotone linear function during the application of a quasi-Newton approach. As we have seen, this will ensure that the model problems have at most one solution. It can further be shown that a solution exists, so that the algorithm is well-defined. Indeed, for (2.1) a well-known result states that if $-g$ is linear and strictly monotone, then a unique solution exists. For (2.4), $B^TZx \le -B^Tp^0$ implies $Zx \ge -p^0$, which has a bounded feasible region, and again a standard result gives existence.

The question then arises how strict monotonicity can be preserved in a quasi-Newton update. Todd [15] shows that, if $-J$ is strictly monotone and $y^Ts < 0$, then

$$J^+ := J + \frac{(y-Js)(y+J^Ts)^T}{(y+J^Ts)^Ts} \tag{5.1}$$

is such that $-J^+$ is strictly monotone. This update can therefore be used in place of Broyden's.

6. COMPUTATIONAL RESULTS

Here we describe some very preliminary computer experimentation on pure trade general equilibrium models. Problems E1, E2 and E3 are the three examples described by Scarf [12] with 5,8 and 10 goods respectively. All have C.E.S. utility functions for all consumers. E4 is a perturbation of E1; w_{33} is changed to 16 from 15, and σ^T to (1,2,.5) from (.9,1.3,.8). E5 and E6 are then rescalings of E4; the unit used to measure commodity 3 is 4 times smaller (E5) or 16 times larger (E6) than in E4.

We tested 10 quasi-Newton and 8 piecewise-linear homotopy methods on each problem. The methods are denoted QjO (quasi-Newton, using function ℓ^j, and original variables) and QjS (quasi-Newton, using function ℓ^j, and dimensionless scaled variables), $j = 0,1,\dots,4$, and similarly PjO and PjS, $j = 0,1,\dots,3$. In all cases we start with the center of the simplex corresponding to p^0 or q^0 equal to e/n and x^0 equal to 0, and the termination criterion is that the maximum component of $\Omega^{-1}g(p)$, denoted $\|\Omega^{-1}g(p)\|_\infty$, does not exceed 10^{-10}.

The quasi-Newton methods initialize J^0 to $-\alpha I$ with $\alpha = 1/2n\|\ell^j(x^0)\|_\infty$, so that the first step goes at most half-way to the boundary of the price simplex. Subsequently, we choose

$$x^{k+1} := x^k + \bar{\lambda}(x^+-x^k), \tag{6.1}$$

where

$$\bar{\lambda} := \max\{\lambda \le 1 \mid p_i^{k+1} \ge .05p_i^k \text{ for all } i\}$$

with $p^k = p^0 + Zx^k$. The function whose zero is sought is ℓ^j, where

$$\ell^j(x) = \begin{array}{lll} Z^T\Pi g(p) & \text{(see (4.9))} & \text{if } j = 0 \\ Z^T h^1(p) & \text{(see (4.13))} & \text{if } j = 1 \\ Z^T h^2(p) & \text{(see (4.14))} & \text{if } j = 2 \\ Z^T g(p) & \text{(see (4.3))} & \text{if } j = 3 \text{ or } 4 \end{array}$$

and $p = p^0 + Zx$. These formulae are modified in the obvious way if scaling is performed, see (4.11), (4.16) and (4.7) for j = 0, j = 1 or 2, and j = 3 or 4 respectively. So far, there appears to be no difference between Q30 (Q3S) and Q40 (Q4S). The distinction is in the update used. While for j = 0,1,2 and 3 the Broyden update is employed, j = 4 uses the new update (5.1). (Although the model does not guarantee that $y^Ts < 0$ at each iteration, this was observed in practice in all examples.)

Table 1 gives the number of function evaluations required. The results on this limited test set are remarkably consistent. In all cases rescaling improves the computational performance, especially for the (deliberately) badly-scaled problems E5 and E6. Problems E4-E6, which only differ in scaling, give identical results as expected for the rescaled methods. Finally, using ℓ^0 (basically Πg) yields a substantial improvement over any of the other formulations, especially when the problems are not rescaled. Methods Q2 and Q3 performed identically, which is not too surprising: if $g(p) + \lambda e \geq -p/\mu$ (recall, we chose $\mu = 10^{-5}$), then $Z^Th^2(p) = Z^Tg(p)$. Finally, we should comment on the two failures. In our primitive implementation, the choice of step-size in (6.1) is the only concession to global convergence. The failure of Q10 on E2 appears related to this, as the iterates tried to converge to a point on the boundary of the price simplex until they were repulsed, when they tried to converge to another boundary point. Also we explicitly updated the inverse of J^k. The failure of Q40 on E5 seems to be related to the near-singularity of several J^k matrices. More sophisticated implementations (see Powell [11]) might eliminate these difficulties.

The piecewise-linear methods all used the PLALGO code (Todd [14]) with default settings (hence Merrill's method with triangulation J_1), except that the grid size was initially 1/n and after each major cycle reduced by a factor .37. The mappings used were those described in Section 4. With the modifications outlined there, method Pj0 (PjS) used $\bar{k}^j$ ($\hat{k}^j$), given by (4.15) ((4.16)) for j = 1,2. For j = 0, these functions were based on $\tilde{f}^1$

and $\tilde{h}^1$ in (4.18), and for j = 3, on $Z^T g(p)$ as for the quasi-Newton methods.

The results are given in Table 2, where an entry p/q means that p linear programming pivots and q function evaluations were required. Once again the beneficial effects of rescaling are demonstrated convincingly. Similarly, P00 and P0S perform much better than the other methods, showing the advantage of the nearly linear function $\Pi' g(p)$. Indeed, method P0S, with guaranteed convergence, requires a number of function evaluations not much greater than those for the best quasi-Newton method, Q0S. The very poor behaviour of all "unscaled" methods on the poorly-scaled problem E5 should also be noted.

These results, while based on limited testing, substantiate the more theoretical discussion in Section 3 and argue for the use of reformulations before applying numerical methods. Also, the new update (5.1), while not designed for this class of problems, seems to perform reasonably well and deserves further investigation.

Table 1

	Problem	E1	E2	E3	E4	E5	E6
Method	Dimension	5	8	10	5	5	5
Q00		20	19	19	22	40	16
Q10		62	*	24	22	79	49
Q20		25	35	23	23	53	24
Q30		25	35	23	23	53	24
Q40		26	25	22	20	*	23
Q0S		10	16	14	10	10	10
Q1S		11	17	15	13	13	13
Q2S		10	17	15	12	12	12
Q3S		10	17	15	12	12	12
Q4S		10	18	15	13	13	13

* Failed to converge

Table 2

	Problem	E1	E2	E3	E4	E5	E6
Method	Dimension	5	8	10	5	5	5
P00		54/58	41/51	82/93	74/77	215/202	23/32
P10		59/65	99/109	75/86	76/82	417/377	39/49
P20		69/74	89/99	69/82	124/127	184/178	41/54
P30		68/77	83/94	82/94	77/83	468/417	41/52
P0S		5/11	24/32	23/32	6/14	6/14	6/14
P1S		10/21	47/58	35/45	10/21	10/21	10/21
P2S		10/20	49/60	34/46	10/22	10/22	10/22
P3S		10/21	51/62	36/46	11/22	11/22	11/22

REFERENCES

[1] K.J. Arrow and F.H. Hahn, *General competitive analysis*, Holden-Day, San Francisco, 1971.

[2] S.A. Awoniyi and M.J. Todd, "An efficient simplicial algorithm for computing a zero of a convex union of smooth functions", *Mathematical Programming* 25 (1983) 83-108.

[3] C.G. Broyden, "A class of methods for solving nonlinear simultaneous equations", *Mathematics of Computation* 19 (1965) 577-593.

[4] G. Debreu, "Excess demand functions", *Journal of Mathematical Economics* 1 (1974) 15-21.

[5] J.E. Dennis and R.B. Schnabel, *Numerical methods for unconstrained optimization and nonlinear equations*, Prentice-Hall, Englewood Cliffs, 1983.

[6] B.C. Eaves, "Where solving for stationary points by LCPs is mixing Newton iterates", in: *Homotopy methods and global convergence*, B.C. Eaves, F.J. Gould, H.-O. Peitgen, and M.J. Todd, eds., Plenum Press, New York and London, 1983, pp. 63-77.

[7] B.C. Eaves, "Finite solution of pure trade markets with Cobb-Douglas utilities", *Mathematical Programming Study* 23 (1985) 226-239.

[8] W. Hildenbrand, "On the "Law of Demand"", *Econometrica* 51 (1983) 997-1019.

[9] W.W. Hogan, "Energy policy models for project independence", *Computers and Operations Research* 2 (1975) 251-271.

[10] L. Mathiesen, "Computational experience in solving equilibrium models by a sequence of linear complementarity problems", *Operations Research* 33 (1985) 1225-1250.

[11] M.J.D. Powell, "A hybrid method for nonlinear equations", in: *Numerical methods for nonlinear algebraic equations*, P. Rabinowitz, ed., Gordon and Breach, London, 1970.

[12] H.E. Scarf, "The approximation of fixed points of a continuous mapping", *SIAM Journal on Applied Mathematics* 15 (1967) 1328-1343.

[13] H.E. Scarf and J.B. Shoven, eds., *Applied general equilibrium analysis*, Cambridge University Press, Cambridge, 1984.
[14] M.J. Todd, "PLALGO: a FORTRAN implementation of a piecewise-linear homotopy algorithm for solving systems of nonlinear equations", Technical Report No. 454, School of Operations Research and Industrial Engineering, Cornell University, Ithaca, NY, USA, 1980 (revised 1983, 1985).
[15] M.J. Todd, "Quasi-Newton updates in abstract vector spaces", *SIAM Review* 26 (1984) 367-377.

The Computation and Modelling of Economic Equilibria
A.J.J. Talman, G. van der Laan (Editors)

COMPUTING "ALL" SOLUTIONS OF SYSTEMS OF POLYNOMIAL EQUATIONS BY SIMPLICIAL FIXED POINT ALGORITHMS

W. FORSTER

Faculty of Mathematical Studies, The University of Southampton, Southampton SO9 5NH, United Kingdom

1. INTRODUCTION

The first announcement of a new algorithm relying only on pivoting and utilizing only homotopy-theory as background appeared in Forster [6]. The main aim of this paper is to present in concise form results which are important in the context of the numerical solution of systems of polynomial equations by simplicial pivoting algorithms. For a historical background and extensive literature on simplicial pivoting algorithms see for example Forster [5].

Using fixed point theorems for existence proofs, i.e. for showing that systems of complicated equations have a solution, can now be regarded as standard technique. Advances in computational techniques allow us to find for example Brouwer and Kakutani fixed points constructively. In many applications we want to be able to find not only one solution but as many solutions as can reasonably be expected taking into consideration theoretical mathematical results. This paper builds on the work of Kuhn [9,10], Kuhn et al. [11], in particular the work on zeroes of polynomials, the work of Nielsen [12], in particular his work on fixed points on a torus, the work of Brooks et al. [2], in particular the work on the Nielsen number of the n-dimensional torus, and on the work of Jiang [8] (best known for the Jiang subgroup of the fundamental group), in particular his work on the least number of fixed points. The material will be developed in the context of homotopy algorithms using triangulations and pivoting.

Homotopy considerations are important in a computational context. The distortions introduced by finite machine accuracy on computers can be viewed as a deformation (homotopy) of the original problem. Therefore results derived by Jiang [8] (using piecewise linear techniques) of the type that to a given map f with Nielsen number N there is a homotopic map with exactly N fixed points can be interpreted in a computational setting in the following way: the original map f (which might possibly have more than N fixed points) was deformed by inaccuracies into a map which has exactly N fixed points. It further means that we cannot expect to obtain better results for the number of solutions we can hope to find by numerical methods (taking into account the inevitable inaccuracies of computers).

2. BROUWER DEGREE AND EXTENSIONS

The search for homotopy-invariants led Brouwer in 1912 to the introduction of a homotopy-invariant integer now called Brouwer degree. Brouwer used combinatorial methods for the definition of his degree. Intuitively the Brouwer degree tells us how often a given map wraps the domain round a sphere.

If we consider the map

$$f\colon S^1 \to C\backslash\{0\} \tag{2.1}$$

from the one-dimensional sphere S^1 into the nonzero complex numbers $C\backslash\{0\}$, then we can determine for example the degree of

$$g = \frac{f}{|f|} : S^1 \to S^1. \tag{2.2}$$

The Brouwer degree enables us to determine the degree of maps from n-dimensional spheres S^n to itself, i.e.

$$\tilde{g} : S^n \to S^n. \tag{2.3}$$

Another generalization of (2.1) was given by Bott [1]. He generalized the map into the nonzero complex numbers $C\backslash\{0\}$ to a map into nonsingular matrices with complex entries; more precise, to maps

$$f : S^{n-1} \to GL(M,C) \tag{2.4}$$

with $2M \geq n$, S^{n-1} the unit-sphere in n-dimensional euclidean space and GL(M,C) the general linear group of all invertible maps from C^M to C^M. Bott gave the famous periodicity theorem for such maps.

Another generalization of (2.2) was given by Nielsen [12]. Brouwer [3] investigated the connection between the degree and the existence of fixed points of maps of spheres into itself. In 1926 Brouwer gave a clarification of some material on the projective plane which was implicitly contained in his earlier papers. As far as Nielsen was concerned Brouwer gave results for the 2-dimensional sphere S^2, i.e. a surface of Euler characteristic 2, the projective plane P^2, i.e. a surface of Euler characteristic 1, and Nielsen derived results for the 2-dimensional torus $T^2 = S^1 \times S^1$, i.e. a surface of Euler characteristic 0. Corresponding results for the n-dimensional torus T^n had to wait until 1975 when Brooks, Brown and Pak gave the result for T^n. The following holds for the Nielsen number N giving the minimum number of fixed points on T^n.
For maps

$$f : T^n \to T^n \tag{2.5}$$

we have

$$N(f) = |L(f)|, \tag{2.6}$$

where L(f) is the Lefschetz number.

3. APPROXIMATION OF FUNCTIONS ON COMPUTERS

The importance of being able to find zeroes of systems of polynomial equations stems from the fact that any function has to be approximated on computers. One widely used approximation is via polynomials. The Stone-Weierstrass approximation theorem states that any continuous function

$$f : C^n \to C \tag{3.1}$$

from a suitable subset of the n-dimensional complex space C^n into C can be uniformly approximated by polynomials in z_i and $\bar{z}_i$ (the complex conjugate of z_i), $i = 1,\ldots,n$. Furthermore, from a topological point of view the map

$$f(z) = z^{\ell} : S^1 \to S^1 \tag{3.2}$$

has Brouwer degree ℓ, and

$$f(z) = \bar{z}^{\ell} : S^1 \to S^1 \tag{3.3}$$

has Brouwer degree $-\ell$.
S^1 is the unit circle in the complex plane C. The degree ℓ of the approximating polynomials and their topological interpretation will play an important role in determining the number of solutions we can approximate.

4. HOMOTOPIES FOR SYSTEMS OF POLYNOMIAL EQUATIONS

If we return for the moment to the case

$$f : S^1 \to S^1, \tag{4.1}$$

or to the problem of finding all roots for a polynomial in a single variable (fundamental theorem of algebra), then this case can be solved by using an algorithm of Kuhn described in Kuhn [9,10] and in [11].
This algorithm uses the fact that the polynomial

$$p(z) = z^n + a_{n-1}z^{n-1} + \ldots + a_0 \tag{4.2}$$

for large z behaves like z^n. With the homotopy

$$p(z,t) = t\, p(z) + [1-t]z^n \tag{4.3}$$

with $0 \le t \le 1$, we obtain

$$\frac{p(z,t)}{z^n} = 1 + t[\ldots]. \tag{4.4}$$

$$\underset{z\to\infty}{\to 0 \text{ as}}$$

The algorithm uses the simple fact that z^n wraps round n times in the $w = p(z)$ plane. With an appropriate labelling function and a suitable triangulation one can then use pivoting to find approximations to all roots. The beauty of this algorithm is that the size of the region and the mesh size necessary to find all roots are given a priori from the coefficients of the polynomial $p(z)$.

We will retain most of these desirable properties and give an algorithm for n polynomials in n variables. The general case of k polynomials in ℓ variables with $k < \ell$ is only a slight generalization. Maps of k polynomials in ℓ variables with $k > \ell$ give systems which under arbitrarily small perturbations have no solution even if the original system has a solution, i.e. we have a numerically ill-posed problem.

We consider systems of polynomial equations

$$p_j : C^n \to C \ , \ 1 \le j \le n \tag{4.5}$$

with

$$p_j(z_1,\dots,z_n) = \sum_{\ell_{j1}=0}^{L_{j1}\max} \cdots \sum_{\ell_{jn}=0}^{L_{jn}\max} a^{(j)}_{\ell_{j1}\dots\ell_{jn}} z_1^{\ell_{j1}} \cdots z_n^{\ell_{jn}} \tag{4.6}$$

where for j, $1 \le j \le n$,

$L_{j1}\max$ is the highest power of z_1 in $p_j(z_1,\dots,z_n)$

...

$L_{jn}\max$ is the highest power of z_n in $p_j(z_1,\dots,z_n)$.

Let us use polar coordinates for all complex variables $z_1,\dots,z_n$ and let us fix the radii of all complex variables. Then we can consider maps

$$p_j(\text{all radii fixed}) : T^n \to T^n \tag{4.7}$$

with T^n the n-dimensional torus

$$T^n = S^1 \times S^1 \times \dots \times S^1 \ (\text{n times}), \tag{4.8}$$

where each S^1 is a circle in a complex plane C.

We define homotopies

$$p_j(z_1,\ldots,z_n,t) = t\, p_j(z_1,\ldots,z_n) + [1-t] z_1^{L_{j1}} z_2^{L_{j2}} \ldots z_n^{L_{jn}} \qquad (4.9)$$

with $0 \le t \le 1$ and $1 \le j \le n$,

where

$$L_{j1} + L_{j2} + \ldots + L_{jn} \qquad (4.10)$$

is the dominating term, i.e., for a particular j, $1 \le j \le n$, the dominating term

$$L_{j1} + L_{j2} + \ldots + L_{jn}$$

is strictly larger than any other term

$$\ell_{j1} + \ell_{j2} + \ldots + \ell_{jn}.$$

We assume that the coefficient of the dominating term of equation j, $1 \le j \le n$,

$$z_1^{L_{j1}} \ldots z_n^{L_{jn}}$$

is equal to 1, i.e.

$$a^{(j)}_{L_{j1}\ldots L_{jn}} = 1 \ , \ 1 \le j \le n. \qquad (4.11)$$

For large

$$z_1^{L_{j1}} z_2^{L_{j2}} \ldots z_n^{L_{jn}}$$

we obtain

$$\frac{p_j(z_1,\ldots,z_n,t)}{z_1^{L_{j1}} z_2^{L_{j2}} \ldots z_n^{L_{jn}}} = 1 + t[\ldots] \qquad (4.12)$$

with $t[\ldots] \to 0$ as $z_1^{L_{j1}} z_2^{L_{j2}} \ldots z_n^{L_{jn}} \to \infty$.

For large $z_1^{L_{j1}} z_2^{L_{j2}} \ldots z_n^{L_{jn}}$ the polynomial p_j behaves like

$$z_1^{L_{j1}} z_2^{L_{j2}} \ldots z_n^{L_{jn}},$$

i.e. it wraps around an n-dimensional torus.
It wraps L_{j1} times around the first circle S^1,
it wraps L_{j2} times around the second circle S^1,
.....
and it wraps L_{jn} times around the n-th circle S^1
in $T^n = S^1 \times S^1 \times \ldots \times S^1$ (n times).

Every system of polynomials can be brought into a form where each polynomial has a dominating term. If there is a polynomial in the system which has no dominating term, then we add a dummy equation

$$p_{n+1}(z_{n+1}) = z_{n+1} = 0. \qquad (4.13)$$

We add to the polynomial with no dominating term a new term in the following way. We take one of the terms with highest degree, multiply this term by z_{n+1} and add this term to the polynomial. Because the solution to $p_{n+1} = 0$ is that the (n+1)-st variable z_{n+1} is zero, the system so obtained has the same solution as the original system. But now we have brought the system into a form with dominating terms. Because we can select any of the terms with highest degree and multiply by z_{n+1}, there are many different ways of achieving systems with dominating terms.

5. LABELLING FUNCTION

We have n equations p_j, $1 \le j \le n$. Each equation

$$p_j : C^n \to C \qquad (5.1)$$

maps from C^n into the complex plane C. To simplify matters we subdivide all the p_j-planes into the same three sectors. We indicate the subdivision into three segments by the argument values β_0, β_1 and β_2. The variable k is a parameter which runs from 0 to n-1.

Label

$$
\begin{array}{lll}
2(n-k) & \text{if} & \beta_0 \le \arg p_n < \beta_1 \text{ and} \\
 & & \beta_0 \le \arg p_{n-1} < \beta_1 \text{ and} \\
 & & \cdots\cdots\cdots\cdot \\
 & & \beta_0 \le \arg p_{n-k+1} < \beta_1 \text{ and} \\
 & & \beta_2 \le \arg p_{n-k} < \beta_0 + 2\pi; \\
2(n-k)-1 & \text{if} & \beta_0 \le \arg p_n < \beta_1 \text{ and} \\
 & & \beta_0 \le \arg p_{n-1} < \beta_1 \text{ and} \\
 & & \cdots\cdots\cdots\cdot \\
 & & \beta_0 \le \arg p_{n-k+1} < \beta_1 \text{ and} \\
 & & \beta_1 \le \arg p_{n-k} < \beta_2; \\
2(n-k)-2 & \text{if} & p_{n-k} = 0; \\
0 & \text{if} & \beta_0 \le \arg p_n < \beta_1 \text{ and} \\
 & & \beta_0 \le \arg p_{n-1} < \beta_1 \text{ and} \\
 & & \cdots\cdots\cdots\cdot \\
 & & \beta_0 \le \arg p_2 < \beta_1 \text{ and} \\
 & & \beta_0 \le \arg p_1 < \beta_1 .
\end{array}
\qquad (5.2)
$$

6. NIELSEN NUMBER

Using results obtained by Nielsen [12] for the 2-dimensional torus and in [2] for the n-dimensional torus we can give the Nielsen number $\bar{N}$ for the minimum number of roots of our system of polynomial equations. If

$$z_1^{L_{j1}} \cdots z_n^{L_{jn}}$$

is the dominating term of the j-th equation, then the minimum number of roots is given by

$$\bar{N} = \left| \det \begin{vmatrix} L_{11} & \cdots\cdots\cdots & L_{1n} \\ L_{21} & \cdots\cdots\cdots & L_{2n} \\ \cdot & \cdots\cdots\cdots & \cdot \\ L_{n1} & \cdots\cdots\cdots & L_{nn} \end{vmatrix} \right| . \tag{6.1}$$

7. MESH SIZE AND RADII OF TORUS

In order for our algorithm to work we need an a priori estimate which connects the mesh size of the triangulation and the radii of the circles which make up the torus T^n. By using techniques related to techniques used in Kuhn [10, page 15 and 16] we obtain

$$\begin{aligned} \mu_j \geq {} & \left[1 - \frac{\max_{J_j} | a_{J_j}^{(j)} |}{R_j - 1}\right] \\ & \times \frac{R_j}{\left[\prod_{i=1}^{n} L_{ji}\max\right]\left[\sum_{i=1}^{n} L_{ji}\max\right] K_j} \; \frac{\sin \alpha}{2 \cos \frac{\alpha}{2}} \end{aligned} \tag{7.1}$$

where μ_j is the mesh size (related to equation j), where

$$a_{J_j}^{(j)} = \sum_{\substack{\ell_{j1}=0 \\ \ell_{j1} + \cdots + \ell_{jn} = J_j}}^{L_{j1}\max} \cdots \sum_{\ell_{jn}=0}^{L_{jn}\max} a_{\ell_{j1}\cdots\ell_{jn}}^{(j)},$$

i.e. $a_{J_j}^{(j)}$ is the sum over all terms such that $\ell_{j1} + \ldots + \ell_{jn} = J_j$, and where

$$R_j > \max_{J_j} | a^{(j)}_{J_j} | + 1,$$

$$K_j = \max_{\ell_{j1}\ldots\ell_{jn}} | a^{(j)}_{\ell_{j1}\ldots\ell_{jn}} |,$$

and

$$\alpha = \min \{\beta_1 - \beta_0, \beta_2 - \beta_1, \beta_0 + 2\pi - \beta_2\}.$$

If equation (7.1) holds for $1 \le j \le n$, there are completely labelled simplices in a region which satisfies all the inequalities for $1 \le j \le n$

$$z_1^{L_{j1}} \ldots z_n^{L_{jn}} > R^{L_{j1}+\ldots+L_{jn}}, \tag{7.2}$$

where $R \ge \max_j R_j$.

If we do not want completely labelled simplices in the region determined by (7.2), then we have to ensure that (7.1) is not satisfied, i.e.

$$\mu_j < \text{right-hand side from (7.1)}. \tag{7.3}$$

a) If we keep for example R fixed, where $R \ge \max_j R_j$, and we take a mesh size μ such that $\mu < \mu_j$ for at least one j, $1 \le j \le n$, then we cannot have completely labelled simplices in a region determined by (7.2). For $R > \max_j R_j$ fixed, equation (7.3) gives the mesh size we need for our algorithm.

b) If we keep for example μ fixed where $\mu < \min_j \mu_j$, and we take all the radii of the n-dimensional torus to be $R > \max_j R_j$, where R_j is determined from (7.1), i.e. from the quadratic equation

$$R_j^2 - R_j [1 + M_j + W_j] + W_j = 0, \tag{7.4}$$

where

$$M_j = \max_{J_j} | a_{J_j}^{(j)} | ,$$

$$W_j = \mu_j \frac{2 \cos \frac{\alpha}{2}}{\sin \alpha} [\prod_{i=1}^{n} L_{ji}\max] [\sum_{i=1}^{n} L_{ji}\max] K_j ,$$

then we cannot have completely labelled simplices in the region described by (7.2).

Remark. What we just said under a) and b) does not mean that there can be no solution (or completely labelled simplex) at infinity. If for the dominating terms

$$z_1^{L_{j1}} \dots z_n^{L_{jn}} < r^{L_{j1}+\dots+L_{jn}} , \quad 1 \le j \le n, \tag{7.5}$$

where $r = \min_j R_j$, then this is the region where we can have completely labelled simplices. Obviously any of the coordinates z_j can go to infinity as long as (7.5) is satisfied.

8. DESCRIPTION OF ALGORITHM

In order to obtain starting simplices it is convenient to work in polar coordinates

$$z_j = r_j \exp(i\varphi_j) , \quad 1 \le j \le n. \tag{8.1}$$

We keep the radius $r_j = R$ (radius of all circles $S^1 \times S^1 \times \dots \times S^1$ on T^n is the same) fixed and consider the n-dimensional cube

$$0 \le \varphi_j \le 2\pi , \quad 1 \le j \le n. \tag{8.2}$$

We pivot along the edges of this cube until we find a 1-simplex with for example label 2n - 1 (for a particular j = s). We search all edges $0 \le \varphi_j \le 2\pi$.
For each of the 1-simplices we have found with at least one label 2n - 1 we pivot on 2-dimensional cubes $0 \le \varphi_j \le 2\pi$ (for particular j = s,t) until we find a 2-simplex with for example label 2n - 3. We search all 2-dimensional cubes $0 \le \varphi_j \le 2\pi$. For each of the 2-simplices we have found with

at least one label 2n - 1 and one label 2n - 3 we pivot on 3-dimensional cubes $0 \le \varphi_j \le 2\pi$ (for particular j = s,t,v) until we find a 3-simplex with for example label 2n - 5. We search all 3-dimensional cubes $0 \le \varphi_j \le 2\pi$.

. . . .

This process is continued until we have found all n-simplices on the n-dimensional cube $0 \le \varphi_j \le 2\pi$, $1 \le j \le n$, which have for example the n labels 2n - 1, 2n - 3,...,1.

We should obtain $\bar{N}$ (Nielsen number) such simplices in the n-dimensional cube $0 \le \varphi_j \le 2\pi$, $1 \le j \le n$.

On this cube all coordinates r_j, $1 \le j \le n$, are kept constant, i.e. $r_j = R = \text{const}$, $1 \le j \le n$.

We now take one of the $\bar{N}$ n-simplices we have found and allow for example r_1 to decrease in the first pivoting step and pivot until we have found an (n+1)-simplex with a label not yet in our set of labels, i.e. n+2 different labels (all the other r_j are kept constant, i.e. $r_j = R = \text{const}$, $2 \le j \le n$).

We then allow for example r_2 to decrease in the first pivoting step and pivot until we have found an (n+2)-simplex again with a label not yet in our set of labels, i.e. n+3 different labels (we have kept $r_j = R = \text{const}$, $3 \le j \le n$).

. . . .

We continue in this way until we have found a 2n-simplex with 2n + 1 different labels, i.e. a completely labelled simplex. The simplices so obtained represent approximations to zeroes of our system of polynomial equations.

9. EXAMPLES

We conclude this paper by giving illustrations for 2 polynomials in 2 variables (case a), and 3 polynomials in 3 variables (case b). We illustrate the labelling function and consider especially what is happening on the starting cube. The figures will show the influence of the dominating terms on the Nielsen number and how this affects the labels of the starting simplices.

a) <u>Two polynomials in two variables</u>

We first illustrate the labelling function using cartesian coordinates in the p_j-planes, $j = 1,2$, in Figure 1.a and 1.b respectively.

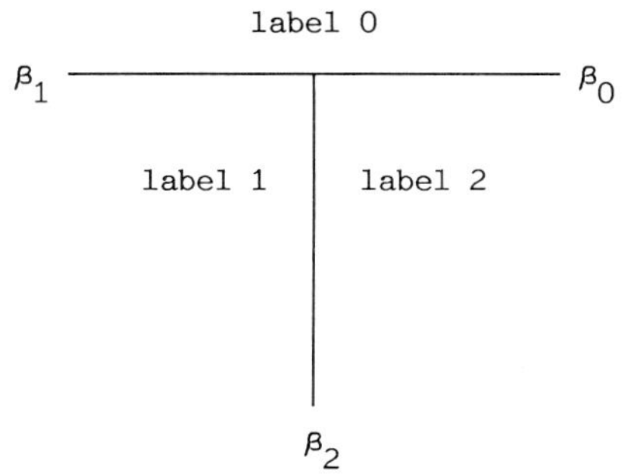

FIGURE 1.a
The labelling function in the p_1-plane, $p_1 = p_1(z_1,z_2)$, in the case a.

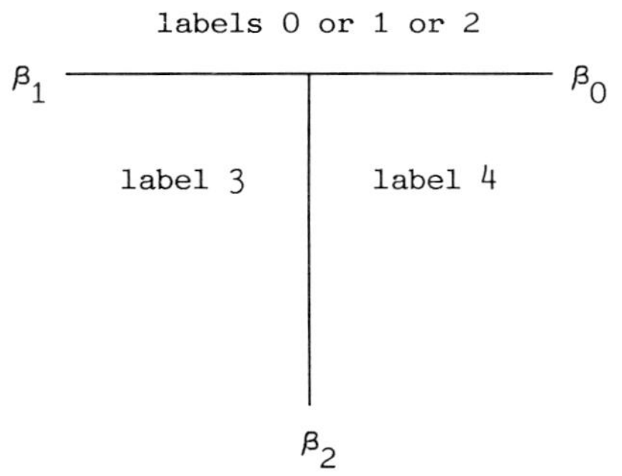

FIGURE 1.b
The labelling function in the p_2-plane, $p_2 = p_2(z_1,z_2)$, in the case a.

In Figure 2 we now illustrate the labelling function using polar coordinates

$$p_j = \rho_j \exp(i\vartheta_j) \ , \ j = 1,2,$$

and concentrate on the argument part, i.e. the dependence on ϑ_1 and ϑ_2.

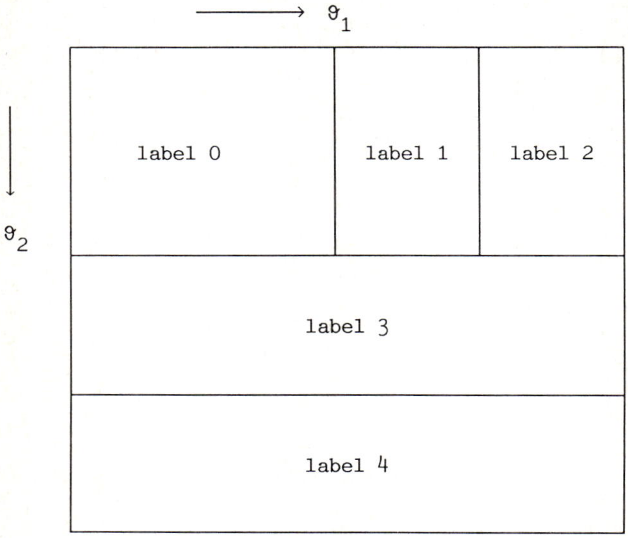

FIGURE 2
The labelling function in the $(\vartheta_1,\vartheta_2)$-plane in the case a.

We first consider an example with nonzero Nielsen number.
We write the dominating terms only.

$$p_1(z_1,z_2) = z_1^4 \, z_2^2 + \ldots$$

$$p_2(z_1,z_2) = z_1 \, z_2^2 + \ldots$$

The Nielsen number $\bar{N}$ is

$$\bar{N} = \left| \det \begin{vmatrix} 4 & 2 \\ 1 & 2 \end{vmatrix} \right| = 6.$$

We obtain for the argument part φ_1, φ_2, i.e. for the starting cube $0 \le \varphi_1 \le 2\pi$, $0 \le \varphi_2 \le 2\pi$, the situation given in Figure 3.

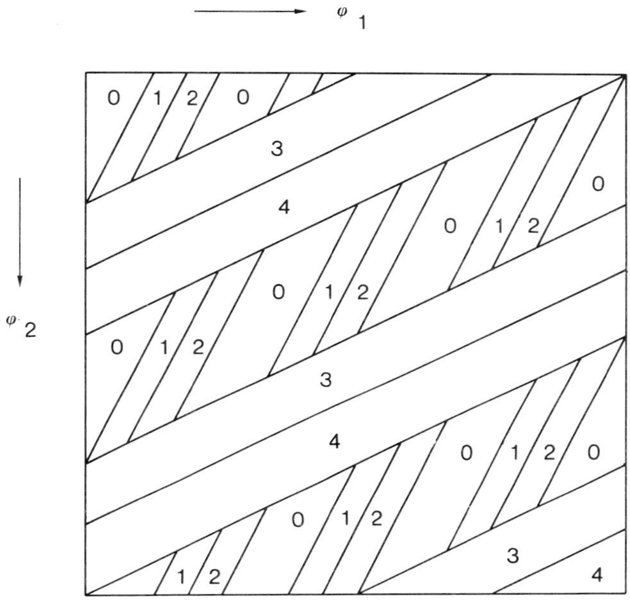

FIGURE 3

The labelling in the (φ_1,φ_2)-plane for the example with nonzero Nielsen number.

Next we consider an example with Nielsen number $\bar{N} = 0$. We take an example with the following dominating terms

$$p_1(z_1,z_2) = z_1^4 z_2^2 + \dots$$

$$p_2(z_1,z_2) = z_1^2 z_2 + \dots$$

The Nielsen number $\bar{N}$ is

$$\bar{N} = \left| \det \begin{vmatrix} 4 & 2 \\ 2 & 1 \end{vmatrix} \right| = 0.$$

We obtain for the argument part φ_1, φ_2, i.e. for the starting cube $0 \le \varphi_1 \le 2\pi$, $0 \le \varphi_2 \le 2\pi$, the situation given in Figure 4.

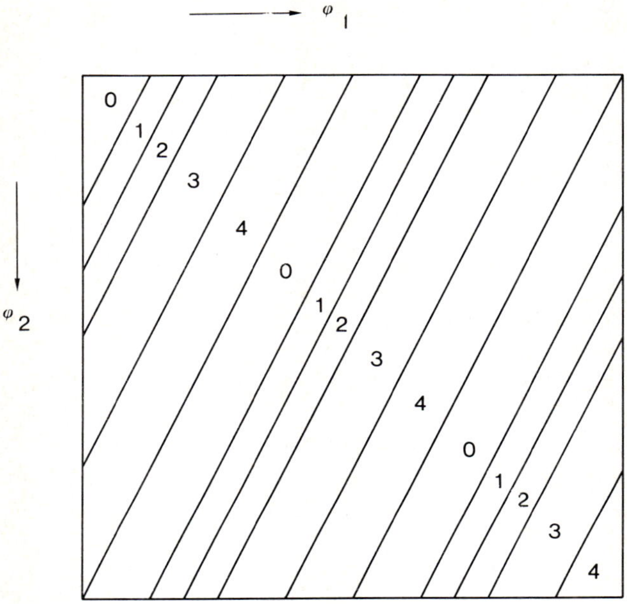

FIGURE 4
The labelling in the (φ_1, φ_2)-plane for
the example with zero Nielsen number.

In the latter case the areas with different labels do not intersect on the starting cube and therefore we cannot find starting simplices.

b) <u>Three polynomials in three variables</u>
The labelling function using polar coordinates

$$p_j = \rho_j \exp(i\vartheta_j), \; j = 1,2,3,$$

is illustrated for this case in Figure 5. In this figure we concentrate only on the argument part, i.e. the dependence on ϑ_1, ϑ_2 and ϑ_3.

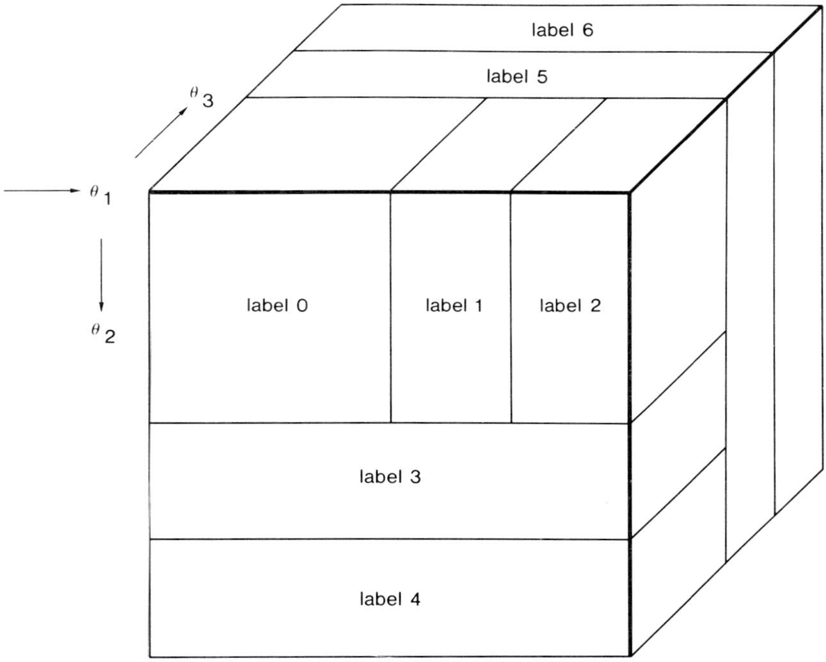

FIGURE 5
The labelling function in the $(\vartheta_1, \vartheta_2, \vartheta_3)$-plane in the case b.

We consider an example with the following dominating terms

$$p_1(z_1, z_2, z_3) = z_1^4 z_2^2 z_3 + \dots$$

$$p_2(z_1, z_2, z_3) = z_1 z_2^2 z_3 + \dots$$

$$p_3(z_1, z_2, z_3) = z_1^3 z_2 z_3 + \dots$$

The Nielsen number $\bar{N}$ is

$$\bar{N} = \left| \det \begin{vmatrix} 4 & 2 & 1 \\ 1 & 2 & 1 \\ 3 & 1 & 1 \end{vmatrix} \right| = 3.$$

We obtain for the argument part φ_1, φ_2, φ_3, i.e. for the starting cube $0 \leq \varphi_j \leq 2\pi$, $j = 1,2,3$, the situation as given in Figure 6.

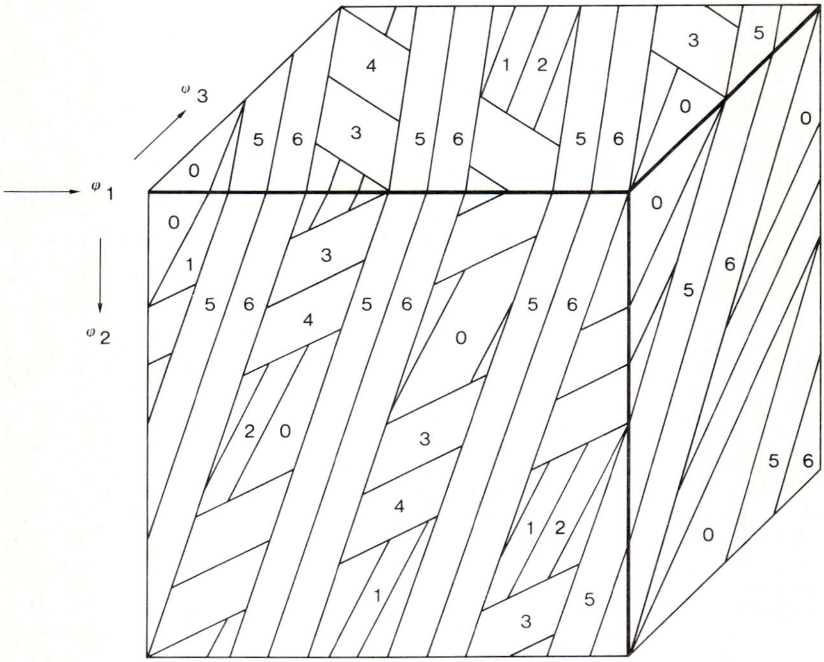

FIGURE 6
The labelling in the $(\varphi_1, \varphi_2, \varphi_3)$-plane.

REFERENCES

[1] R. Bott, "The stable homotopy of the classical groups", *Mathematische Annalen* 70 (1959) 313-337.
[2] R.B.S. Brooks, R.F. Brown and J. Pak, "Nielsen number of maps of tori", *Proceedings of the A.M.S.* 52 (1975) 398-400.
[3] L.E.J. Brouwer, "Uber Abbildung von Mannigfaltigkeiten", *Mathematische Annalen* 71 (1912) 97-115.
[4] L.E.J. Brouwer, "On transformations of projective spaces", *Koninklijke Nederlandse Akademie van Wetenschappen te Amsterdam, Proc.* 29 (1926) 864-865.
[5] W. Forster, ed., *Numerical solution of highly nonlinear problems,* North-Holland, Amsterdam, 1980.
[6] W. Forster, "Utilizing the Nielsen number for finding multiple solutions of systems of nonlinear equations by simplicial fixed point algorithms", in: *Abstracts of the IIASA workshop on nondifferentiable optimization: motivations and applications,* International Institute for Applied Systems Analysis, Laxenburg, Austria, 1984, pp. 50-55.
[7] W. Forster, "A guaranteed minimum number of solutions for systems of nonlinear equations solved by simplicial algorithms", Discussion Paper, University of Southampton, Southampton, UK, 1984, to appear.
[8] B.J. Jiang, "On the least number of fixed points", *American Journal of Mathematics* 102 (1980) 749-763.
[9] H.W. Kuhn, "A new proof of the fundamental theorem of algebra", *Mathematical Programming Study* 1 (1974) 148-158.
[10] H.W. Kuhn, "Finding roots of polynomials by pivoting", in: *Fixed points - algorithms and applications,* S. Karamardian, ed., Academic Press, New York, 1977, pp. 11-39.
[11] H.W. Kuhn, Z. Wang and S. Xu, "On the cost of computing roots of polynomials", *Mathematical Programming* 28 (1984) 156-163.
[12] J. Nielsen, "Uber die Minimalzahl der Fixpunkte bei den Abbildungstypen der Ringflächen", *Mathematische Annalen* 82 (1921) 83-93.

The Computation and Modelling of Economic Equilibria
A.J.J. Talman, G. van der Laan (Editors)

CONSEQUENCES OF INCREASED FOODGRAIN PRODUCTION ON THE BANGLADESH ECONOMY*

M.A. KEYZER

Centre for World Food Studies, Free University, De Boelelaan 1105, 1081 HV Amsterdam, The Netherlands

1. INTRODUCTION

Plan-formulation has become universally based on macro-economic models of different types. Policy parameters, plan targets and objectives, international prices and capital flows constitute some of the exogenous variables within which the model-builders have to prepare consistent forecasts of sectoral production, prices, income levels and other relevant variables. For Bangladesh, it is often argued that over-ambitious targets of the earlier plans may have biased investment allocations into sectors which have not adequately supported growth and income creation. The general equilibrium model for the Third Five-Year-Plan (TFYP-model, 1985-1990) has been developed and used to simulate the implications of various policy-scenarios and assess their consistency with targets and objectives. It is currently being applied for monitoring plan realizations.

This paper provides an informal outline of the model and assesses the effectiveness of alternative policies in dealing with the consequences of increased foodgrain production, i.e. of the switch on the rice market from an import to an autarky regime. It is shown how an increase in food distribution to vulnerable groups can be used as an effective demand policy to stabilize foodgrain prices, as long as foreign donors are willing to

* Paper prepared under UNDP-project no. BGD/83/029. The UNDP-project team which has developed the model consists of Salauddin Ahmad, Willem van der Geest, Michiel Keyzer and Mustafa Mujeri, in cooperation with Walter Kennes, Geert Overbosch, Herman Stolwijk and Willem van Veen from the Centre for World Food Studies, Amsterdam, The Netherlands.

provide increased balance of payments aid. However, when the donors are only willing to provide increased foodgrain aid, this policy appears to lose most of its effectiveness.

The paper is structured as follows. In Section 2 an informal outline of the model is provided. In Section 3 further details are given on the component of the model which relates to market clearing. Finally, Section 4 deals with the assessment of the consequences of increased foodgrain production.

2. MAIN FEATURES OF THE TFYP-MODEL

2.1. Main components

The TFYP-model is a dynamic simulation model with a time increment of one year. Initially, the simulations started in 1980/81 and the period 1980/81 - 1984/85 was the pre-plan testing phase. On basis of these results revisions were introduced and the model was updated incorporating 1984/85 data as far as available.

In modeling the Bangladesh economy two main components are distinguished, the supply- and the exchange-component. The supply-component describes how at given prices production and investment plans are made in the economy. Given these plans, at the end of the gestation-period, production capacity is generated. The exchange-component describes what happens then. Thus, the supply-component contains the lagged relations of the model, while the exchange-component describes the economic interactions within the year, including market clearing. This section provides an informal overview of the model. Full details can be found in [1] and [6]. A more aggregated version of the exchange component is described in Keyzer [2].

2.2. Demand- and price-adjustment

The owners of the commodities and of production capacities are subdivided into ten social classes, covering the whole Bangladesh population. Each class buys consumption and investment goods in amounts which vary with the income earned and the price of the commodities. The excess of demand over supply is imported (or exported) as long as this import (or export) is permitted by the government and profitable for the trader. This is the case for imports as long as the retail price can cover the cost of bringing it to the retail market. Exports are said to be profitable as long as the cost of bringing the commodity to the border is covered by the price received at the border. If neither exports nor imports are profitable, there is a situation of autarky in which a price-adjustment takes place which restores the balance between supply and demand. This price-adjustment in turn affects the revenue of the classes which sell the commodity and thereby the demand for other commodities. The exchange-component shows the final outcomes of these linkages on consumer demand, on nutrition, on investment for each social class, and also on government revenue and expenditure, at given prices in the international market.

2.3. Production capacity and supply in agriculture and manufacturing industry

Supply capacity is the main determinant of long-run growth. In the short-run, growth can be stimulated by a rise in effective demand but if this does not lead to expansion of capacity the maximum degree of capacity utilization will eventually be reached in some sectors and growth will be curbed.

Capacity is created through net investment in land, buildings and equipment. Once capacity has been created the producer can make the decisions on utilization of capacity. In agriculture this typically involves the decision as to which crop to grow and which inputs to buy. In manufacturing industry, which is more specialized, there is less scope for choice. The producer will maximize the rate of capacity utilization (at least as long as price exceeds variable cost). This degree of capacity utilization is largely technologically determined. Due to power failures, management and maintenance problems, capacity will be underutilized.

2.4. Supply-adjustment in the construction and service sector

It would, however, be unrealistic to assume that all production takes place with a lag and is fixed during the exchange. Trade services, housing services, transportation, food processing of all kinds, constitute activities which cannot be performed in advance, yielding outputs to be kept in stock. The technology of these activities is such that production only takes place at the moment when demand must be satisfied. The price of the output is set by the producer as long as he can adjust to demand. When supply capacity reaches an upper bound for him and his competitors, then the price will rise above the predetermined (mark-up over cost) level. Such a constrained short-run supply-adjustment to effective demand has been specified only for domestic non-agricultural commodities, i.e., which are not tradeable internationally. (For reasons to be explained in Section 3 these commodities will be called input-output commodities, abbreviated as IO-commodities). Production of these commodities requires an input of internationally tradeable commodities. Thus, any boost in the demand for domestic commodities has its cost in terms of foreign exchange. This combination of supply-adjustment and price-adjustment regimes on one single market, makes it possible to explore the scope for macro-economic stabilization policies through effective demand management.

2.5. Government policies

The model does not limit to the representation of macro-economic stabilization policies. It also represents government operation on commodity markets and income redistribution policies. On the commodity markets, quota on international trade can be imposed and buffer stocks can be kept for selected commodities. These market policies are strongly related to redistributive policies, since most of these serve the purpose of affecting income distribution.

The food-rationing schemes under which individuals are allowed to buy a certain amount of food at a low price are an important component of income redistribution policies. There are also other transfers such as a subsidy on wages repatriated by citizens abroad but these are small relative to other public expenditures, which are dominated by government consumption (mainly salaries of civil servants) and investments. Interest payments on domestic and foreign debt are of increasing significance.

On the receipts-side foreign aid plays a predominant role. Aid is mainly given in kind and thus falls to a large extent outside the government financial sphere, except food aid which is resold with profit in the government-owned ration shops and on the open market, thus yielding government revenue. Further sources of government finance are provided by taxes on foreign trade, taxes on domestic sales, and direct taxes. A quantitative presentation will not be given here, as the aim of the present section only is to give a summary list of features which are represented in the TFYP-model.

3. STRUCTURE OF THE EXCHANGE-COMPONENT

3.1. The supply-demand balancing module

In this section the structure of the exchange-component will be outlined in more detail. Emphasis will be put on the specification of the supply-demand balancing module because it deals with market regimes and regime switches, such as the switch from import to autarky. As mentioned earlier it is on such a switch for the rice market that attention will be focussed in Section 4.

In the supply-demand balancing module, net revenue from trade with the outside world is being maximized subject to a commodity balance and capacity constraints, and given domestic final demand. Clearing prices result as dual variables, which can be passed on to the income formation and to the behavioural equations which then in turn update domestic final demand, and other coefficients to be used in the next round by the trade module. Thus, a cycle is obtained. The equilibrium solution follows naturally as the fixed-point of this cycle, i.e. as a set of values such that all variables remain unchanged from one cycle to the next.

The supply-demand balancing module is formulated as a linear program. It distinguishes between production activities, and buying/selling activities. Upper bounds are imposed on these activities which reflect production capacities and trade quota. An overhead charge is imposed on production, which may reflect a mark-up or an excise tax. Clearing prices emerge as dual variables associated to the commodity balance.

The net revenue maximizing problem is formulated as follows:

$$\max_{q_c, s_r^+, s_r^- \geqq 0} \; - \Sigma_c \hat{v}_c q_c + \Sigma_r (\bar{p}_r^- s_r^- - \bar{p}_r^+ s_r^+) \quad \text{(net revenue from trade with outside)}$$

subject to:

$$(B-A)q - (I+T^-)s^- + (I-T^+)s^+ \geqq d \qquad (p) \qquad \text{(commodity balance)}$$

$$\underline{q}_c \leqq q_c \leqq \bar{q}_c \qquad c=1,\ldots,C \qquad (\psi_c^-, \psi_c^+) \qquad \text{(bounds on production)}$$

$$0 \leqq s_r^- \leqq \bar{s}_r^- \qquad r=1,\ldots,R \qquad (\mu_r^-) \qquad \text{(bounds on selling)} \qquad (3.1)$$

$$0 \leqq s_r^+ \leqq \bar{s}_r^+ \qquad r=1,\ldots,R \qquad (\mu_r^+) \qquad \text{(bounds on buying activities)}$$

$s^- = \Sigma_r s_r^-$, $s^+ = \Sigma_r s_r^+$, $q = \Sigma_c q_c$,

where variables in brackets are associated shadow prices and xy denotes the inner product of a row vector x and a column vector y. Prices and other dual variables are row vectors, other variables are column vectors, and I is the m×m identity matrix. The symbols in (3.1) have the following meaning and dimension:

symbol	meaning	dimension
A	input matrix	m × n
B	output matrix	m × n
d	domestic final demand	m × 1
p	clearing price	1 × m
$\bar{p}_r^-$	selling price (regime r)	1 × m
$\bar{p}_r^+$	buying price (regime r)	1 × m
q_c	activity level	n × 1
$\underline{q}_c$, $\bar{q}_c$	lower, resp. upper bound on q_c	n × 1
s_r^-, $\bar{s}_r^-$	realized, resp. maximum sale activity r	m × 1
s_r^+, $\bar{s}_r^+$	realized, resp. maximum purchase activity r	m × 1
T^-	input requirements for selling	m × m
T^+	input requirements for buying	m × m
$\hat{v}_c$	overhead charge	1 × n
μ_r^-	premium on upper bound of selling regime r	1 × m
μ_r^+	premium on upper bound of buying regime r	1 × m
ψ_c^-	premium on lower bound on capacity rental activity c	1 × n
ψ_c^+	premium on upper bound on capacity rental activity c	1 × n

The corresponding tableau is:

variables	q_c	s_r^-	s_r^+	
objective	$-\hat{v}_c$	$\bar{p}_r^-$	$-\bar{p}_r^+$	
constraints:	$-(B-A)$	$(I+T^-)$	$-(I-T^+)$	$\leqq -d$
	I	0	0	$\leqq \bar{q}_c$
	$-I$	0	0	$\leqq -\underline{q}_c$
	0	I	0	$\leqq \bar{s}_r^-$
	0	0	I	$\leqq \bar{s}_r^+$

(3.2)

This leads to the dual program (all dual variables are taken to be row vectors):

$$\max\ pd - \Sigma_c \psi_c^+ \bar{q}_c + \Sigma_c \psi_c^- \underline{q}_c - \Sigma_r(\mu_r^+ \bar{s}_r^+ + \mu_r^- \bar{s}_r^-)$$

subject to

$$p(B-A) + \psi_c^- - \psi_c^+ \leqq \hat{v}_c$$

$$p(I+T^-) + \mu_r^- \geqq \bar{p}_r^- \qquad (3.3)$$

$$p(I-T^+) - \mu_r^+ \leqq \bar{p}_r^+$$

and to the following first-order complementarity conditions ($x \geqq 0 \perp y \geqq 0$ is equivalent to $x \geqq 0$, $y \geqq 0$, $xy = 0$):

commodity balance with free disposal

$$(B-A)q - (I+T^-)s^- + (I-T^+)s^+ \geqq d \perp p \geqq 0$$

$$s^+ = \Sigma_r s_r^+,\ s^- = \Sigma_r s_r^-,\ q = \Sigma_c q_c \qquad (3.4)$$

bounds on production activities and trade

$$q_c \leqq \bar{q}_c \perp \psi_c^+ \geqq 0$$

$$q_c \geqq \underline{q}_c \perp \psi_c^- \geqq 0$$

$$s_r^+ \leqq \bar{s}_r^+ \perp \mu_r^+ \geqq 0 \qquad (3.5)$$

$$s_r^- \leqq \bar{s}_r^- \perp \mu_r^- \geqq 0$$

zero overprofit-conditions on production activities and trade

$$p(B-A) - \psi_c^+ + \psi_c^- \leqq \hat{v}_c \perp q_c \geqq 0$$

$$p(I+T^-) + \mu_r^- \geqq \bar{p}_r^- \perp s_r^- \geqq 0 \qquad (3.6)$$

$$p(I-T^+) - \mu_r^+ \leqq \bar{p}_r^+ \perp s_r^+ \geqq 0.$$

These overprofit-conditions constrain the prices which may emerge as a solution. We observe the following:

i) as long as production is not at bound, the value of the output of a production activity will equal the value of the input plus overhead charge (mark-up pricing)

ii) as long as the selling price is lower than the cost of buying at clearing level and 'shipping' to the border, no export adjustment will take place

iii) as long as the clearing price is lower than the cost of shipping from border to the retail market plus the buying price, then no import adjustment will take place.

Clearly, when neither import nor export adjustment takes place, clearing prices will be determined domestically, i.e. the market will behave as in autarky, the situation which will be of interest to us in the next section.

In the following we shall call any change in the optimal basis of the linear program (3.1) a regime-switch and the characterization of the corresponding situation on a particular market will be called a regime (say, an autarky regime, a supply-adjustment regime, etc.).

3.2. A simplification in order to obtain a unique solution for the linear program

Linear programs tend to suffer from a weakness which hampers their practical application and which we shall address first. This is that it may have infinitely many primal solutions (solution on a face of the constraint-set instead of a corner). This problem is troublesome. From a theoretical point of view, it points to an underspecification since the model generates an infinity of primal solutions without assigning a likelihood to any specific one. From a practical point of view solutions on a face are hard to find and the algorithm (say, the simplex algorithm) will select one corner-solution and jump from one corner to another under a change in parameters. The model will then behave in a discrete fashion which may be very disturbing not only for interpretation of results from model simulation, but also for econometric estimation of parameters.

We therefore introduce four assumptions which impose a special structure on the linear program, as is commonly done, say in the solution of transportation problems, in order to avoid multiplicity of the primal solution. We do not need to rule out multiple dual solutions, for reasons which will be explained below.

<u>Assumption 3.1</u>. All production sectors fall into either of the following two categories:

1) <u>IO-sectors</u>, each of which produces one single commodity i not produced by any other IO-sector and for which there exists no trade activity ($\bar{s}^{--}_{ir} = \bar{s}^{-+}_{ir} = 0$) but at least one regime with unbinding capacity, $\bar{q}_c = +\infty$ for $c = C$.
   Commodities produced by IO-sectors are called IO-commodities, the other ones are called non-IO-commodities
2) <u>non-IO-sectors</u>, for which $\underline{q}_{hc} = \bar{q}_{hc}$ for $c = 1$ and which have no further production-adjustment regime: $\bar{q}_{hc} = \underline{q}_{hc} = 0$, for $c = 2,\ldots,C$.

<u>Assumption 3.2</u>. Selling prices fall, buying prices and rental prices rise with regime for all commodities and sectors (downward-sloping export demand, upward-sloping import supply):

$$\bar{p}^{+}_{r+1} \geqq \bar{p}^{+}_{r}$$

$$\bar{p}^{-}_{r+1} \leqq \bar{p}^{-}_{r} \qquad \text{for } r = 1,\ldots,R-1,\ \bar{p}^{-}_{R} > 0 \text{ and } \bar{p}^{-}_{1} < \bar{p}^{+}_{1}$$

$$\hat{v}_{c+1} \geqq \hat{v}_{c} \qquad \text{for } c = 1,\ldots,C-1.$$

Assumption 3.3. Each IO-commodity requires directly or indirectly a positive amount of some non-IO-commodity.

Assumption 3.4. Import of non-IO-goods is possible: $(I_2 - T^{+}_{2})s^{+}_{2} > 0$ has a non-negative solution where subscript 2 indicates the non-IO-commodities.

Figure 1 illustrates the price relations which emerge from the LP under Assumption 3.2. The border prices which appear in this diagram can be defined for imports as $p^{B+} = p(I-T^{+})$ and for exports as $p^{B-} = p(I+T^{-})$, i.e. as the value it would have at the border if the commodity were to be imported or exported.

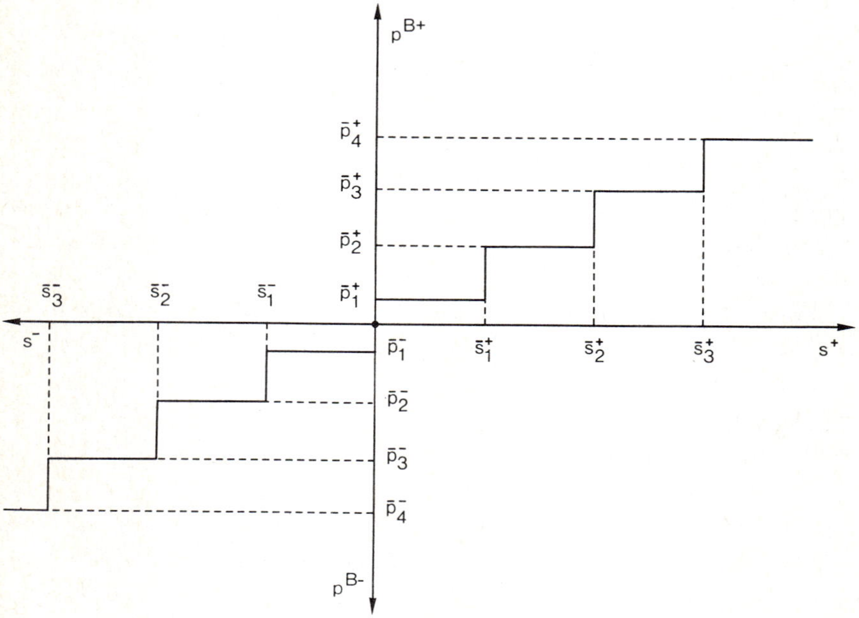

FIGURE 1
Border price of imports and exports related to buying and selling activities, for one selected commodity, with four regimes.

It can be seen that, as far as the dual LP solution is concerned, set-valuedness is not ruled out. Assumption 3.1 is drastic because it implies that no change in basis can ever take place as a consequence of a change in the coefficients of the objective, which satisfies Assumption 3.2. As a matter of fact the only change in basis which can occur is a switch between rental activities and between buying and selling activities under a change in final demand. We observe that the model always has a feasible solution and, as long as each product requires some input (a standard assumption), this solution is bounded. Assumption 3.3 ensures that when non-IO-prices are positive, IO-prices are positive as well.

Finally, we make a simplifying assumption which ensures that surplusses can be disposed of at a positive price.

<u>Assumption 3.5</u>. For non-IO-commodities, selling regime $r = R$ operates with zero trade and zero transportation cost. Instead of T^- we write T_r^-, with $T_r^- = 0$ for $r = R$ and $T_r^- = T^-$ for $r = 1,\ldots,R-1$. Furthermore, purchase is always possible, $\bar{s}_R^{+} = +\infty$.

Thus, the model has become very rigid. This rigidity is only seemingly a disadvantage, which disappears when the parameters of the linear program are made price- and activity-level-dependent.

3.3. Price and quantity feedbacks to the linear program

The linear program, as specified above contains objective-coefficients, constraint-coefficients and resource-levels as fixed parameters. In several economic applications it would be unrealistic to keep these parameters at levels which are independent of the activity levels and shadow prices which result from the linear program itself. Thus, feedbacks need to be specified which relate LP-outcomes to LP-parameters. The combination of the LP with its feedbacks will then yield the exchange-component of the TFYP-model, i.e., a static Applied General Equilibrium model.

The supply-demand balancing component is represented through a linear program, which operates through a constrained maximization of the net revenue from selling to the outside world. Given technical input-output coefficients, bounds on net-selling and on available capacity, final demand, and given prices for external trade, the component generates prices of commodities and the rental price of capacity. It may also be observed that the equilibrium model obtained in this way consists of the first-order, i.e., linear complementarity, conditions of the LP with some of the LP-parameters as nonlinear functions of primal and dual variables. Thus, the exchange-component of the TFYP-model falls within the class of nonlinear complementarity problems and can be solved as such (cf. Appendix). We discuss here which feedback mechanisms are considered, as illustrated in Figure 2.

1) Primary income distribution

Based on the outcomes of the trade-component, income from trade and production is distributed among social classes and government. The distribution is based on exogenous (or lagged) shares which are supposed to reflect resource-ownership.

2) Tax and transfers

After-tax income is generated by deducting income tax from primary income, which may be negative for some or all social classes. This is done for each actor, social class as well as government, according to a tax function.

3) Aggregate savings, consumption and investment by actor

Based on after-tax income and prices, aggregate savings, consumption and investment are determined through behavioural equations.

4) Consumption and investment by commodity and actor

Static utility maximization subject to the budget constraint is applied to determine investment and consumption by commodity which feed into the trade component as final demand.

5) Foreign trade, balance of payments deficit and the adjustment of the tax rate

Based on the outcome of the trade component, import, export and balance of payments deficit can be determined for given trade prices. The tax-rate is subsequently adjusted to satisfy the balance of payments restriction.

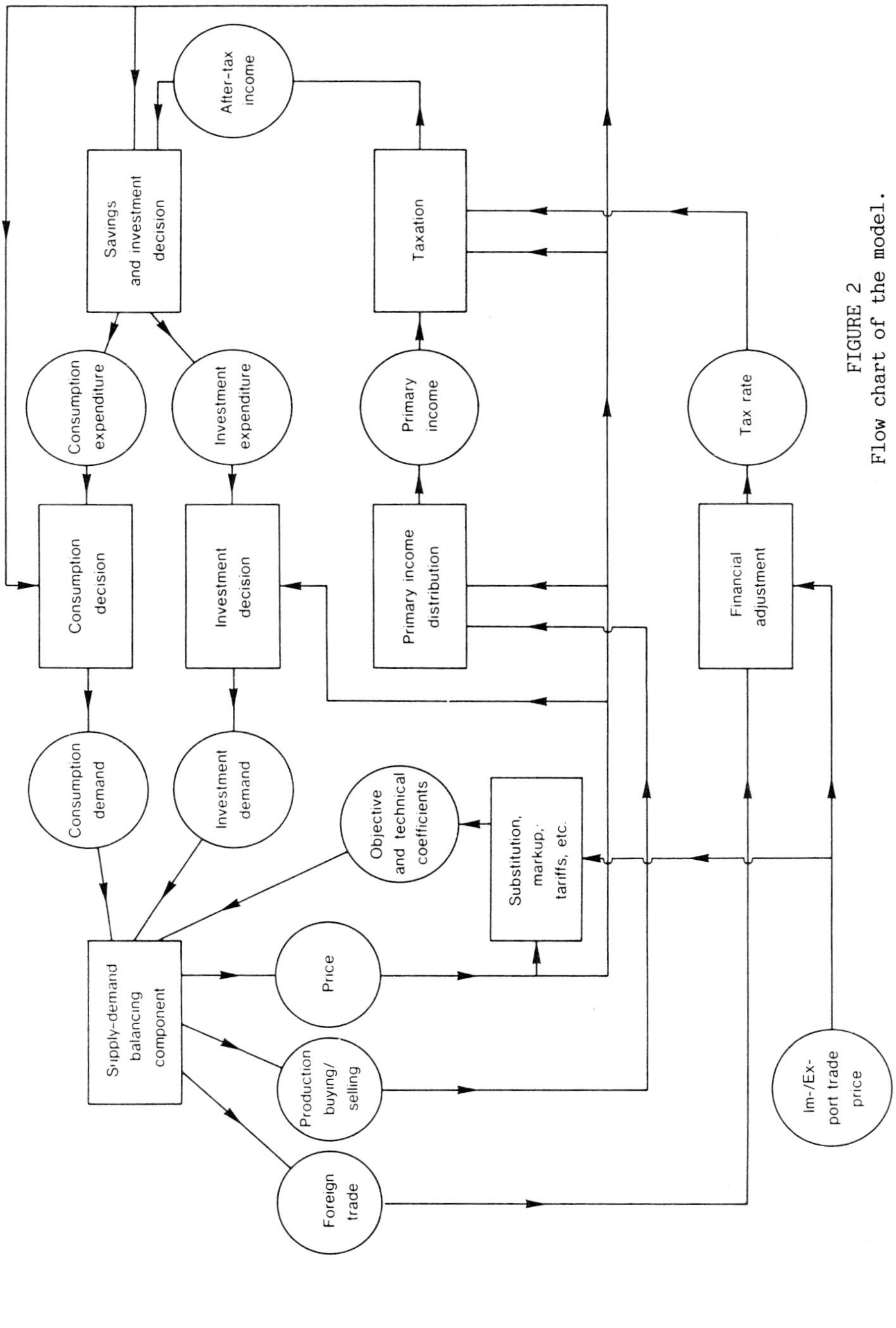

FIGURE 2
Flow chart of the model.

6) Substitution, decreasing returns, price expectations, mark-up and tariffs
New coefficients of the trade component are calculated on the basis of the prices which have been obtained.

Further details and proofs can be found in Keyzer [3], to appear in [5].

4. CONSEQUENCES OF INCREASED FOODGRAIN PRODUCTION

4.1. A rice surplus

It is not uncommon to think of Bangladesh as a food deficit country. It may therefore come as a surprise that simulation exercises with the TFYP-model suggest that in the near future rice surplus is going to be an issue to be coped with. Not that all Bangladesh people would be well-fed. Some would have enough rice, while others would not have sufficient purchasing power to buy it.

4.2. Increased foodgrain production through improved water control

Bangladesh has two main resources: labour and land. Any development strategy for the country will have to focus on improving the productivity of these resources, i.e., land development and education. This paper addresses an issue related to consequences of land development in Bangladesh. Land development can be looked at as improvement of water control. In the summer season this consists of drainage and flood control, in the winter season of irrigation. Stabilization of water availability thoughout the year reduces yield variability of crops, permits to harvest throughout the year and to cultivate rice-HYV (high yielding variety) and in winter also wheat-HYT. Although water control is not a sufficient condition for agricultural growth it is widely seen to be the most binding constraint in Bangladesh. Fertilizer availability needs to be expanded as well but fortunately the country has limited reserves of natural gas which are currently being tapped for ureum production. If availability of seeds, pesticides, agricultural extension and storage capability is expanded accordingly, and with normal weather, it would be possible to expand (gross) foodgrain production by around 800,000 tons per year on average in the Plan-years, starting from a 84/85 level of 15.8 million ton (a bad year). With a population of around 100 million and reaching 112 million in 1990 this amounts to a growth in foodgrain production of 4.6 per cent together with a population growth of around 2.3 per cent. Not a bad record at all, if it is realized. But such a possible succes generates problems of its own.

4.3. Switch from import regime to self-sufficiency in rice

Over the past decade Bangladesh has received large amounts of food aid (around 300 million US$ in the fiscal year 1984/85), mainly consisting of wheat. For this reason, but also because wheat prices have fallen with respect to rice inside Bangladesh as well as on the international market, the share of wheat in total foodgrain consumption has augmented sharply.

In 1976/77 average foodgrain consumption per caput was 146 kg of which 11.5 kg wheat consumption. In 1984/85 these figures are 170 kg of which 35.2 kg wheat. Wheat production was up from 230 thousand metric tons to 1175 thousand tons. Wheat can only be produced in the winter season, since the summer is too warm and humid and even in winter not all land suitable for rice cultivation is suitable for wheat. The summer season accounts for slightly less than 75 per cent of the foodgrain production. Jute is the only serious competitor for rice in the summer season and then only on a very restricted area. Moreover, since Bangladesh is the world's largest exporter of jute, an increase in jute production easily leads to a fall in prices. In short, significant growth in crop production cannot be envisaged without expansion of rice production. This expansion can be realized through improved water control and higher yields but combined with the sharp increase of the share of wheat in foodgrain consumption, this leads to self-sufficiency in rice. This change is bound to have an impact on the price of rice unless perfect substitutability is assumed on the production side in the winter season between wheat and rice.

In Bangladesh import of foodgrains is largely handled by government. Nevertheless pricing appears to satisfy this equality with competitive trade margins. For rice the tariff is zero in 1984/85 and there is an import margin of around 8.5 per cent of the trade price.

As could be seen from (3.6) when self-sufficiency is reached retail price becomes the equilibrating price between domestic supply and demand. The price may in principle fall until export becomes profitable. Even when no tariffs are levied and when trade price on export equals trade price on import, there will be a self-sufficiency band within which it does not pay for the trader to either import or export. Since the average rice consumption per head is already at a high level, an increase in rice production per caput may easily lead to a price fall, which will have serious macroeconomic consequences, due to the predominant role of rice in the national economy. The first effect of a fall in the price of rice will be a lower agricultural income which has a depressing effect on effective demand for rice but also for services. This multiplier impact is then magnified due to Keynesian effects. Obviously the fall in the rice price causes an increase in real income outside agriculture, but there the marginal propensity to consume rice is lower because the income is somewhat higher. Moreover the multiplier effect on the service sectors negatively affects income, especially for the informal classes. In short, the economy shows signs of contraction when self-sufficiency in rice has been reached.

4.4. Effective demand management

How should economic policy react to this contraction? There are basically two lines of thinking, a 'supply-side' and a 'Keynesian' approach. The supply-sider might claim that a low food price reduces wage costs, and increases savings by the urban classes, thus permitting to reduce industrial protection and to embark on an industry-oriented strategy. Economic history can offer a lot of cases in which food self-sufficiency has been the prerequisite and starting signal for successful industrialization. Unfortunately, it seems that Bangladesh is not ready for such a strategy (see [6]). In such a situation it is not unreasonable to turn temporarily to the demand-side of the economy and see which effective-demand management policies can keep prices of the surplus goods from falling to excessively low levels. Such a fall should be avoided because low rice prices have severe consequences on farm incomes and through incomes on effective demand for services and other domestic commodities. They do hardly reduce production, since land and labour have no alternative use in the summer season which could substantially substitute for paddy production. Econometric evidence suggests that, even in winter season, substitutability between wheat and rice acreage is limited.

Four categories of policy measures currently exist which could possibly help to avoid an excessive fall in paddy prices: stock accumulation, rationing, procurement, and rural works. Through rationing, special groups (mainly civil servants and vulnerable groups) receive cards which allow them to buy a specific volume of wheat and rice at a ration price which is set once a year. The difference between retail and ration price, multiplied by the ration volume is then the subsidy. In other forms of rationing labourers in rural work programmes are being paid a wage in kind which may be considered to include a subsidy component. Similarly, under procurement schemes wheat and rice are bought at harvest time at a support price and sold in the ration system (which is mainly supplied through food aid) and on the open market or kept in stock. In the past procurement volumes have been modest and were limited by handling capacity.

How do rationing, rural works and procurement operate as macro economic stabilization measures? In their present set-up they hardly do. Rural works clearly generate income and effective demand but the level of activity is mainly determined by availability of projects, not by stabilization considerations. Rationing stabilizes effective demand when relative foodgrain prices are rising (1 per cent price increase generates around 2.5 per cent increase in subsidy) but is destabilizing when foodgrain prices are falling (since the same reaction applies). Procurement does protect farmers against falling prices but is severely constrained on the volume side.

There are basically two ways to dampen the price fall for rice, the building-up of stocks and increasing purchasing power of social classes with high marginal propensity to consume rice, i.e., of the poor. It seems that rationing for vulnerable groups can help in this respect, provided the ration subsidy is stabilized. Expansion of rural works remains constrained by project availability and should not become an aim in itself. Procurement subsidy would become very costly and not reach the poor if all the food procured for the rationing system was to be purchased at a procurement price well above the market price. Stock accumulation must take place in future years in order to improve government's capability to cope with natural disasters, but is not an effective way of coping with surplus production in the long-run.

Before proceeding with the discussion of the simulation runs performed, it may be useful to investigate the types of impact to be expected on the basis of the market clearing structure of the TFYP-model. Although general equilibrium solutions cannot fully be understood in a partial setting, it is possible to analyze first-round effects on a commodity by commodity basis. Figure 3 illustrates this. Clearly, an increase in rationing would increase the income of the poor and thus shift their incomes upwards. This would cause the supply-demand equilibrium to shift from A to B. In what we call a tied aid scheme this food would be imported so that the net import schedule would shift to the right also. Since consumers would not spend all their extra income on foodgrains, the upward shift of the demand curve would tend to be smaller than the shift of the net import curve. Thus, price will tend to shift to the new equilibrium C which lies below A, making the price stabilization policy counterproductive. This is indeed the type of result obtained from simulation.

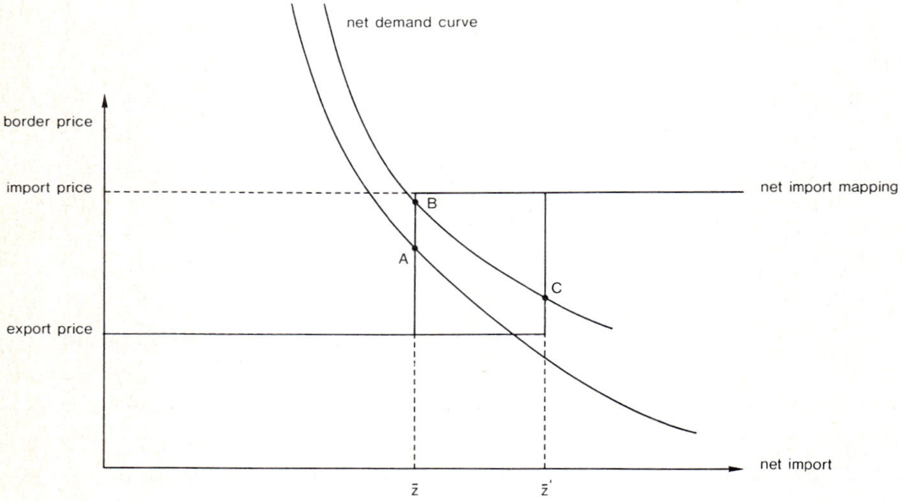

FIGURE 3
Possible consequences of increased rationing; A: original solution, B: solution with increased rationing, untied aid, C: solution with increased rationing, tied aid.

4.5. Tied versus untied aid; consequences of increased rationing

It may be helpful to list some conflicting views on the impact of ration subsidy or more generally food aid as a background against which results from simulation runs will be presented. For the sake of clarity the views will be expressed in such simple terms that it would be unfair to attribute them to any author

i) food aid does not reach the poor; it is often used to pay civil servants and soldiers, or sold on the open market to supplement government budget
ii) food aid does not help because it depresses agricultural prices and thus agricultural production
iii) food aid through income support does not help because it does not increase production and fuels inflation
iv) it is from an administrative point of view very difficult to extend the coverage of food aid.

First some general remarks on the first point. Of the 7800 million taka food aid received in the fiscal year 1984/85, Tk 1940 is directly given as food subsidy to the poor and Tk 2000 as the non-subsidy component of the Food-for-Work Programme (see [7]). Thus, roughly speaking one half of the aid directly reaches the poor. Would an increase in food ration subsidy depress prices or conversely, would it fuel inflation? To study this, three simulation runs were performed. First, a 3 per cent yearly growth in subsidy to the poor, then a 25 per cent (the base-run scenario), and finally a 35 per cent rate. The subsidy can be seen as an extension of the coverage of the ration system. To avoid the destabilizing effects mentioned earlier the subsidy would be determined through income entitlements. It would not necessarily be distributed through ration shops only, but possibly through free meals in schools and hospitals. Moreover, for the 25 per cent-case a tied aid-variant was run also, in which food in kind is distributed which was obtained from food aid imports and no accomodating balance of payment aid is provided. It is assumed that the public investment is adjusted so as to keep the trade deficit equal in each year to the one realized under untied aid. The results may be summarized as in Table 1 for the end-year 1989/90 (exchange rate 26 taka/US$, population 112.5 million of which 22.6 landless and 11.9 rural informal).

We first compare the three schemes with untied aid and then compare tied aid with untied aid.

The main impact of increased rationing is on income distribution. The two poorest classes, which are the main recipients of ration subsidy, gain significantly although they are still far from reaching the commonly accepted minimum requirement of 2020 calories (see [7]). Thus an important increase in ration subsidy would indeed help the poor. It could only to a limited extent be achieved through an increase in food aid (wheat) but would rather require balance of payment aid. Of each taka of subsidy provided, about three quarters should be financed through balance of payments aid and only about 15 per cent be given as direct food aid. The impact on wheat and rice production is as could be expected, but it is rather small. At first-sight it would seem that there are important multiplier effects, Tk. 2.2 increase in household receipts being generated for every taka increase in ration. But prices are affected as well, so that the impact on average real national income is very limited.

Table 1. Outcomes for the year 1989/1990

Yearly increase in subsidy	3% untied	25% untied	35% untied	25% tied
Flexible ration subsidy (1)	2000.	5282.	7785.	3993.
Trade deficit (1)	47461.	49856.	51666.	49856.
Household receipts (1)	380239.	387489.	393032.	352350.
Foodgrain production in 1000 mt (2):				
wheat	2161.	2137.	2120.	1966.
rice	15532.	15547.	15559.	15590.
Wheat import:				
in 1000 mt	1581.	1688.	1767.	2479.
million taka c.i.f.	7239.	7730.	8092.	11350.
Real income per caput (3):				
landless	2346.	2457.	2541.	2313.
rural informal	2679.	2731.	2772.	2990.
national average	3626.	3653.	3672.	3738.
Calory intake (4):				
landless	1682.	1720.	1748.	1741.
rural informal	1795.	1811.	1823.	1951.
national average	2002.	2012.	2020.	2067.
Retail price of rice (5)	7.75	7.91	8.04	6.28

(1) million taka
(2) net of seed and waste
(3) taka per head, national deflator
(4) calories per head per day
(5) taka per kg

Turning to a comparison between untied and tied aid (Table 1, second and fourth column, and Table 2), one might, at a first glance, be tempted to conclude that tied aid works better, since average calory consumption is higher, although the poorest people, i.e. the landless farmer, lose. Table 2 gives evidence to the contrary. Farmers lose significantly with respect to non-farmers as can be understood from the drastic fall in their prices of wheat and rice. The rice price is indeed much lower than in the 3% case, for reasons which were explained in Figure 3. The most severe consequence is, however, a significant fall in the ratio of domestic savings

Table 2. Tied versus untied aid, 25% yearly increase in subsidy, year 1989/90

	untied	tied
Ratio of per caput income to national average:		
(80 million) farmers	.89	.86
(32.5 million) non-farmers	1.26	1.30
Retail price of wheat	5.17	3.56
Ratio of domestic savings to total investment	.36	.32

over total investment which is caused by a fall in the savings rate of farmers. This ratio is already very low in the base-run, reflecting the fact that most investment is financed from aid. This is also the reason why the impact of tied food aid is not as negative in the short run: investments take place anyhow, even in agriculture.

In summary, calculations seem to suggest that most of the alleged negative consequences of food aid should not be attributed to the food aid itself but rather to the policy package which is often associated with it. Furthermore, it appears that increased rationing would dampen the fall in the price of rice resulting from increased efforts in irrigation and drainage, but the Keynesian multiplier effects seem to be modest in real terms.

APPENDIX. A SKETCH OF THE ALGORITHM USED FOR SOLVING THE EXCHANGE-COMPONENT

A.1. The model as a non-linear complementarity problem

It was explained in Section 3.3 that the exchange-component can be written as a non-linear complementarity problem. Consider $G : R^m_+ \to R^m$, then the non-linear complementarity problem can be written as:

$$G_i(x) \geqq 0, \; x_i \geqq 0, \; x_i G_i(x) = 0, \quad i = 1,\dots,m. \tag{A.1}$$

Typically, $G_i(x) = 0$ and $x_i > 0$ for, say, $i \in I_1$, and $G_i(x) > 0$, $x_i = 0$ otherwise. For $i \in I_1$, x_i adjusts (for example a price-adjustment) and otherwise $G_i(x)$ adjusts. Let $G(x)$ and x be partitioned accordingly by $(G_1(x), G_2(x))$ and (x_1, x_2), then

$$\begin{aligned} & x_1 > 0, \; G_1(x_1, x_2) = 0 \\ & x_2 = 0, \; G_2(x_1, x_2) > 0. \end{aligned} \tag{A.2}$$

A.2. Principle of the algorithm

The algorithm applies an artificial slack-technique (also called homotopy- or continuation-technique). It solves the complementarity problem through a sequence of optimizations which involve fixed-point calculations. It operates as follows:

i) set $K := 0$, assume an initial partitioning and a guessed value x^{*0}

ii) set $K := K+1$

set $\lambda := 1$ and $s^K := G^K(x^{*K-1})$

iii) solve

$\min \lambda$

$\lambda \geqq 0$

subject to:

$$\begin{aligned} & x_1 \geqq 0, \; G_1^K(x_1, x_2) - \lambda s_1^K = 0 \\ & x_2 = 0, \; G_2^K(x_1, x_2) - \lambda s_2^K \geqq 0 \end{aligned} \tag{A.3}$$

iv) when iii) finds a solution x^{*K} with $\lambda = 0$, stop (complementarity problem has been solved). Otherwise perform a pivot (set x_i at zero and adjust G_i or vice versa) and go to ii).

Obviously the main issue involved is to approximate $G_1^K(x_1, x_2) - \lambda s_1^K = 0$. This is achieved through an iterative adjustment of x_1, i.e., through a search for a fixed-point x_1^{*K} of $x_1 = F^K(x_1,x_2,\lambda s_1^K)$, where F^K is defined in such a way that $G_1^K(x_1^{*K}, x_2) = \lambda s_1^K$. The main practical advantage of this type of algorithm is that it permits to accept a high degree of imprecision in the solution of (A.3) as long as the final solution has not been reached. In fact any sequence $\{s^K\}$ such that $\|s^K\| - \|s^{K-1}\| \geq \varepsilon_1$ and $x_1^{*K} \geq -\varepsilon_2$ is acceptable. Thus, it is possible to pivot whenever the violation of x_1 is not too severe, even when the value of x_1 is not (yet) a precise approximation of the fixed point of F^K, i.e., the algorithm proceeds through a sequence of truncated fixed-point iterations.

A.3. The fixed-point calculation

We consider the adjustment scheme:

$$x_1^{k+1} = F^K(x_1^k, x_2, \lambda s_1^K), \; k = 0,1,\ldots \; . \qquad (A.4)$$

Observe that when one makes sufficiently small steps in λ, only local convergence properties of F are required. The Ostrowski-theorem provides sufficient conditions for such a convergence.

Definition A.1. Let $F : D \subset R^n \rightarrow R^n$. Then x^* is a point of attraction of the iteration (A.4), if there is an open neighbourhood S of x^* such that $S \subset D$ and, for any $x^0 \in S$, the iterates $\{x^k\}$ defined by (A.4) all lie in D and converge to x^*.

Theorem A.2. (Ostrowski theorem [4, p. 300]). Suppose that $F : D \subset R^n \rightarrow R^n$ has a fixed-point x^* in the interior of D and that it is differentiable at x^*. Let $F'(x^*)$ be the Jacobian matrix at x^*. Now if $\rho(F'(x^*)) < 1$, then x^* is a point of attraction of the iteration (A.4) (ρ is the spectral radius).

As long as the ball of convergence around x^* is not too small, one can proceed with the algorithm by decreasing λ with a small step size and recalculating the artificial slack s^k, not only when a pivot is to be taken, but also as soon as a sufficient reduction in $\|x_1 - F^K(x_1,x_2,\lambda s_1^K)\|$ has been obtained. It may be observed that, while the conditions of the Ostrowski theorem appeared to be satisfied in virtually all models to which the algorithm was ever applied, the global Jacobi-type iteration scheme $x_1^{k+1} = F^K(x_1^k, x_2, 0)$ did often not converge.

In several economic applications global convergence results can be obtained through the Kantorovitch-lemma (or its generalization, the Schröder-theorem). One then must distinguish between positive and negative artificial slacks and alternate the reduction in each of them, i.e.

$$x^{k+1} \geqq F^K(x_1^k,\ x_2,\ \lambda^+ s_1^{+K} - \lambda^- s_1^{-K}). \tag{A.5}$$

This permits to obtain after a reduction in, say, from λ^+ to $\lambda^{+'}$:

$$x^{k+1} \geqq F^K(x_1^k,\ x_2,\ \lambda^{+'} s_1^{+K} - \lambda^- s_1^{-K}).$$

When sufficiently is known about the directional derivatives of $G^K(x_1,\ x_2)$ a mapping F^K can be constructed which satisfies the isotonicity properties required for the convergence of the Kantorovitch-iteration scheme.

Definition A.3. A mapping $F : D \subset R^n \rightarrow R^m$ is isotone on $D_0 \subset D$ if $F(x) \leqq F(y)$ whenever $x \leqq y$, $(x,y) \in D_0$.

Lemma A.4. (Kantorovitch-lemma). Let $F : D \subset R^n \rightarrow R^n$ be isotone on D and suppose that $x^0 \leqq y^0$, $\langle x^0, y^0 \rangle \subset D$, $x^0 \leqq F(x^0)$, $y^0 \geqq F(y^0)$. Then the sequences $x^{k+1} = F(x^k)$, $y^{k+1} = F(y^k)$, $k = 0,1,\ldots,$ satisfy $x^k \geqq x^{k-1}$, $x^k \rightarrow x^*$, $k \rightarrow \infty$, $y^k \leqq y^{k-1}$, $y^k \rightarrow y^*$, $k \rightarrow \infty$ and $x^* \leqq y^*$. Moreover, if F is continuous on $\langle x^0, y^0 \rangle$, then $x^* = F(x^*)$, $y^* = F(y^*)$, and any fixed point $u \in \langle x^0, y^0 \rangle$ of F is contained in $\langle x^*, y^* \rangle$.

We observe that (A.5) will also converge locally when the conditions of the Ostrowski theorem are satisfied.

In practical applications it has proven advisable to start with adjustment scheme (A.4) and large reductions in λ, to reduce step size in λ when this step size creates problems, and to turn to (A.5) when the step size has become too small. The approach discussed here has not only extensively been applied in national modeling at the Centre for World Food Studies but was also used for solving the international general equilibrium model of IIASA's Food and Agriculture Program. In the latter application it has proven to operate significantly faster (about 40 per cent) than non-smooth optimization used earlier, with higher accuracy and lower cost per iteration (because no gradient is needed).

REFERENCES

[1] S. Ahmad, W. v.d. Geest, M.A. Keyzer and M. Mujeri, "An applied general equilibrium model for the third five-year-plan of Bangladesh", *Bangladesh Journal of Political Economy* 7 (1987) 35-99.

[2] M.A. Keyzer, "Short-run impact of trade liberalization measures on the economy of Bangladesh: exercises in comparative statics for the year 1977", in: *General equilibrium trade policy models,* T.N. Srinivasan and J. Whalley, eds., MIT-Press, Cambridge, 1984.

[3] M.A. Keyzer, "An applied general equilibrium model with price rigidities", Working paper SOW 85-11R, Centre for World Food Studies, Amsterdam, The Netherlands, 1986.

[4] J.M. Ortega and W.C. Rheinboldt, *Iterative solution of non-linear equations in several variables,* Academic Press, New York, 1970.

[5] K.S. Parikh, et al., *The BLS: A system of linked national models for food policy analysis,* Nijhoff, The Hague, to appear in 1987.

[6] UNDP, "Macro model for third five-year-plan", BGD/83/029, Vol. I-III, Dhaka, Bangladesh, 1985.

[7] World Bank, "Bangladesh: economic trends and development administration", Report number 4822, Vol. II, Statistical Appendix, Washington, USA, 1984.

The Computation and Modelling of Economic Equilibria
A.J.J. Talman, G. van der Laan (Editors)

ADJUSTMENT PROCESSES FOR FINDING ECONOMIC EQUILIBRIA*

G. van der LAAN

Department of Economics and Econometrics, Free University, De Boelelaan 1105, 1081 HV Amsterdam, The Netherlands

A.J.J. TALMAN

Department of Econometrics, Tilburg University, P.O. Box 90153, 5000 LE Tilburg, The Netherlands

In this paper we deal with adjustment mechanisms which lead to an economic equilibrium starting from an arbitrarily chosen price vector. This problem goes back to Walras, who was concerned with the problem of finding for a pure exchange economy a price adjustment mechanism leading from an initial price system to an equilibrium. It should be noticed that convergence of the Walrasian tatonnement process can be proved if certain conditions are satisfied, for example, Revealed Preferences. Although this condition may be satisfied for many excess demand functions in operational economic models, it has been shown that any continuous function on the unit price simplex satisfying Walras' law can be realized as the excess demand function for some pure exchange economy.
A more advanced method of price adjustment is the Global Newton method. However, also for this method convergence may not hold for an arbitrarily chosen initial point.
We give several adjustment processes which can start anywhere and always lead to an equilibrium point. It appears that these processes can serve as a convergent alternative for the classical Walrasian tatonnement process. The paths traced by the various processes are governed by maintaining complementarity conditions between the prices and the value of the corresponding excess demands. In particular we present a process in which the excess demands successively become equal to zero. More precisely, by increasing the prices of the commodities with excess demand, decreasing the prices of the commodities with excess supply, and adjusting the prices of the commodities in equilibrium in order to keep them so, all markets successively reach their equilibrium. However, to assure convergence, we allow for a market to lose temporarily its equilibrium. This protects the process from cycling or leaving the price space.

---

* This research is part of the VF-program "Equilibrium and Disequilibrium in Demand and Supply", which has been approved by the Netherlands Ministry of Education and Sciences.

1. INTRODUCTION

In this paper we deal with adjustment mechanisms which lead to an economic equilibrium, starting from an arbitrarily chosen initial point. This problem goes back to Walras, who was concerned with the problem of finding for a pure exchange economy a price adjustment mechanism leading from an initial price system to an equilibrium price system. A straightforward choice for such a mechanism in case z is a continuously differentiable function is the differential equation

$$\frac{dp}{dt} = z(p), \tag{1.1}$$

where, for an economy with n+1 commodities indexed $j = 1,\dots,n+1$, $z(p) = (z_1(p),\dots,z_{n+1}(p))^\top$ is the excess demand at price $p = (p_1,\dots,p_{n+1})^\top$. From Walras' law we know that the inner product $p^\top z(p) = 0$ for all p and hence z(p) is a vector field tangent to the set of prices

$$B = \{p \in \mathbb{R}^{n+1}_{+} \mid \sum_{j=1}^{n+1} p_j^2 = 1\}.$$

When starting at a point p^0 in B, the differential equation has a solution curve of points on B. Unfortunately, the solution curve may fail to converge to a vector of equilibrium prices, even when the set of initial price systems is restricted to points near the boundary or, by contrast, to points close to an equilibrium price system. So, neither global nor local convergence can be guaranteed. Stated differently, the mechanism is not effective in the sense of Saari and Simon [18], who took a mechanism to be effective if the solutions converge to an equilibrium point for almost all initial price systems in some subset of the manifold on which z(p) is given. Counterexamples have been given by Scarf [19]. In these examples each solution curve leads in the limit to a cycle around the unique equilibrium point p^*.

It should be noticed that convergence of the Walrasian tatonnement process can be proved if certain conditions are satisfied. For example, if z(p) has the property of Revealed Preferences, $p^{*\top} z(p) > 0$ for all $p \neq p^*$, then the Lyapunov function $V(p) = \Sigma_{j=1}^{n+1} (p_j - p_j^*)^2$ monotonically declines along the solution path of (1.1), implying that the path will converge to p^*. Other sufficient conditions for convergence of the tatonnement process are Gross Substitutability or Diagonal Dominance (for example see Arrow and Hahn [1]). In this paper we want to give processes which converge for any excess demand function. It has been shown by several authors (for example see Sonnenschein [23] and Debreu [2]) that any smooth vector field on B satisfying Walras' law can be realized as the excess demand function for some pure exchange economy. In the last ten years general equilibrium theory has also been concerned with problems which lead to more general excess demand functions. For instance, Drèze [5] proved the existence of an equilibrium for a pure exchange economy with prices between upper and lower bounds. In this proof a vector of variables $q = (q_1,\dots,q_{n+1})^\top$ defines for each j either a price p_j (between the bounds) or a quantity constraint on either the demands or supplies of the j-th commodity. From these prices and quantities induced by q, the excess demand z(q) is obtained, while an equilibrium is induced by a vector q^* for which $z(q^*) = 0$. Also in this case we may consider the differential equation

$$\frac{dq}{dt} = z(q)$$

as a mechanism leading from an initial point q^0 to an equilibrium point q^*. However, in this case the excess demand function is typically not continuously differentiable. And if so, the question arises under which conditions does this mechanism converge? For excess demand functions under quantity rationing we cannot use the properties of, for instance, Revealed Preferences and Gross Substitutability. Suppose we say that z(q) prevails Revealed Preferences if $q^{*\top}z(q) > 0$ for all $q \neq q^*$. Even when this holds, it is not clear whether there is a Lyapunov function which monotonically declines along the solution path. Because we do not have $q^\top z(q) = 0$ as in the case of prices, the function $V(q) = \Sigma_{j=1}^{n+1} (q_j - q_j^*)^2$ cannot be used. So, it is hard to derive convergence conditions for tatonnement processes which adjust quantities.

A more advanced method of price adjustment is the Global Newton method of Smale [22], which has the form

$$Dz(p)\frac{dp}{dt} = -\lambda(p)z(p) \tag{1.2}$$

with Dz(p) the n×n Jacobian matrix of $(z_1,\dots,z_n)^\top$ evaluated at $(p_1,\dots,$

$p_n)^\top$ with $p_{n+1} = 1$ the price of the numeraire commodity. The scalar $\lambda(p)$ is a real valued function depending on the behaviour of z near the boundary of $\mathbb{R}^n_+$. A relevant choice is $\lambda(p) = \det Dz(p)$. The Global Newton process (1.2) is effective in the sense that when the eigen values of $Dz(p)$ are non-zero at a zero of z, it converges to a solution point starting from almost all points on the boundary of $\mathbb{R}^n_+$. In a more recent paper, Keenan [6] showed that the Global Newton process also converges locally. However, Keenan also argued that convergence may not hold for an arbitrarily chosen starting point. So the question arises whether there is a process which will converge globally, in the sense that it converges to an equilibrium point for any arbitrarily chosen initial price system. In Saari and Simon [18], it is shown that for such processes not only knowledge of the excess demands z(p) is required (as in the tatonnement process) but also knowledge of the gradients of all of its component functions, except for the numeraire commodity. Clearly, in (1.2) the Jacobian $Dz(p)$ is used and hence the gradients. On the other hand, the Global Newton process can be rewritten as

$$\frac{dz(p)}{dt} = -\lambda z(p). \tag{1.3}$$

So, along the trajectory of the process the prices are adjusted in such a way that the changes in the excess demands z(p) are proportional to z(p) itself. A well-known example of such a trajectory is the path traced by the algorithm of Scarf [20, 21]. When starting in the vertex $(0, 0, \ldots, 0, 1)^\top$ of the n-dimensional unit simplex

$$S^n = \{p \in \mathbb{R}^{n+1}_+ \mid \sum_{j=1}^{n+1} p_j = 1\}$$

a path of prices in S^n is followed which is characterized by the property that for all prices p on the path

$$z_j(p) = z_k(p) \text{ for all } j, k \neq n+1.$$

So, as in the Global Newton method the changes in the components of z are proportional to z itself. It has been recognized by several authors that the path followed by Scarf's algorithm coincides with the path traced by the Global Newton process when the latter is started at $(0, 0,\ldots,0, 1)^T$.

In this paper we define several adjustment processes which can start anywhere in (the interior of) S^n and will be shown to converge to an equilibrium if the function z is continuously differentiable on S^n and some regularity condition is satisfied. These processes are governed by maintaining complementary conditions on the components of both p and z(p) along the path. Much attention will be paid to the economic interpretation of the processes when they are applied to find a Walrasian equilibrium price vector in a pure exchange economy or to reach a supply-constrained equilibrium. One of these processes will have some similarities with the classical Walras tatonnement process in the sense that at the starting point the prices of the commodities with excess demand are increased, while the prices of the commodities with excess supply are decreased. These price changes will be not proportional to the excess demands but are relative to the initial price system. In this way the starting point is left in one out of $2^{n+1}-2$ directions depending on the sign pattern of the excess demands at the starting point. Relative to the initial price system, the process keeps the prices of the commodities with excess demand larger than all other prices and it keeps the prices of the commodities with excess supply relatively smaller than all other prices. Other processes to be defined in this paper leave the starting price system by increasing the price of the commodity with the largest excess demand and by decreasing some or all other prices, in order to keep the sum of the prices equal to one. In this way the initial price system can be left in n+1 directions. The process by which the price of the commodity with the largest excess supply is decreased and some or all other prices are increased will be discussed as well. All the processes to be defined in this paper can be approximated by simplicial algorithms (see for example [3] and [15]). These algorithms follow a piecewise linear path in a simplicial subdivision of S^n obtained from the corresponding process with z replaced by its piecewise linear approximation with respect to that underlying simplicial subdivision.

This paper is organized as follows. The notions of an excess demand function and a supply-constrained equilibrium are dealt with in Section 2. In Sections 3 and 4 the adjustment processes are defined. Section 3 discusses the processes in which the initial price system can be left in n+1 directions and Section 4 deals with the process which shows similarities with the classical Walras tatonnement process. The existence proofs of the paths of points followed by all these processes can be found in Section 5.

2. EXCESS DEMAND FUNCTIONS

In this paper we deal with excess demand functions on the n-dimensional unit simplex $S^n = \{p \in \mathbb{R}_+^{n+1} | \Sigma_i p_i = 1\}$. In case of a competitive exchange economy with n+1 commodities, S^n is the price simplex with the sum of the prices normalized to one. Suppose we have an economy with m consumers and for each consumer $i = 1,\ldots,m$ holds

a) the consumption set X^i is a compact, convex subset of $\mathbb{R}_+^{n+1}$, containing the set

$$\{x \in \mathbb{R}^{n+1} | 0 \leq x_j \leq \Sigma_i w_j^i,\ j = 1,\ldots,n+1\},$$

where $w^i = (w_1^i,\ldots,w_{n+1}^i)^\top$ is the vector of initial endowments of consumer i

b) $w_j^i > 0$ for all j

c) the preference relation $\succsim_i$ is continuous, monotonic and strictly convex.

Let $x^i(p)$ be the demand of consumer i given price $p \in S^n$, i.e. $x^i(p)$ is a maximal element for $\succsim_i$ subject to $x \in X^i$ and $p^\top x \leq p^\top w^i$. Then the total excess demand $z(p) = \Sigma_{i=1}^m (x^i(p) - w^i)$ is a continuous function on S^n and satisfies

i) for all $p \in S^n$, $p^\top z(p) = 0$ (Walras' law)

ii) $z_j(p) \geq 0$ if $p \in S_j^n = \{p \in S^n | p_j = 0\}$ (nonnegative excess demand if $p_j = 0$).

In the next sections we allow for more general excess demand functions.

Definition 2.1. A continuous function $z: S^n \to \mathbb{R}^{n+1}$ is an excess demand function if

i) for all $p \in S^n$, there exists a nonnegative vector $y(p)$ with $y_j(p) > 0$ if $p_j > 0$, such that $y^\top(p) z(p) = 0$

ii) $z_j(p) \geq 0$ if $p \in S_j^n$.

By defining the continuous function f from S^n into itself by

$$f_j(p) = [p_j + \max\{0, z_j(p)\}]/c(p) \qquad j = 1,\ldots,n+1$$

with $c(p) = 1+\Sigma_j \max\{0, z_j(p)\}$, it follows from Brouwer's fixed point theorem that any excess demand function $z:S^n \to \mathbb{R}^{n+1}$ has a zero point p^*, i.e. $z(p^*) = 0$. In the case of the classical Walrasian excess demand function, p^* is the vector of equilibrium prices. In the next example we consider an economy in which prices are bounded.

Example. Let $E = (\{X^i, \succsim_i, w^i\}_{i=1}^m)$ be an exchange economy with m consumers and n+1 commodities. Suppose the conditions a)-c) above hold. Now assume that the set of admissible prices is given by

$$P = \{p \in \mathbb{R}_+^{n+1} | 0 < \underline{p}_j \le p_j \le \bar{p}_j \text{ for all } j\}.$$

Clearly, P does not necessarily contain a vector p^* such that $z(p^*) = 0$. However, Drèze [5] defined an equilibrium concept with quantity constraints on the excess supplies and excess demands. The existence of an equilibrium with only quantity constraints on the supplies, is proven by van der Laan [13, 14] and Kurz [11].

Definition 2.2. A supply-constrained equilibrium is an allocation x^i, $i = 1,\ldots,m$, a price vector $p \in P$ and a rationing scheme $\ell \le 0$ such that

i) for all i, x^i is a maximal element for $\succsim_i$ in the set $B^i(p,\ell) = \{x \in X^i | p^\top x \le p^\top w^i,\ x-w^i \ge \ell\}$

ii) $\Sigma_i x^i = \Sigma_i w^i$

iii) $\ell_j = -\infty$ if $p_j > \underline{p}_j$, $j = 1,\ldots,n+1$

iv) $\ell_j = -\infty$ for at least one j.

We now construct an excess demand function such that a zero point yields a supply-constrained equilibrium. For $q \in S^n$, let $p(q)$ and $\ell(q)$ be defined by

$$p_j(q) = \max[\underline{p}_j, \tilde{q}_j \bar{p}_j] \qquad j = 1,\ldots,n+1$$

and

$$\ell_j(q) = -\min[\tilde{q}_j\bar{p}_j/\underline{p}_j, 1]w_j \qquad j = 1,\ldots,n+1,$$

where $\tilde{q}_j = q_j/\max_h q_h$ and $w_j = \Sigma_i w_j^i$, $j = 1,\ldots,n+1$. Now, let $x^i(q)$ be maximal for $\underset{\sim i}{>}$ in the set $B^i(q) = \{x \in X^i | p^\top(q)x \leq p^\top(q)w^i$ and $x-w^i \geq \ell(q)\}$, and let $z(q) = \Sigma_i(x^i(q) - w^i)$. From the conditions a)-c) it follows that $x^i(q)$ is a continuous function of q and satisfies $p^\top(q)x^i(q) = p^\top(q)w^i$. Hence, z is a continuous function from S^n into R^{n+1} satisfying $y^\top(q)z(q) = 0$ for all $q \in S^n$ with $y(q) = p(q) > 0$. Finally, $q_j = 0$ implies $\ell_j(q) = 0$ and hence $z_j(q) \geq 0$. So, z is an excess demand function. Clearly, $x^i(q^*)$, $i = 1,\ldots,m$, $p(q^*)$ and $\ell(q^*)$ induce a supply-constrained equilibrium if $z(q^*) = 0$.

The example shows that Definition 2.1 covers excess demand functions z which may arise both from an economy with flexible prices (Walrasian) and from an economy with bounded prices. Also the existence of a Drèze equilibrium can be shown by constructing an excess demand function on the unit simplex.

3. CONVERGENT ADJUSTMENT PROCESSES WITH n+1 RAYS

In this section we describe several adjustment processes to find a zero point of an excess demand function on S^n which, in principle, can start anywhere and always lead to such an equilibrium point. In addition to describing the paths of points followed by these processes, we also discuss their economic interpretation. It appears that the processes can serve as a convergent alternative for the classical tatonnement process in the case of a Walrasian economy. The existence of the paths we describe in this section will be examined in Section 5.

First, for some $v \in S^n$, we consider the homotopy function H from $S^n \times [0,1]$ to $Q^n = \{x \in \mathbb{R}^{n+1} | \Sigma_i x_i = 0\}$ given by

$$H(p,t) = t\hat{z}(p) + (1-t)(v-p),$$

where $\hat{z}_j(p) = z_j(p) - \Sigma_i z_i(p)/n+1$, $j = 1,\ldots,n+1$. Assuming that 0 is a regular value of H, we can easily show that for continuously differentiable excess demand functions z, $H^{-1}(0)$ contains a curve of points (p,t) starting at (v,0). If we replace condition ii) of Definition 2.1 by $\hat{z}_j(p) \geq 0$ it follows that the curve cannot cross $\mathrm{bd}(S^n) \times [0,1]$ and reaches a point $(p^*,1)$. Clearly, $H(p^*,1) = 0$ implies $\hat{z}(p^*) = 0$, so that for $j = 1,\dots,n+1$, $z_j(p^*) = \Sigma_i z_i(p^*)/n+1$. According to $y^T(p)z(p) = 0$ for all p, we conclude that p^* must be a zero (equilibrium) point of z.

For a point (p,t), $0 < t < 1$, in $H^{-1}(0)$ we have that

$$\hat{z}(p) = \lambda(p-v)$$

with $\lambda = (1-t)/t > 0$. So, the path in $H^{-1}(0)$ starting in (v,0) can, in the case of a Walrasian economy, be interpreted economically as a path of prices along which the difference of the current price system p and the initial price v is proportional to the relative excess demand, being the difference between the excess demand and the average excess demand of the goods. This path of points can be followed approximately by the Sandwich method devised by Kuhn and MacKinnon [10] and independently proposed for problems on $\mathbb{R}^n$ by Merrill [17]. In this algorithm the set $S^n \times [0,1]$ is simplicially subdivided. Starting with the unique simplex containing (v,0), a sequence of adjacent (n+1)-dimensional simplices is generated which leads to a simplex yielding an approximate equilibrium point $(\hat{p},1)$. The path will be followed more accurately if the mesh of the subdivision decreases. Therefore, if a more accurate approximation is required, the algorithm can be restarted with a finer subdivision in order to follow a new curve with v being the last found approximate solution.

Another simplicial restart algorithm on S^n to find economic equilibria was proposed by van der Laan and Talman [15]. Instead of a path of (n+1)-dimensional simplices in $S^n \times [0,1]$, their algorithm generates a path of simplices in S^n of varying dimension. From the starting point v, being a zero-dimensional simplex, for varying t a path of adjacent t-dimensional simplices is followed, $0 \le t \le n$, until an n-dimensional simplex yielding an approximate solution is found. Again, the accuracy can be improved by restarting at the approximate solution using a finer subdivision. The path of points followed approximately by this simplicial algorithm leaves the starting point in one out of n+1 different directions or rays. This specific ray is determined by the component j for which $z_j(v)$ is minimal. In the case that z is an excess demand function arising from a Walrasian economy, this component corresponds to the commodity with lowest excess demand (highest excess supply) at prices v. Along the ray corresponding to this component, the price of this commodity is lowered, whereas the prices of some of the other commodities are raised, in order to keep the sum of the prices equal to one. The price of commodity j is lowered until for a second commodity, say k, z_k becomes equal to z_j. Since $\min_h z_h(p) \le 0$ for all p and $z_j(p) \ge 0$ if $p_j = 0$, lowering p_j must yield a price vector p for which $z_k(p) = z_j(p) \le 0$ for some $k \ne j$. From this point on, the price of commodity k is also lowered and a path of prices is followed along which $z_k(p) = z_j(p) = \min_h z_h(p)$, until a price vector is reached for which a third commodity also has minimal excess demand, etc. To be sure that such a price vector will indeed be found, we have to protect the procedure against cycling or leaving S^n. To clarify this and the way in which the process in general proceeds, we formalize the description. Therefore, let $\mathcal{T}$ be the collection of subsets of $I_{n+1} = \{1,\dots,n+1\}$ and let $a(1),\dots,a(n+1)$ be n+1 vectors in Q^n such that any set of n of these vectors a(j) are linearly independent. For simplicity's sake we assume v to be in the interior of S^n.

Definition 3.1. For any $T \in \mathcal{T}$, the subset A(T) of S^n is given by

$$A(T) = \{p \in S^n | p = v + \sum_{j \in T} \lambda_j a(j),\ \lambda_j \ge 0 \text{ for all } j \in T\}.$$

Observe that $A(\emptyset) = \{v\}$, $A(I_{n+1}) = S^n$ and that for any $T \ne I_{n+1}$, A(T) is a t-dimensional convex polyhedron in S^n, where $t = |T|$ denotes the cardinality of the set T. Moreover, for any $T \in \mathcal{T}$, we define the set C(T) by

$$C(T) = \{p \in S^n | z_i(p) = \min_h z_h(p),\ i \in T\}.$$

Clearly, $C(\emptyset) = S^n$ and $C(I_{n+1}) = \{p \in S^n | z_i(p) = \min_h z_h(p)$ for all $i \in I_{n+1}\} = \{p^* \in S^n | z(p^*) = 0\}$, since $y^T(p)z(p) = 0$ for all p. So, $A(\emptyset) \cap C(\emptyset) = \{v\}$ and $A(I_{n+1}) \cap C(I_{n+1})$ is the set of all equilibrium points. In Section 5 we show that under some conditions the union B over all sets $B(T) = A(T) \cap C(T)$, $T \in \mathcal{T}$, contains a curve of points in S^n starting in $B(\emptyset) = \{v\}$ and ending with an element of the set $B(I_{n+1})$ of equilibrium points, if the vectors a(i), i = 1,...,n+1, are chosen in such a way that they are equal to b(i) - e(i), with e(i) the i-th unit vector in $\mathbb{R}^{n+1}$ and b(i) some vector in S^n. The variable dimension restart algorithm follows this curve approximately by a sequence of adjacent t-simplices in A(T) for varying $T \in \mathcal{T}$. Let us consider in more detail the curve in B having v as one of its end points. Suppose that for some unique j the starting point v is in the set C({j}). Then the curve starting in v leaves v along the one-dimensional set A({j}), lowering the price of commodity j, until for some k, $k \neq j$, a price vector in C({j,k}) is reached. So, by increasing λ_j from zero, the ray

$$v + \lambda_j(b(j) - e(j)), \quad \lambda_j \geq 0$$

is followed from v, until a point $\tilde{p}$ is reached such that for some $k \neq j$,

$$z_k(\tilde{p}) = z_j(\tilde{p}) = \min_h z_h(\tilde{p}).$$

Then the region A({j,k}) is entered by increasing the coefficient λ_k of $b(k) - e(k)$ from zero, and a path of prices p in A({j,k}) is followed from $\tilde{p}$ on which $z_k(p)$ is equal to $z_j(p)$ but less than the excess demand of the other goods, i.e., the path in B({j,k}) is followed starting at $\tilde{p}$. Following this path, two things can occur. Firstly, a price $\hat{p}$ can be reached for which a third commodity, say ℓ, also has minimal excess demand. Then the process continues along the curve in B({j,k,ℓ}) starting in $\hat{p}$. Secondly, the curve can hit the boundary of A({j,k}). Then, from the definition of A({j,k}), either one of the prices p_j or p_k is equal to zero, or one of the variables λ_j or λ_k is equal to zero. Since $z_i(p) \geq 0$ if $p_i = 0$, it is not possible that the path in A({j,k}) on which $z_j(p) = z_k(p) = \min_h z_h(p)$ crosses the boundary $p_j = 0$ or $p_k = 0$ without finding another index ℓ for which $z_\ell(p) = \min_h z_h(p)$. So, if the curve hits the boundary of A({j,k}), then either λ_j or λ_k is equal to zero, i.e., the path hits either the ray A({k}) or A({j}). Suppose λ_j becomes equal to zero. Now, λ_j is not further decreased but is kept equal to zero, and the process continues in A({k}) with prices p such that $z_k(p) = \min_h z_h(p)$.

Economically, decreasing the variable λ_j below zero is not very appropriate, since $\lambda_j < 0$ implies an increase of the price of commodity j whereas the excess demand of commodity j is negative. So decreasing λ_j below zero would imply that the excess demand of commodity j is kept at the minimum while its price increases. Instead of doing so, λ_j is kept equal to zero and the excess demand of commodity j is forced to become larger than the minimum excess demand. This protects the process from cycling and leaving S^n.

In general, for varying $T \subset I_{n+1}$, the process follows a path of prices p in $B(T) = A(T) \cap C(T)$. Clearly, if $p \in B(T)$, we have the complementarity property

$$\lambda_i \geq 0 \text{ and } z_i(p) = \min_h z_h(p) \quad \text{for all } i \in T$$

and

$$\lambda_i = 0 \text{ and } z_i(p) \geq \min_h z_h(p) \quad \text{for all } i \notin T,$$

where $p = v + \Sigma_{i=1}^{n+1}\lambda_i(b(i) - e(i))$. Since $b(i) \in S^n$, we conclude that the sum of the prices of the goods with minimal excess demand is smaller than the sum of the initial prices v_i of these goods. As soon as a price p on the path in $B(T)$ is generated for which a commodity j, $j \notin T$, has excess demand equal to the excess demand of the goods in T, the process continues along a curve in $B(T \cup \{j\})$, i.e., also λ_j is increased from zero causing a relative decrease in the price of commodity j. If, on the other hand, λ_k becomes zero for some $k \in T$, then the process continues along a curve of $B(T\backslash\{k\})$, keeping λ_k equal to zero and forcing the excess demand of commodity k to become higher than the minimum excess demand. An example of the path followed by this process is given in Figure 1. In this example B consists of three curves. One curve is the loop L in $B(\{1,2\})$. The second curve is the path C having two end points in $B(I_{n+1}) = C(I_{n+1})$, each being an equilibrium point. The third curve is the path P having an end point in $B(\emptyset) = A(\emptyset) = \{v\}$ and an end point in $B(I_{n+1})$, being an equilibrium point. Starting in $\{v\}$, the latter path is followed by the process until the equilibrium point is reached. Observe that the process cannot cycle or reach bd S^n. Even when v had been chosen within the loop L, cycling cannot occur because the curves in B depend on the starting point v. If v lies inside L then each ray $A(\{j\})$, $j \in I_{n+1}$, crosses L, which prevents the process from cycling. In Figure 2 the path followed by the process is given in case v lies inside L.

The fact that there is a curve in B from v to an equilibrium point p^* proves the well-known intersection theorem of Knaster, Kuratowski and Mazurkiewicz [7] stating that $C(I_{n+1})$ is nonempty.

The path P from v to p^* can be followed approximately by a sequence of adjacent simplices of varying dimension, where in a t-dimensional region

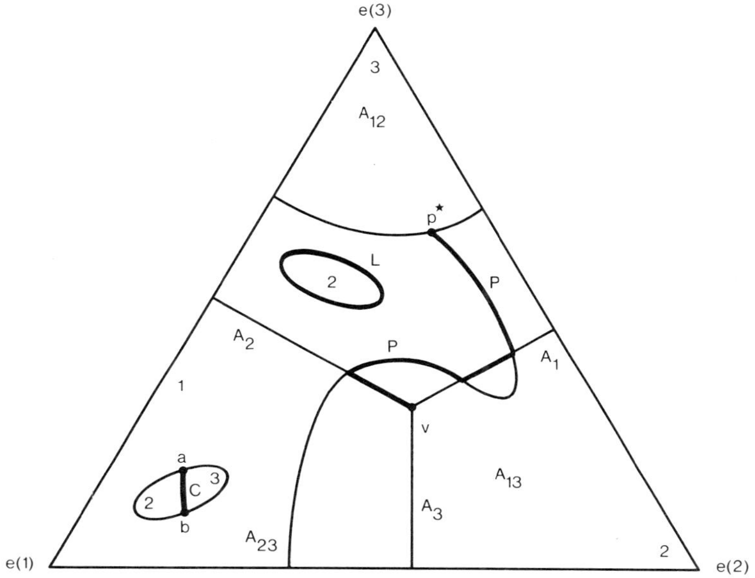

FIGURE 1

The sets $C(\{i\})$ are denoted by i, i = 1,2,3; $C(T) = \cap_{i \in T} C(\{i\})$. The sets $A(\{i\})$ and $A(\{i,j\})$ are denoted by A_i and A_{ij} respectively, i,j ∈ {1,2,3}. B consists of a path P from v to p^*, a path C from a to b and the loop L.

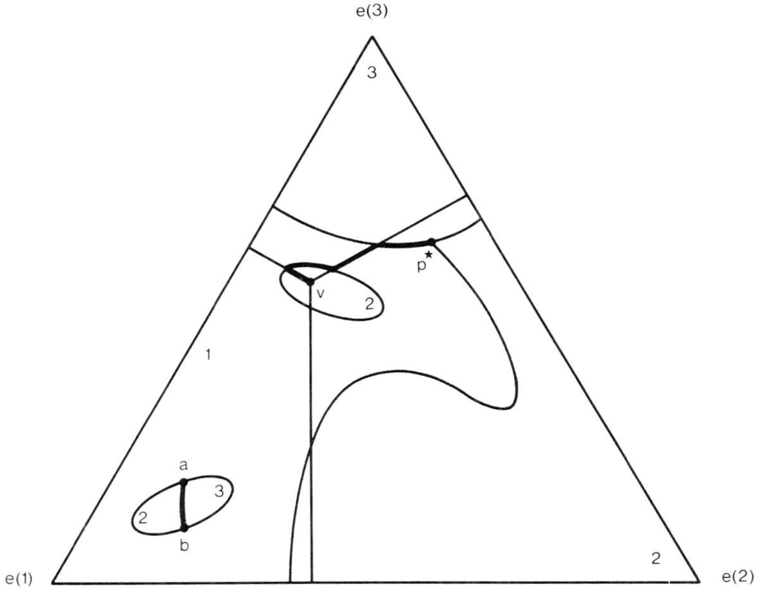

FIGURE 2

B consists of a path from v to p^* and one from a to b.

A(T) the path is followed by adjacent t-dimensional simplices. Therefore, we need a triangulation or simplicial subdivision of S^n which for each T induces a subdivision of A(T) in t-dimensional simplices. A well-known triangulation of S^n is the Q-triangulation (see for example Todd [24]). This triangulation subdivides the sets A(T) if and only if b(i) = e(j) for some $j \neq i$. Since any set of n vectors a(i) must be linearly independent we require that $b(i_1) \neq b(i_2)$ for all $i_1 \neq i_2$. A typical choice is b(i) = e(i+1) with i+1 = 1 if i = n+1 (see [12] and [15]). In this case a decrease of the price of a commodity i with the smallest excess demand is compensated by an increase of the price of commodity i+1 in order to keep the sum of the prices equal to one. Clearly, economically it is rather unsatisfactory that a decrease of a price of one commodity is compensated by an increase of the price of just one other commodity.

A triangulation leading to a more attractive interpretation has been given in [16]. Further, Doup and Talman [3] presented a simplicial subdivision of S^n which gives a triangulation of the t-dimensional sets A(T) in t-simplices when b(j) is chosen to be equal to v for all j. Then the sets A(T) can be written as

$$A(T) = \{p \in S^n | p = v + \sum_{j \in T} \lambda_j (v - e(j)),\ \lambda_j \geq 0,\ j \in T\}$$

$$= \{p \in S^n | p = (1+b)v - \sum_{j \in T} \lambda_j e(j)\ ,\ \lambda_j \geq 0,\ j \in T\} \qquad (3.1)$$

with $b = \Sigma_{j \in T} \lambda_j$. So, leaving v along the ray A({j}) with j the index of the commodity with the smallest excess demand, the price of commodity j is decreased whereas all other prices are increased with the same rate, i.e., the prices of the other goods are increased proportionally to their initial values and are therefore kept relatively equal to each other. In general, for a price vector $p \in A(T)$

$$p_j \leq (1+b)v_j \qquad \text{if } j \in T$$

and

$$p_j = (1+b)v_j \qquad \text{if } j \notin T.$$

So, if $p \in B(T) = A(T) \cap C(T)$, for the commodities k not in T

$$p_k/v_k = \max_h p_h/v_h \text{ and } z_k(p) \geq \min_h z_h(p)$$

whereas for all k in T

$$p_k/v_k \leq \max_h p_h/v_h \text{ and } z_k(p) = \min_h z_h(p).$$

That means that the prices of the goods with minimal excess demand are, relative to the initial prices, lower than the prices of the other goods. From an economic viewpoint, this seems to be rather attractive and appealing. Doup and Talman [3] showed that this is also computationally efficient. However, they followed the path obtained by increasing the price with the highest excess demand (see also [12]) instead of the path obtained by decreasing the price of the commodity with the smallest excess demand. In fact, the paths discussed in this section can be reversed by redefining A(T) and C(T) by

$$A'(T) = \{p \in S^n | p = v + \sum_{j \in T} \lambda_j (e(j) - b(j)),\ \lambda_j \geq 0 \text{ for all } j \in T\}$$

and

$$C'(T) = \{p \in S^n | z_i(p) = \max_h z_h(p) \text{ for all } i \in T\},$$

where b(j) again lies in S^n, $j = 1,\ldots,n+1$. Under some conditions, the union B' over all sets $B'(T) = A'(T) \cap C'(T)$, $T \subset I_{n+1}$, contains a unique path leading from v in $B'(\emptyset)$ to an equilibrium point in $B'(I_{n+1})$. Along this curve in B', the price of the commodity with the highest excess demand is initially increased while the prices of some or of all the other commodities are lowered. In general, if $p \in B'(T)$, we have the complementarity property

$$\lambda_i \geq 0 \text{ and } z_i(p) = \max_h z_h(p) \text{ for } i \in T$$

and

$$\lambda_i = 0 \text{ and } z_i(p) \leq \max_h z_h(p) \text{ for } i \notin T,$$

where $p = v + \Sigma_{j=1}^{n+1}\lambda_j(e(j) - b(j))$.

Again we may take the vector $b(j)$ equal to $e(j+1)$. However, the most interesting choice is $b(j) = v$ for all j. Then the set $A'(T)$ becomes

$$A'(T) = \{p \in S^n | p = v + \sum_{j \in T} \lambda_j(e(j) - v),\ \lambda_j \geq 0 \text{ for all } j \in T\}$$

$$= \{p \in S^n | p = (1-b)v + \sum_{j \in T} \lambda_j e(j),\ \lambda_j \geq 0 \text{ for all } j \in T\}$$

with $b = \Sigma_{j \in T}\lambda_j$. Therefore, for any price vector p in some $B'(T)$ we have for some $0 \leq b \leq 1$

$$p_j \geq (1-b)v_j \text{ and } z_j(p) = \max_h z_h(p) \text{ if } j \in T$$

and (3.2)

$$p_j = (1-b)v_j \text{ and } z_j(p) \leq \max_h z_h(p) \text{ if } j \notin T.$$

So, for a point p on the curve from v to p^* all prices of the commodities with highest excess demand are not minimal, relative to the initial price system v, whereas for all other commodities the relative prices have not been changed compared with the initial price system. As soon as, relative to the starting price, the price of a commodity with highest excess demand becomes equal to the prices of the commodities not having maximum excess demand, then that price is not further decreased but kept relatively equal to these prices. In addition, the excess demand of this commodity is forced to decrease from the maximal excess demand. Again the condition $z_i(p) \geq 0$ if $p_i = 0$ is sufficient to assure that the curve in B' starting in v does not break down at a point $p \in \text{bd } S^n$. If for some T a point $p \in B'(T)$ with $p_i = 0$ for some i is reached, then $b = 1$ in (3.2), i.e., $p_j = 0$ for all j not in T. So, if $p_k > 0$ then $k \in T$ and $z_k(p) = \max_h z_h(p)$. However, this implies that $\max_h z_h(p) = 0$. Since $z_i(p) \geq 0$ for all i with $p_i = 0$, we obtain that $z(p) = 0$. Hence, if a point p on the boundary is reached this point is an equilibrium point and hence an end point of the path (see Figure 3).

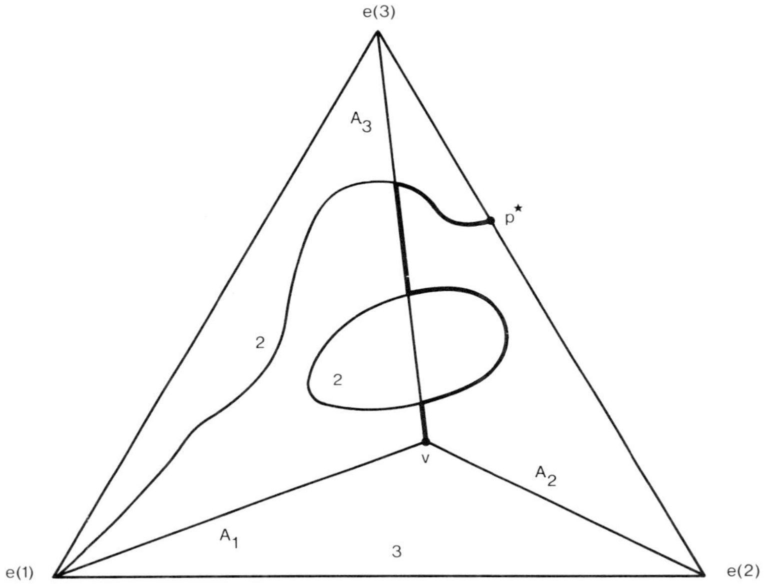

FIGURE 3
The path in B' starting at v ends at an equilibrium point p^* in bd S^n; $C(\{1\}) = C(I_{n+1}) = \{p^*\}$.

For the processes discussed in this section we have seen that during the process the index $j \in T$ is deleted from T as soon as λ_j becomes zero, i.e., when the price of commodity j relative to the initial price v_j rises above (in case of minimal excess demands) or falls below (in case of maximal excess demands) a certain level. This means that during the process the initial price system is taken into consideration. In fact, this prevents the process from cycling or leaving S^n, and hence the process converges for any starting point. This property does not hold for the Global Newton method, so that for this method the set of admissible starting points is restricted.

A drawback of the processes discussed in this section is that either the prices of the commodities with the highest excess supplies or the prices of the commodities with the highest excess demands are adjusted, but not simultaneously. In the next section we present a process in which all prices are adjusted simultaneously.

4. A NEW CONVERGENT ADJUSTMENT PROCESS

In the previous section we described several adjustment processes to find an equilibrium point. In these processes the starting point could be left in one out of n+1 directions, namely the n+1 rays $A(\{j\})$ (or $A'(\{j\})$). In this section we describe a process in which the starting point can be left in one out of $2^{n+1} - 2$ directions. At the initial price system all prices are adjusted simultaneously, the prices of the commodities with excess demand being increased and the prices of the commodities with excess supply being decreased.

To describe the process, let Ω be the set of all sign vectors in $\mathbb{R}^{n+1}$ having at least one component equal to +1 and one component equal to -1. Further, for $s \in \Omega$ we define

$$I(s) = \{i \in I_{n+1} | s_i = 0\}.$$

Each $s \in \Omega$ induces an $(|I(s)|+1)$-dimensional subset of S^n given by

$$A(s) = \{p \in S^n | p_i/v_i = \min_h p_h/v_h \text{ if } s_i = -1 \text{ and}$$

$$p_i/v_i = \max_h p_h/v_h \text{ if } s_i = 1\}, \qquad (4.1)$$

where v is again the initial price system in the interior of S^n. So, $A(s)$ is the set of prices in S^n such that, relative to v, p_i is minimal if s_i is negative, and p_i is maximal if s_i is positive. When $s_i = 0$, the price p_i may vary between the relative lower and upper bounds. Observe that the number of different sign vectors s in Ω for which $I(s)$ is empty is equal to $2^{n+1} - 2$, implying that there are $2^{n+1} - 2$ rays along which the initial price system can be left. From v there is a ray to each face of S^n. For n=2 the sets $A(s)$, $s \in \Omega$, are illustrated in Figure 4.

The process will leave v along the ray $A(s^0)$ with $s^0 = \text{sgn } z(v)$, simultaneously causing a relative decrease of the prices of the commodities with negative excess demand (positive excess supply) and a relative increase of the prices of the commodities with positive excess demand. The process continues along this ray until for one of the commodities, say i, the excess demand becomes equal to zero. Then s_i becomes equal to zero and the process continues in the corresponding region $A(s)$, i.e., the price of the commodity i is not further increased or decreased relative to v, but

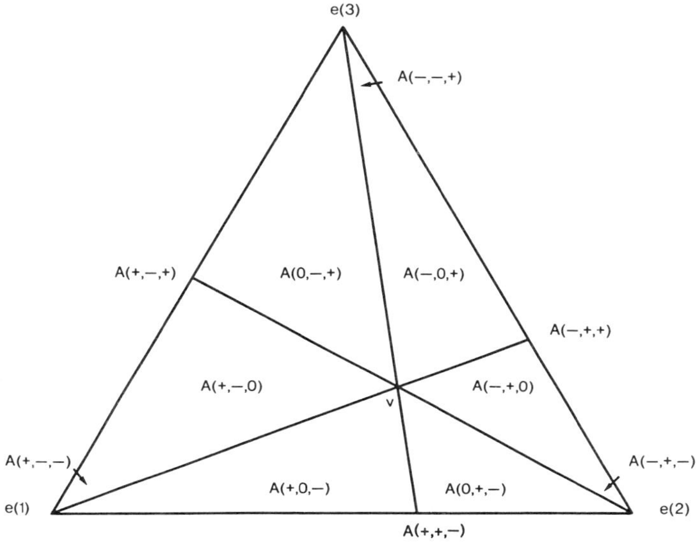

FIGURE 4
The sets $A(s)$, $s \in \Omega$, $n=2$; $A(s)$ is given by $A(s_1, s_2, s_3)$.

may vary between the relative upper and lower bounds while the excess demand is kept equal to zero. In general, for varying s in Ω, the process traces a path of prices in $A(s)$ such that

$$p \in C(s) = \text{cl}(\{p' \in S^n | \text{sgn } z(p') = s\})$$

where $\text{cl}(S)$ is the closure of the set S. So, for various s in Ω, a path of prices p in $B(s)$ is followed with $B(s) = A(s) \cap C(s) =$

$$\{p \in S^n | p_i/v_i = \min_h p_h/v_h \text{ and } z_i(p) \le 0 \text{ if } s_i = -1,$$

$$\min_h p_h/v_h \le p_i/v_i \le \max_h p_h/v_h \text{ and } z_i(p) = 0 \text{ if } s_i = 0,$$

$$p_i/v_i = \max_h p_h/v_h \text{ and } z_i(p) \ge 0 \text{ if } s_i = +1\}.$$

In fact, the process follows a path of prices such that, relative to the initial price system v, the price of a commodity with negative excess demand is kept minimal and the price of a commodity with positive excess demand is kept maximal, while the prices of the commodities in equilibrium may vary between the relative bounds. As soon as the process reaches a price p in B(s) for which the excess demand of a commodity i becomes zero for some i with $s_i \neq 0$, then the process continues in B(s') with $s'_i = 0$ and $s'_j = s_j$ for all $j \neq i$. On the other hand, when for some p in B(s) the relative price p_i/v_i of a commodity i with zero excess demand ($s_i = 0$) reaches the upper or lower bound, then the process continues in B(s') with $s'_i = 1$, $s'_i = -1$, respectively, and $s'_j = s_j$ for all $j \neq i$. As will be proved in the next section, the sets B(s) can be linked together in this way and the union B of B(s) over all sign vectors s in Ω contains a curve leading from the initial price system v to an equilibrium price system p^* (see Figures 5 and 6). In the figures the curves along which $z_i = 0$ have been drawn for i = 1, 2 and 3. Figure 5 shows the simple case in which B consists of one curve going from v to the equilibrium price p^*. In Figure 6, B consists of a curve P from v to p^*, a curve C between the two equilibria a and b in A(+1, -1, 0) and the loop L in A(0, -1, +1). Observe that $z_i(p) \geq 0$ if $p_i = 0$ and that sgn $z_i(p)$ changes if the curve $z_i = 0$ is crossed. So, corresponding to the fact that C is in A(+1, -1, 0), along the curve C we have that $z_1 > 0$, $z_2 < 0$ and $z_3 = 0$.

We now show that a path in B(s), $s \in \Omega$, cannot leave S^n. Suppose that for some s in Ω, p is a point in B(s) on the boundary of S^n, implying that $p_i = 0$ for at least one i. Hence $\min_h p_h/v_h = 0$ and therefore $p_j = 0$ for all indices j with $s_j = -1$. Since $s_j = -1$ implies $z_j(p) \leq 0$ and $p_j = 0$ implies $z_j(p) \geq 0$, we must have $z_j(p) = 0$ for all j with $s_j = -1$. For all k with $s_k = 0$ we have that $z_k(p) = 0$. Finally for all h with $s_h = +1$, $z_h(p) \geq 0$ and $p_h > 0$, so that $z_h(p) = 0$ since $y^T(p)z(p) = 0$ for all p. Hence, if the process reaches a point p on boundary S^n, then an equilibrium point is reached.

In these two sections we have described convergent processes for finding an equilibrium point of an excess demand function. Along the path traced by such a process the prices and excess demands satisfy a complementarity property. In particular, the process described in this section is rather interesting. Analogous to the classical tatonnement process, at the starting point the prices of the commodities with positive excess demand are increased and the prices of the commodities with negative excess demand are decreased. As soon as an excess demand becomes equal to zero, this commodity is kept in equilibrium, unless the price of such a commodity reaches the relative upper or lower bound on which the prices of the commodities with positive and negative excess demands

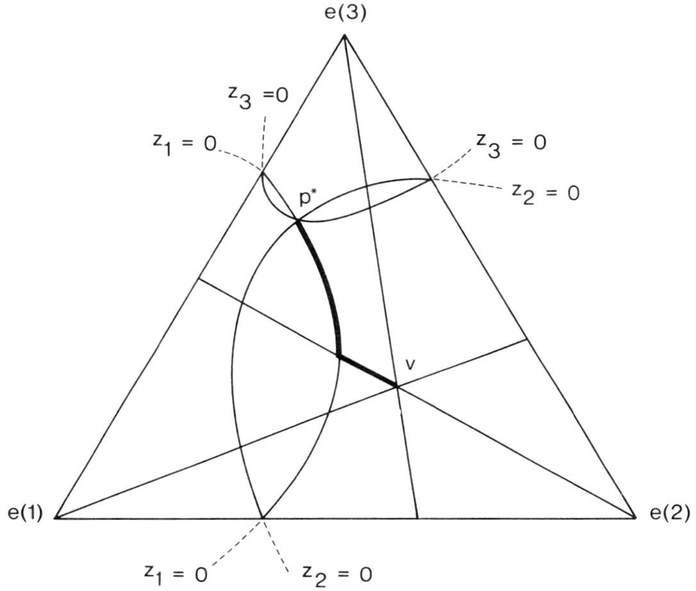

FIGURE 5

B consists of the curve from v to p^*.

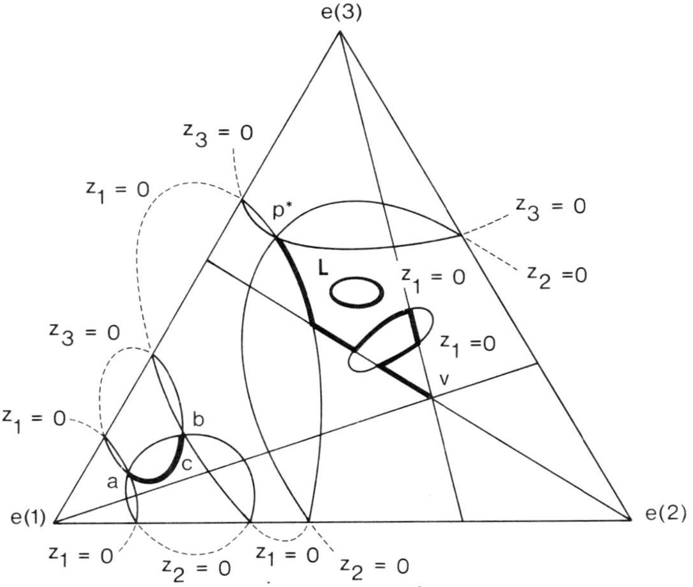

FIGURE 6

B consists of a curve P from v to p^*, a curve C in A(+1, -1, 0) from a to b and the loop L in A(0, -1, +1).

respectively are kept. In this case the price is kept on the relative upper or lower bound while the excess demand is forced to become positive or negative respectively. Increasing (decreasing) the price of a commodity with zero excess demand above (below) the relative prices of the commodities with positive (negative) excess demand does not seem to be very satisfactory. Since this is prevented by taking into consideration the initial price system v, the process is protected from cycling or leaving S^n. So, again we see that the starting point v plays a very essential role. In fact, the convergence of the process is assured by memorizing the starting point during the process.

Until now we have only discussed the economic interpretation of the adjustment processes in case of a Walrasian pure exchange economy. The second application mentioned in Section 2, the computation of a supply-constrained equilibrium, gives very similar interpretations of the various adjustment processes. In the process described in this section, the accounting prices q_j are increased, relative to the initial accounting prices v_j, if the corresponding excess demands $z_j(q)$ are positive, while the other accounting prices are decreased relative to the initial prices. When a price $p_j(q)$ becomes equal to $\underline{p}_j$, the price p_j is not further decreased but is kept equal to $\underline{p}_j$ and commodity j becomes rationed. The rationing becomes stronger when the accounting price q_j decreases, causing a decrease in the supply of the corresponding commodity j which has an excess supply. In general, the accounting prices of the goods with excess demand are kept maximal relative to the initial price system and the accounting prices of the goods with excess supply minimal, whereas the accounting prices of the goods having zero excess demand are allowed to vary between $\max_h q_h/v_h$ and $\min_h q_h/v_h$. When the accounting price q_j induces a real price equal to $\underline{p}_j$, commodity j is rationed whereas commodity h has maximal real price $\bar{p}_h$ if it has the highest accounting price. Notice the role of the starting accounting price system v. If, for some j, q_j is maximal at the initial point, $p_j(q)$ is equal to $\bar{p}_j$ although commodity j might have an excess supply. If so, then q_j is immediately decreased, relative to the initial accounting price. On the other hand, when at the initial system $p_h(q) = \underline{p}_h$ for some h and commodity h is rationed, this commodity might have an excess demand. The process will then immediately increase q_h in order to relax the rationing, and after that, to increase the real price

$p_j(q)$ from p_h until eventually $\bar{p}_h$ is reached. Similar interpretations can be given for the adjustment processes given in Section 3.

Finally, we remark that the path followed by the process given in this section can also be generated approximately by a sequence of simplices of varying dimension. For a detailed description we refer to [4].

5. EXISTENCE PROOFS

In the previous sections we have described paths of points leading from an arbitrarily chosen starting point v, in the interior of the unit simplex S^n, to an equilibrium point. In this section we present the existence proofs of these paths. We assume that the function z is continuously differentiable. To give the proofs, we need the concept of a primal-dual pair of subdivided manifolds, abbreviated PDM. This concept has been introduced in Kojima and Yamamoto [8]. Here we only give the basic tools and some theorems. For a complete discussion of the PDM-theory and the detailed proofs we refer to [8] and [9]. The existence of the paths is obtained from defining an appropriate PDM.

An m-cell in $\mathbb{R}^k$ is an m-dimensional convex polyhedral set being the intersection of a finite number of closed half spaces in $\mathbb{R}^k$. If a cell D is a face of a cell E, we write $D < E$. If we let $\mathcal{M}$ be a (finite) collection of m-dimensional cells in $\mathbb{R}^k$, then the collection of faces $\{D|D < E, E \in \mathcal{M}\}$ is denoted by $\bar{\mathcal{M}}$ and the union of all m-cells E, $E \in \mathcal{M}$, by $|\mathcal{M}|$. The collection $\mathcal{M}$ of m-cells is called a subdivided m-manifold if

a) for all D, $E \in \mathcal{M}$, $D \cap E = \emptyset$ or $D \cap E$ is a common face of both D and E
b) each (m-1)-cell in $\bar{\mathcal{M}}$ lies in at most two m-cells of $\mathcal{M}$
c) $\mathcal{M}$ is locally finite, i.e., each point x in $|\mathcal{M}|$ has a neighbourhood which intersects with only a finite number of cells in $\mathcal{M}$.

The boundary of $\mathcal{M}$, denoted by $\partial\mathcal{M}$, is the collection of all (m-1)-cells of $\bar{\mathcal{M}}$ which lie in only one m-cell of $\mathcal{M}$. A subdivided 2-manifold with 7 cells is pictured in Figure 7. Observe that we allow a cell to be unbounded.

Now, let $\mathcal{P}$ and $\mathcal{D}$ be two subdivided m-manifolds and d a dual operator such that

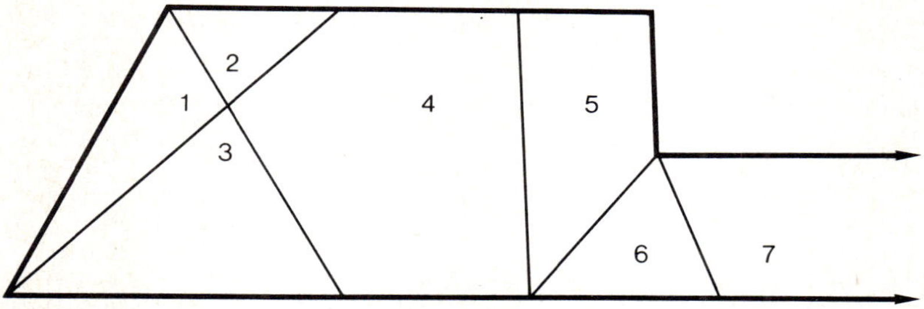

FIGURE 7
A subdivided m-manifold of 7 m-cells, m=2. The boundary is heavily drawn.

1) $|\mathcal{D}|$ is a bounded polyhedral set

2) d is an operator from $\bar{\mathcal{P}} \cup \bar{\mathcal{D}}$ into itself such that $X^d \in \bar{\mathcal{D}}$ for all $X \in \bar{\mathcal{P}}$ and $Y^d \in \bar{\mathcal{P}}$ for every $Y \in \bar{\mathcal{D}}$

3) if $Z \in \bar{\mathcal{P}} \cup \bar{\mathcal{D}}$ then $(Z^d)^d = Z$ and $\dim Z + \dim Z^d = m$

4) if $X_1, X_2 \in \bar{\mathcal{P}}$ and $X_1 < X_2$ then $X_2^d < X_1^d$

5) if $Y_1, Y_2 \in \bar{\mathcal{D}}$ and $Y_1 < Y_2$ then $Y_2^d < Y_1^d$.

Then the triplet ($\mathcal{P}$, $\mathcal{D}$, d) is a primal-dual pair of subdivided manifolds with degree m. $\mathcal{P}$ and $\mathcal{D}$ respectively are the primal and dual subdivided manifolds of the PDM. We say that Z^d is the dual of Z for each $Z \in \bar{\mathcal{P}} \cup \bar{\mathcal{D}}$. The dual operator is one-to-one and onto, and its inverse is d itself. An example of a PDM is given in Figure 8.

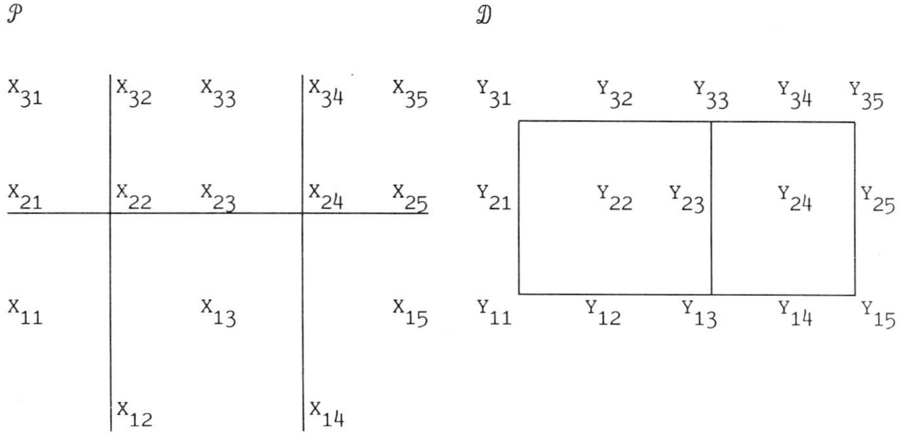

FIGURE 8
A PDM with degree 2 with $X^d_{ij} = Y_{ij}$, $1 \le i \le 3$ and $1 \le j \le 5$.

Next we define the collection of m-cells $\mathcal{L}$ by $\mathcal{L} = \langle \mathcal{P}, \mathcal{D}, d \rangle$ where

$$\langle \mathcal{P}, \mathcal{D}, d \rangle = \{X \times X^d | X \in \bar{\mathcal{P}}\} = \{Y^d \times Y | Y \in \bar{\mathcal{D}}\}. \quad (5.1)$$

<u>Lemma 5.1</u>. If $(\mathcal{P}, \mathcal{D}, d)$ is a PDM with degree m, then $\mathcal{L}$ is a subdivided m-manifold with no boundary, i.e., $\partial \mathcal{L} = \emptyset$. Moreover, $|\mathcal{L}|$ is a closed subset.

If $D = X \times Y$ is an (m-1)-cell of $\bar{\mathcal{L}}$ with $X \in \bar{\mathcal{P}}$ and $Y \in \bar{\mathcal{D}}$ and E is an m-cell of $\mathcal{L}$ having D as one of its faces, then either $E = X \times X^d$ or $E = Y^d \times Y$. With respect to the m-manifold $\mathcal{L} = \langle \mathcal{P}, \mathcal{D}, d \rangle$ defined in (5.1), we define the subdivided (m+1)-manifold $\mathcal{K}$ by

$$\mathcal{K} = \{Z \times \mathbb{R}_+ | Z \in \mathcal{L}\}. \quad (5.2)$$

Since $\partial \mathcal{L} = \emptyset$, we must have $|\partial \mathcal{K}| = |\mathcal{L}| \times \{0\}$. More precisely,

$$\partial \mathcal{K} = \{Z \times \{0\} | Z \in L\}.$$

Finally, let h be a piecewise continuously differentiable (abbreviated PC^1) function from $|\mathcal{K}|$ to an m-dimensional linear subspace L^m of $\mathbb{R}^k$, i.e., the restriction of h to each (m+1)-cell of $\mathcal{K}$ can be extended to a continuously differentiable function on an open neighbourhood of the cell. For a regular value c in L^m of h, the set

$$h^{-1}(c) = \{x \in |\mathcal{K}| \,\big|\, h(x) = c\}$$

does not intersect with any face D in $\bar{\mathcal{K}}$ of dimension less than m. From Sard's theorem we know that almost every c in L^m is a regular value.

Theorem 5.2. Let $\mathcal{K}$ be a subdivided (m+1)-manifold as defined above and let $h: |\mathcal{K}| \to L^m$ be a PC^1 function on $\mathcal{K}$. If c is a regular value of h, then $h^{-1}(c)$ is a disjoint union of piecewise smooth paths and loops satisfying

i) if $E \in \mathcal{K}$ and $h^{-1}(0) \cap E \neq \emptyset$ then $h^{-1}(0) \cap E$ is a disjoint union of smooth 1-manifolds

ii) each loop has no intersection with $|\partial \mathcal{K}|$

iii) $x \in h^{-1}(0)$ is an end point of a path if and only if $x \in |\partial \mathcal{K}|$

iv) if $|\mathcal{K}|$ is a closed set, then every open or semiclosed path is unbounded.

We will apply Theorem 5.2 for an appropriately chosen subdivided (n+1)-manifold $\mathcal{K}$ and PC^1 function h to deduce that $h^{-1}(0)$ corresponds to a set B (or B') defined in the Sections 3 and 4 and that $h^{-1}(0)$ contains a path in $|\mathcal{K}|$ corresponding to a path from v to an equilibrium point. First, let us consider the process described in Section 3 where the starting point v is left by decreasing the price of the commodity with the highest excess supply. The primal of the corresponding PDM is completely determined by the sets $A(T)$ defined in (3.1) as subsets of the affine hull of S^n, i.e.,

$$A(T) = \{p \in U^n | p = (1+b)v - \sum_{j \in T} \lambda_j e(j),\ \lambda_j \geq 0,\ j \in T,\ b \geq 0\},$$

with $U^n = \{x \in R^{n+1} | \Sigma_{i=1}^{n+1} x_i = 1\}$. The dual is induced by the sets $C(T)$, $T \subset I_{n+1}$. More precisely, the subdivided n-manifold $\mathcal{P}$ is defined by

$$\mathcal{P} = \{A(T) \mid T \subset I_{n+1} \text{ and } |T| = n\},$$

i.e., $\mathcal{P}$ is the collection of the n-dimensional cones A(T) in U^n. Clearly, $\bar{\mathcal{P}} = \{A(T) \mid T \subset I_{n+1}\}$ is the collection of all cones A(T), $|T| \le n$, in U^n. The dual subdivided n-manifold $\mathcal{D}$ consists of the n-cell Y_0 defined by

$$Y_0 = \{y \in Q^n \mid y_j \le 1 \text{ for all } j \in I_{n+1}\}.$$

Defining the sets Y(T), $T \subset I_{n+1}$, $T \ne I_{n+1}$, by

$$Y(T) = \{y \in Q^n \mid y_j = 1,\ j \in T, \text{ and } y_j \le 1,\ j \notin T\},$$

we obtain that $\bar{\mathcal{D}} = \{Y(T) \mid T \underline{\subset} I_{n+\underline{1}} \text{ and } |T| \le n\}$. Observe that $Y_0 = Y(\emptyset)$. The dual operator between $\mathcal{P}$ and $\mathcal{D}$ is defined by

$$A^d(T) = Y(T) \text{ and } Y^d(T) = A(T) \text{ for all } T \subset I_{n+1},\ |T| \le n.$$

Notice that dim A(T) = $|T|$ and that dim Y(T) = n - $|T|$ so that dim A(T) + dim Y(T) = n for all $T \subset I_{n+1}$, $|T| \le n$. By verifying all the conditions of a PDM we immediately get the next corollary.

Corollary 5.3. The triplet ($\mathcal{P}$, $\mathcal{D}$, d) is a PDM with degree n.

The PDM defined above is illustrated in Figure 9 for n=2.

Now, let < $\mathcal{P}$, $\mathcal{D}$, d > be the n-manifold corresponding to ($\mathcal{P}$, $\mathcal{D}$,d) and let $\mathcal{K}$ be defined as in (5.2), i.e.,

$$\mathcal{K} = \{A(T) \times Y(T) \times \mathbb{R}_+ \mid T \subset I_{n+1},\ |T| \le n\}.$$

Notice that $\partial\mathcal{K} = \{A(T) \times Y(T) \times \{0\} \mid T \subset I_{n+1},\ |T| \le n\}$. To define a PC^1 function h on $\mathcal{K}$ we extend the function z to a continuously differentiable function from U^n to $\mathbb{R}^{n+1}$. Then we define the function h: $|\ \mathcal{K}\ | \to \mathbb{R}^{n+1}$ by

$$h(p,y,t) = y - t\,\bar{z}(p) \qquad (p,y,t) \in |\ \mathcal{K}\ |, \tag{5.3}$$

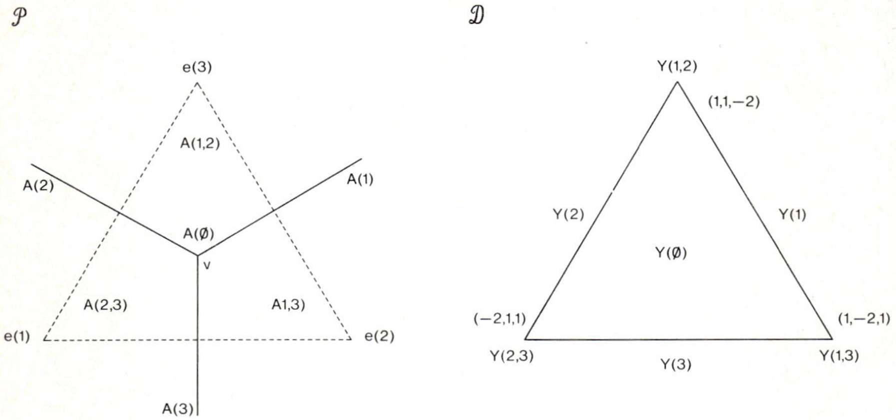

FIGURE 9
The PDM induced by the (n+1)-ray algorithm on minimal excess demands, n=2. The sets A({i}), A({i,j}), Y({i}), Y({i,j}) are denoted by A(i), A(i,j), Y(i) and Y(i,j), $1 \le i \ne j \le 3$.

where $\bar{z}_j(p) = z^m(p) - z_j(p)$, $j = 1,\ldots,n+1$, with $z^m(p) = (n+1)^{-1}\Sigma_{j=1}^{n+1} z_j(p)$ being the average excess demand. Since y lies in Y_0 and therefore in Q^n and since by definition $\Sigma_{j=1}^{n+1} \bar{z}_j(p) = 0$, implying that $t\bar{z}(p)$ also lies in Q^n, h is a PC^1 function from the (n+1)-manifold $|\mathcal{K}|$ to the n-dimensional linear subspace Q^n. Therefore, we may apply Theorem 5.2 to obtain the next corollary.

Corollary 5.4. If z is a continuously differentiable function and if 0 is a regular value of the function h defined in (5.3), then $h^{-1}(0)$ consists of piecewise smooth loops and paths having 0, 1 or 2 end points, each of them lying in $|\partial \mathcal{K}|$.

Lemma 5.5. The intersection of $h^{-1}(0)$ and $|\partial \mathcal{K}|$ consists of the single point (v,0,0).

Proof. Since $|\partial \mathcal{K}| = |\mathcal{L}| \times \{0\}$ we must have t=0 for any end point (p,y,t). Then (5.3) implies $y = t\,\bar{z}(p) = 0$ so that y lies in the interior of $Y(\emptyset)$. Hence, $p \in A(\emptyset) = \{v\}$, i.e. p=v, which proves the lemma.

□

The lemma says that the point $(v,0,0)$ is the only end point of a path in $h^{-1}(0)$ so that this path is a semi-closed unbounded path, whereas all other paths in $h^{-1}(0)$, if any, are open and unbounded, according to Theorem 5.2. The path in $h^{-1}(0)$ having the point $(v,0,0)$ as end point will be denoted by P. Observe that $|\mathcal{K}|$ is indeed closed. Consequently, the path P goes to infinity in at least one of the $2(n+1)+1$ components of (p,y,t).

Lemma 5.6. If the point (p,y,t) belongs to $h^{-1}(0)$ then $p \notin \text{bd } S^n$.

Proof. Suppose that p lies in bd S^n for some (p,y,t) in $h^{-1}(0)$. Since v lies in the interior of S^n and $A(\emptyset) = v$, there must exist a nonempty subset T of I_{n+1} such that $p \in A(T)$. Moreover, $p_j = 0$ implies $j \in T$. Since $y \in Y(T)$ we have according to (5.3)

$$z_h(p) = z^m(p) - 1/t \qquad \text{for all } h \in T$$

and

$$z_h(p) \geq z^m(p) - 1/t \qquad \text{for all } h \notin T,$$

so that, for all $h \in T$, $z_h(p) = \min_k z_k(p) \leq 0$. However, $p_j = 0$ implies $z_j(p) \geq 0$, and hence $z_h(p) = \min_k z_k(p) = 0$, for all $h \in T$. Since $p_j > 0$ for all $j \notin T$, this implies $z(p) = 0$ and so $y = t\bar{z}(p) = 0$ which contradicts the fact that T is nonempty and therefore at least one y_j is equal to one.

□

From this lemma it follows that no path in $h^{-1}(0)$ can cross bd S^n. Therefore, and because the point v lies inside S^n, the path P in $h^{-1}(0)$ which originates in the point $(v,0,0)$ must stay in the compact set S^n in the components of p and in the compact set Y_0 in the components of y. Consequently, along the unbounded semi-closed path P the variable t must go to infinity whereas (p,y) converges to a limit point (p^*, y^*). However, $h(p,y,t) = 0$ implies

$$\bar{z}_j(p) = y_j/t \leq 1/t \qquad \text{for all } j$$

so that if t goes to infinity $\bar{z}_j(p^*) \leq 0$, $j \in I_{n+1}$, and hence $z(p^*) = 0$. The path P therefore approaches a limit point $(p^* y^*)$ in $S^n \times Y_0$ with $z(p^*) = 0$ when t goes to infinity, i.e., P leads from the point (v,0,0) to an equilibrium point. We now prove that if the point (p,y,t) lies in $h^{-1}(0)$ and $p \in S^n$, then p lies in the set B defined in Section 3.

Theorem 5.7. Let (p,y,t) be a point in $h^{-1}(0)$ with $p \in S^n$, then there is a $T \subset I_{n+1}$, $|T| \leq n$, such that

$$p \in B(T) = A(T) \cap C(T).$$

Proof. Since $(p,y,t) \in |\mathcal{K}|$, there is a $T \subset I_{n+1}$, $|T| \leq n$, such that $p \in A(T)$ and $y \in Y(T)$. Consequently, since $y = t\bar{z}(p)$,

$$z_j(p) = z^m(p) - 1/t \qquad \text{for all } j \in T$$

and

$$z_j(p) \geq z^m(p) - 1/t \qquad \text{for all } j \notin T,$$

implying that $z_j(p) = \min_h z_h(p)$ for all $j \in T$. Hence $p \in C(T) \cap A(T)$.

□

Note that we allow T to be empty in which case $p = v \in A(\emptyset)$, $0 \leq t \leq (\max_h \bar{z}_h(v))^{-1}$ and $y = t\bar{z}(v) \in Y_0$. From Theorem 5.7 it follows that along the path P in $h^{-1}(0)$, starting in (v,0,0), a path of prices p in B is traced. The latter path starts in v, leads to an equilibrium price p^*, and is the primal projection of the path P in $|\mathcal{K}|$. With primal and dual projection of (a path in) $h^{-1}(0)$ we mean the set of points $\{p \in S^n | (p,y,t) \in h^{-1}(0)\}$ and $\{y \in Y_0 | (p,y,t) \in h^{-1}(0)\}$ respectively.

Corollary 5.8. The set B is the primal projection of $h^{-1}(0)$ and contains a path of prices leading from v to an equilibrium point p^*. This path is the primal projection of the path P. Moreover, any path or loop in $h^{-1}(0)$ corresponds to a path with two end points or a loop in B, being its primal projection.

We implicitly assume that the point v is not an equilibrium. Moreover, since v lies in the interior of S^n, the regularity assumption on h implies that $z(v) \neq 0$. However, if $z(v) = 0$, then the path P still exists and is equal to the ray $\{(v,0,t) | t \geq 0\}$, having the point v as primal projection. In case $z(v) \neq 0$, along the path P starting in $(v,0,0)$ first y_j is increased from 0 to 1 with j the index for which the excess demand is minimal. Simultaneously t is increased from 0 to $(\bar{z}_j(v))^{-1}$ to keep $y_j - t\bar{z}_j(v)$ equal to zero while for $i \neq j$ the component y_i is kept equal to $t\bar{z}_i(v)$. In this way, a (linear) path in $A(\emptyset) \times Y(\emptyset) \times \mathbb{R}_+$ is traced from $(v,0,0)$ to the point $(v,\bar{z}(v)/\bar{z}_j(v), 1/\bar{z}_j(v))$ in $A(\{j\}) \times Y(\{j\}) \times \mathbb{R}_+$. Then the path P smoothly continues in $A(\{j\}) \times Y(\{j\}) \times \mathbb{R}_+$ keeping y_j equal to 1 and t equal $(\bar{z}_j(p))^{-1}$, until a point (p,y,t) is reached for which $z_i(p)$ becomes equal to $z_j(p) = \min_h z_h(p)$ for some $i \neq j$, and so $y_i = y_j = 1$. Then the path P continues in $A(\{i,j\}) \times Y(\{i,j\}) \times \mathbb{R}_+$ keeping y_i and y_j equal to one and t equal $(\bar{z}_j(p))^{-1} = (\bar{z}_i(p))^{-1}$. In general, the path P in $h^{-1}(0)$ traces in $A(T) \times Y(T) \times \mathbb{R}_+$, for various $T \subset I_{n+1}$, a smooth path of points (p,y,t) such that $y_j = 1$ for all $j \in T$ and $y_i < 1$ for all $i \notin T$. So $t\bar{z}_j(p) = 1$ for all $j \in T$ and $t\bar{z}_i(p) < 1$ for all $i \notin T$, implying that $\bar{z}_j(p) = \max_h \bar{z}_h(p)$, $j \in T$, while $t = (\max_h \bar{z}_h(p))^{-1}$. When $|T| < n$, an end point in $A(T) \times Y(T) \times \mathbb{R}_+$ is reached if either y_h becomes equal to 1 for some $h \notin T$ or p lies in $A(T\backslash\{k\})$ for some $k \in T$. In the first case the path P continues in $A(T \cup \{h\}) \times Y(T \cup \{h\}) \times \mathbb{R}_+$ keeping y_h equal to 1 whereas in the second case P continues in $A(T\backslash\{k\}) \times Y(T\backslash\{k\}) \times \mathbb{R}_+$ by decreasing y_k away from 1. The second case can also occur when $|T| = n$, in which case the parameter t can also go to infinity, yielding an equilibrium point. Notice that if $|T| = n$, then $y_j = -n$ for the unique index j not in T, whereas $y_i = 1$ for all $i \neq j$. The path P in $h^{-1}(0)$ is illustrated in Figure 10 for n=2. In this figure the path P lies in $A(T) \times Y(T) \times \mathbb{R}_+$ for subsequently $T = \emptyset$, $\{2\}$, $\{1,2\}$, $\{1\}$ and $\{1,3\}$. When $T = \{1,2\}$ or $\{1,3\}$, the vector y on the path P is equal to $(1,1,-2)^\top$ and $(1,-2,1)^\top$ respectively.

The proof of the existence of the path in the set B' from v to an equilibrium point is very similar to the proof given above. We only need to replace the function h from $|\mathcal{K}|$ to Q^n by

$$h'(p,y,t) = y + t\bar{z}(p) \qquad (p,y,t) \in |\mathcal{K}|.$$

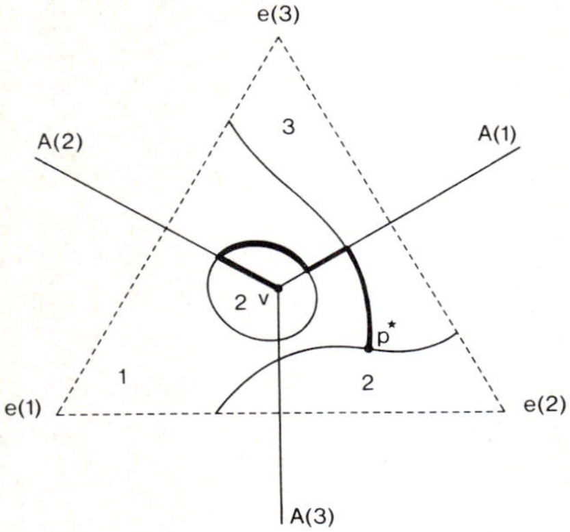

FIGURE 10a
The primal projection of P.

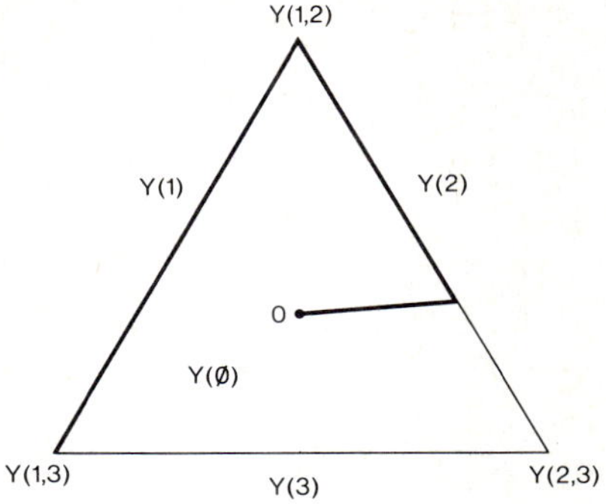

FIGURE 10b
The dual projection of P.

Then, again, if z is a continuously differentiable function and 0 is a regular value of h', there is a piecewise smooth path P' in $h'^{-1}(0)$ starting in (v,0,0) and approaching an equilibrium point for t going to infinity. Moreover, the set B' is the primal projection of the set $h'^{-1}(0)$ and the primal projection of the path P' on S^n is the path in B' which connects the point v with an equilibrium point p^*.

What remains to be proved is the existence of a path from v to an equilibrium point in S^n as described in Section 4. First we define the appropriate PDM and then a PC^1 mapping whose set of zero points yields the path. The primal subdivided n-manifold $\mathcal{P}$ of the PDM is completely determined by the n-dimensional cones A(s), s ∈ Ω. More precisely,

$$\mathcal{P} = \{A(s) | s \in \Omega \text{ and } |I(s)| = n-1\}$$

where

$$A(s) = \{p \in U^n | p_i/v_i = \min_h p_h/v_h \text{ for all } i \text{ with } s_i = -1$$

$$p_i/v_i = \max_h p_h/v_h \text{ for all } i \text{ with } s_i = +1\}.$$

Notice that $s \in \Omega$ and $|I(s)| = n-1$ imply that s is a sign vector in $\mathbb{R}^{n+1}$ with n-1 zero elements, one element equal to +1 and one element equal to -1, so that indeed $\dim A(s) = n$.

Clearly, the collection $\bar{\mathcal{P}}$ of faces of $\mathcal{P}$ is equal to

$$\bar{\mathcal{P}} = \{A(s) | s \in \Omega\} \cup A(\emptyset),$$

where $A(\emptyset) = \{v\}$. The dual subdivided n-manifold $\mathcal{D}$ consists of the n-cell $Y(\emptyset)$ defined by

$$Y(\emptyset) = \{y \in Q^n | \Sigma_j y_j^+ \leq 1\},$$

where, for $a \in R$, $a^+ = \max(0,a)$. Defining the sets $Y(s)$, $s \in \Omega$, by

$$\begin{aligned} Y(s) = \{y \in Q^n | & y_j \geq 0 \text{ if } s_j = +1,\ y_j = 0 \text{ if } s_j = 0, \\ & y_j \leq 0 \text{ if } s_j = -1,\ j = 1,\dots,n+1, \\ & \text{and } \sum_{\{j|s_j=+1\}} y_j = +1\} \end{aligned}$$

we conclude that $\bar{\mathcal{D}} = \{Y(s) | s \in \Omega^0\}$ where $\Omega^0 = \Omega \cup \{\emptyset\}$. Each $Y(s)$, $s \in \Omega$, is an $(n - |I(s)| - 1)$-dimensional face of $Y(\emptyset)$, whereas each $A(s)$, $s \in \Omega$, is an $(|I(s)| + 1)$-dimensional cone in U^n so that, for all $s \in \Omega^0$, $\dim A(s) + \dim Y(s) = n$. Clearly, the triplet $(\mathcal{P}, \mathcal{D}, d)$ is a PDM with degree n and the dual operator d defined by

$$A^d(s) = Y(s) \text{ and } Y^d(s) = A(s) \text{ for all } s \in \Omega^0.$$

The PDM is pictured in Figure 11. Recall that the number of one-dimensional cones A(s) is equal to $2^{n+1} - 2$.

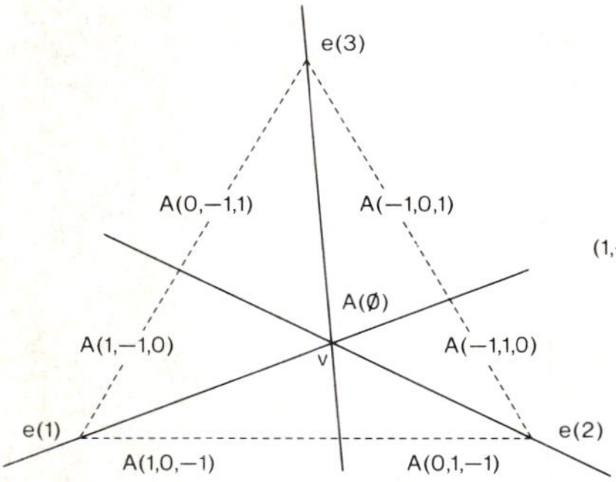

FIGURE 11a

The collection $\bar{\mathcal{P}}$.

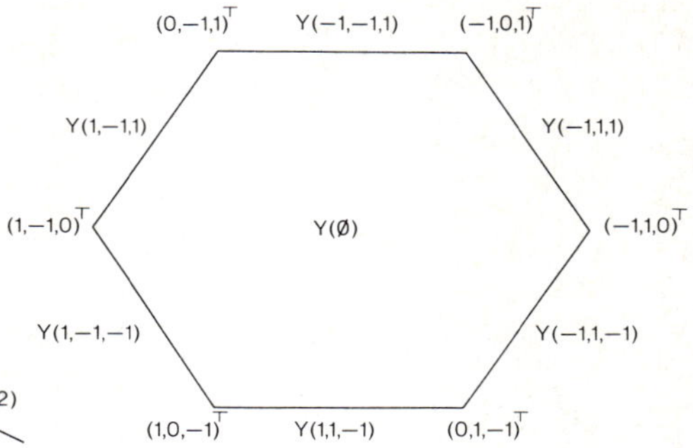

FIGURE 11b

The collection $\bar{\mathcal{D}}$.

Again the collection $\mathcal{L} = \{X \times X^d | X \in \bar{\mathcal{P}}\}$ of n-cells is a subdivided n-manifold with empty boundary and $|\mathcal{L}|$ closed. Furthermore, the collection $\mathcal{K} = \{Z \times \mathbb{R}_+ | Z \in \mathcal{L}\}$ is a subdivided (n+1)-manifold with

$$\partial \mathcal{K} = \{A(s) \times Y(s) \times \{0\} | s \in \Omega^0\}.$$

With z again extended to a continuously (differentiable) function from U^n to $\mathbb{R}^{n+1}$, we define the function $g\colon |\mathcal{K}| \to \mathbb{R}^{n+1}$ by

$$g(p,y,t) = y - t[p.z(p)] \qquad (p,y,t) \in |\mathcal{K}|, \tag{5.4}$$

where $p.z(p) = (p_1z_1(p), p_2z_2(p),\ldots,p_{n+1}z_{n+1}(p))^{\top}$, $p \in U^n$. Since $p^{\top}z(p) = 0$ the result is that $\Sigma_j[p.z(p)]_j = \Sigma_j p_j z_j(p) = 0$. Hence, g is a PC^1 mapping from $|\mathcal{K}|$ to Q^n if z is a continuously differentiable function from U^n to $\mathbb{R}^{n+1}$. If 0 is a regular value of g, $g^{-1}(0)$ consists, according to Theorem 5.2, of a disjoint union of piecewise smooth loops and paths. Furthermore, analogous to Lemma 5.5, the point (v,0,0) is the only end point of a path in $g^{-1}(0)$ so that this path, denoted by G, is a semiclosed unbounded path, whereas all other paths in $g^{-1}(0)$ are unbounded and open.

Lemma 5.9. For all (p,y,t) in $g^{-1}(0)$, $p \notin \text{bd } S^n$.

Proof. Suppose that p lies in the boundary of S^n. Then there is an s in Ω^0 with $p \in A(s)$ and $y \in Y(s)$. Since $p \neq v$ we must have $s \in \Omega$. Moreover, $p \in \text{bd } S^n$ and $p \in A(s)$ imply that $p_j = 0$ for all j with $s_j = -1$ and that $p_j > 0$ for all j with $s_j = +1$. However, this implies $z_j(p) = 0$ for all j because $p^T z(p) = 0$, sgn $z(p) = s$ and $z_j(p) \geq 0$ if $p_j = 0$. Therefore, since $g(p,y,t) = y-t[p.z(p)] = 0$, we also have $y = 0$, i.e. y lies in the interior of $Y(\emptyset)$ and in no $Y(s')$, $s' \in \Omega$. This contradicts the fact that $s \in \Omega$.

□

The lemma says that the paths in $g^{-1}(0)$ cannot cross bd S^n. Since both S^n and $Y(\emptyset)$ are compact, it follows that along the path G in $g^{-1}(0)$ originating in (v,0,0) the variable t goes to infinity and that (p,y) goes to a limit point (p^*,y^*) in $|\mathcal{L}|$. According to (5.4)

$$p_j^* z_j(p^*) = 0 \qquad \text{for } j = 1,\ldots,n+1.$$

This implies that, for all j, $p_j^* = 0$ or $z_j(p^*) = 0$. If we let s^* be the sign vector in Ω with the smallest number of nonzero elements such that p^* lies in $A(s^*)$, then $p_j^* = 0$ implies that $s_j^* = -1$ and therefore $z_j(p^*) \leq 0$. However, $p_j^* = 0$ also implies $z_j(p^*) \geq 0$. Hence, $z_j(p^*) = 0$ for all $j = 1,\ldots,n+1$. Consequently, the path G in $g^{-1}(0)$ starting at (v,0,0) leads, for t going to infinity, to an equilibrium point p^* in S^n. Moreover, as will be shown in the next theorem the set B, being the union of all sets B(s), $s \in \Omega$, is the primal projection of $g^{-1}(0)$.

Theorem 5.10. Let (p,y,t) be a point in $g^{-1}(0)$ such that p lies in S^n. There is an $s \in \Omega$ such that

$$p \in B(s) = A(s) \cap C(s).$$

Proof. Since $(p,y,t) \in g^{-1}(0)$ there is an element s in Ω^0 such that

$$p \in A(s) \text{ and } y \in A^d(s) = Y(s).$$

If $p = v$, then p lies in $B(s^0)$ with $s^0 = \text{sgn } z(v) \in \Omega$. So, suppose $p \neq v$, so that $s \in \Omega$. Then $p_j z_j(p) = 0$ if $s_j = 0$,

$$p_j z_j(p) = y_j/t \geq 0 \qquad \text{when } s_j = +1$$

and

$$p_j z_j(p) = y_j/t \leq 0 \qquad \text{when } s_j = -1.$$

From Lemma 5.9 we know that $p \notin \text{bd } S^n$, so that $p_j > 0$ for all j. Therefore, $\text{sgn } p_j z_j(p) = \text{sgn } z_j(p)$, $j = 1,\ldots,n+1$, and so p lies in C(s).

□

Corollary 5.11. The union B of B(s), over all s in Ω, contains a path of points in S^n going from v to an equilibrium point p^*. This path is the primal projection of the path G in $g^{-1}(0)$.

Since for a point (p,y,t) in $g^{-1}(0)$ we have that

$$t \sum_{j=1}^{n+1} (p_j z_j(p))^+ = \sum_{j=1}^{n+1} y_j^+ = 1,$$

it follows that the homotopy-parameter t in (5.4) is equal to

$$t = (\Sigma_{j=1}^{n+1} p_j z_j^+(p))^{-1}.$$

When $p = v$, then $(p,y,t) \in G$ for all t, $0 \leq t \leq (\Sigma_{j=1}^{n+1} v_j z_j^+(v))^{-1}$, and $y = tv.z(v) \in Y(\emptyset)$. If $t = (\Sigma_{j+1}^{n+1} v_j z_j^+(v))^{-1}$, then $(v,y,t) \in G$ with

$$y = v.z(v)/\Sigma_{j=1}^{n+1} v_j z_j^+(v) \in Y(s^0),$$

where s^0 is equal to sgn z(v). Notice that we assume that s^0 does not contain any zero. In the case $z(v) = 0$ the path G is the ray $\{(v,0,t)|t \geq$

0}. The primal and dual projection of the path G are illustrated in Figure 12. The sequence of sign vectors s, $s \in \Omega$, for which G passes $A(s) \times Y(s) \times \mathbb{R}_+$ is $(1,-1,1)^T, (1,-1,0)^T$, $(1,-1,-1)^T$ and $(1,0,-1)^T$. When p is equal to v, y goes from the point 0 to b, while p goes from v to w if y goes from b to c. Notice that the point b is equal to

$$b = v.z(v)/(v_1 z_1(v) + v_3 z_3(v)) \in Y(1,-1,1)$$

and that $c = (1,-1,0)^T$. When p goes from w to u, y is equal to c and $z_3(p) = 0$. Finally, p goes from u to q if y goes from c to d and y = d if p goes from q to the equilibrium point p^*.

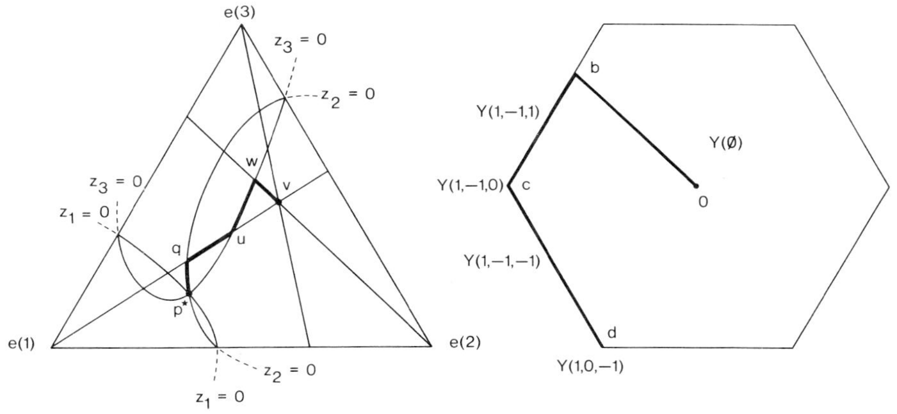

FIGURE 12a
The primal projection of G.

FIGURE 12b
The dual projection of G.

Finally, it is to be noted that the theory above can easily be generalized when we allow v to lie on the boundary of S^n or when we drop the condition that $p_j = 0$ implies $z_j(p) \geq 0$. In the latter case a path of points can be shown to exist from v to a point p^* for which $z(p^*) \leq 0$.

REFERENCES

[1] K. Arrow and F. Hahn, *General competitive analysis*, Holden-Day, San Francisco, 1972.

[2] G. Debreu, "Excess demand functions", *Journal of Mathematical Economics* 1 (1974) 15-23.

[3] T.M. Doup and A.J.J. Talman, "A new variable dimension simplicial algorithm to find equilibria on the product space of unit simplices", Research Memorandum 146, Tilburg University, Tilburg, The Netherlands, 1984, to appear in Mathematical Programming.

[4] T.M. Doup, G. van der Laan and A.J.J. Talman, "The $(2^{n+1}-2)$-ray algorithm: a new simplicial algorithm to compute economic equilibria", Research Report 132, Free University, Amsterdam, The Netherlands, 1984, to appear in Mathematical Programming.

[5] J. Drèze, "Existence of an exchange equilibrium under price rigidities", *International Economic Review* 16 (1975) 301-320.

[6] D. Keenan, "Further remarks on the global Newton method", *Journal of Mathematical Economics* 8 (1981) 159-166.

[7] B. Knaster, C. Kuratowski and S. Mazurkiewicz, "Ein Beweis des Fixpunkt Satzes für n-dimensionale Simplexe", *Fundamenta Mathematicae* 14 (1929) 132-137.

[8] M. Kojima and Y. Yamamoto, "Variable dimension algorithms: basic theory, interpretations and extensions of some methods", *Mathematical Programming* 24 (1982) 177-215.

[9] M. Kojima and Y. Yamamoto, "A unified approach to the implementation of several restart fixed point algorithms and a new variable dimension algorithm", *Mathematical Programming* 28 (1984) 288-328.

[10] H.W. Kuhn and J.G. MacKinnon, "Sandwich method for finding fixed points", *Journal of Optimization Theory and Applications* 17 (1975) 189-204.

[11] M. Kurz, "Unemployment equilibrium in an economy with linked prices", *Journal of Economic Theory* 26 (1982) 100-123.

[12] G. van der Laan, with the collaboration of A.J.J. Talman, *Simplicial fixed point algorithms*, Mathematical Centre Tracts 129, Mathematisch Centrum, Amsterdam, 1980.

[13] G. van der Laan, "Equilibrium under rigid prices with compensation for the consumers", *International Economic Review* 21 (1980) 63-73.

[14] G. van der Laan, "Simplicial approximation of unemployment equilibria", *Journal of Mathematical Economics* 9 (1982) 83-97.

[15] G. van der Laan and A.J.J. Talman, "A restart algorithm for computing fixed points without an extra dimension", *Mathematical Programming* 17 (1979) 74-84.

[16] G. van der Laan and A.J.J. Talman, "An improvement of fixed point algorithms by using a good triangulation", *Mathematical Programming* 18 (1980) 274-285.

[17] O.H. Merrill, "Applications and extensions of an algorithm that computes fixed points of certain upper semi-continuous point to set mappings", Ph.D. Dissertation, University of Michigan, Ann Arbor, MI, USA, 1971.

[18] D.G. Saari and C.P. Simon, "Effective price mechanisms", *Econometrica* 46 (1978) 1097-1125.

[19] H. Scarf, "Some examples of global instability of the competitive equilibrium", *International Economic Review* 1 (1960) 157-172.

[20] H. Scarf, "The approximation of fixed points of a continuous mapping", *SIAM Journal of Applied Mathematics* 15 (1967) 1328-1343.

[21] H. Scarf, *The computation of economic equilibria,* Yale University Press, New Haven, 1973.
[22] S. Smale, "A convergent process of price adjustment and global Newton methods", *Journal of Mathematical Economics* 3 (1976) 107-120.
[23] H. Sonnenschein, "Market excess demand functions", *Econometrica* 40 (1972) 549-563.
[24] M.J. Todd, *The computation of fixed points and applications,* Springer, Berlin, 1976.

The Computation and Modelling of Economic Equilibria
A.J.J. Talman, G. van der Laan (Editors)

SIMPLICIAL ALGORITHMS FOR SOLVING THE NONLINEAR COMPLEMENTARITY PROBLEM ON THE SIMPLOTOPE*

T.M. DOUP**

A.H. van den ELZEN***

A.J.J. TALMAN

Department of Econometrics, Tilburg University, P.O. Box 90153, 5000 LE Tilburg, The Netherlands

Interesting problems like the search for a Nash equilibrium strategy vector in a noncooperative game or a price equilibrium vector in an international trade model can be formulated as a nonlinear complementarity problem on the simplotope. In this paper we present a new variable dimension simplicial algorithm for solving this problem. This algorithm, called the exponent-ray algorithm, can start anywhere and finds an approximate solution by generating a sequence of simplices of varying dimension.
The exponent-ray algorithm differs from existing algorithms, the sum- and the product-ray algorithm, in the number of rays along which it can leave the starting point. However, the main difference among the algorithms lies in their interpretation as adjustment procedures. Characteristic for the exponent-ray algorithm is that it considers all the components of the current function value (simultaneously) whereas the other two algorithms only consider part of these components. The exponent-ray algorithm seems to be very interesting for economic applications because its behaviour then reveals the structure of a market in which prices are adjusted simultaneously.
The examples considered concern the problems of finding equilibria in noncooperative games and in international trade economies. Computational results show that in case of the international trade economies the exponent-ray algorithm performs better than the sum-

---

* This research is part of the VF-program "Equilibrium and disequilibrium in demand and supply", which has been approved by the Netherlands Ministry of Education and Sciences.

** This author is financially supported by the Netherlands Organization for the advancement of pure research (Z.W.O.), Grant 46-98.

*** This author is financially supported by the Co-operation Centre Tilburg and Eindhoven Universities, The Netherlands.

ray algorithm and is competitive to the product-ray algorithm. In case of noncooperative games the product-ray algorithm performs best.

1. INTRODUCTION

We consider the nonlinear complementarity problem (NLCP) with respect to (w.r.t) a function z on the simplotope. A simplotope is the product space of, say N, unit simplices S^{n_j}, where for j = 1,...,N,

$$S^{n_j} = \{x_j \in \mathbb{R}_+^{n_j+1} \mid \Sigma_{k=1}^{n_j+1} x_{jk} = 1\}$$

is the n_j-dimensional unit simplex. Let S be the simplotope $\Pi_{j=1}^N S^{n_j}$, then an element x in S is denoted by $x = (x_1,\ldots,x_N)$ with $x_j \in S^{n_j}$, j = 1,...,N. Let $z : S \to \Pi_{j=1}^N \mathbb{R}^{n_j+1}$ be a continuous function with z(x), denoted by $z(x) = (z_1(x),\ldots,z_N(x))$ with $z_j(x) \in \mathbb{R}^{n_j+1}$, such that z satisfies $x_j^T z_j(x) = 0$ for all x in S and j = 1,...,N. The nonlinear complementarity problem on S w.r.t. z consists of finding a vector x^* in S such that $z_j(x^*) \leq 0$ for all $j \in I_N := \{1,\ldots,N\}$, also denoted by $z(x^*) \leq 0$. Observe that such a solution point x^* satisfies the complementarity condition $x^*_{jk} z_{jk}(x^*) = 0$ for all indices (j,k).

Some interesting problems can be stated in such a form. First we mention the problem of finding a Nash equilibrium in a noncooperative N-person game. In this context S is the mixed strategy space of the game and z_j is the expected excess profit function for player j, j = 1,...,N. A solution of this NLCP gives a Nash equilibrium strategy vector of the game. Another example concerns the search for equilibrium prices in an international trade model with domestic goods, traded within only one country, and internationally traded common goods. The formulation of such a problem as an NLCP on S with respect to a continuous function is shown in van der Laan [7]. Again, a solution to that NLCP on S induces equilibrium prices for the economy. A special case of the NLCP on S is the case when N = 1. The equilibrium price problem in a pure exchange economy can be modelled as an NLCP on one unit simplex. The unit simplex is then interpreted as the price space of the economy, whereas the function z is the excess-demand function of the economy.

Both for the NLCP on S and the NLCP on S^n, variable dimension simplicial restart algorithms have been developed to approximate a solution.

These algorithms generate in a simplicial subdivision of S (or S^n), starting from an arbitrary grid point, a sequence of adjacent simplices of varying dimension which terminates with a simplex that approximates a solution. Improvements of the accuracy of the approximation are obtained by decreasing the mesh of the underlying triangulation and restarting the algorithm in the approximation.

For solving the NLCP on S^n there are the algorithms of van der Laan, Talman and Van der Heyden [11] (see also [8]), Doup and Talman [1], and Doup, van der Laan and Talman [3]. These algorithms differ from each other in the number and in the direction of the rays along which the starting point can be left. In the algorithm on S^n of [11] there are n+1 rays, one to each facet of S^n. Also in the algorithm in [1] there are n+1 rays, but now one to each vertex of S^n, while for the exponent-ray algorithm in [3] there are $2^{n+1}-2$ rays, one to each face of the unit simplex.

In van der Laan and Talman [10] several convergent adjustment processes for solving the NLCP on the unit simplex were described. Each of these processes is related to one of the algorithms mentioned above in the sense that the path generated by each process can be followed arbitrarily close with the corresponding algorithm by taking the mesh of the triangulation small enough. In [10] it is shown that these processes have an attractive economic interpretation when applied to the problem of finding equilibrium prices in a pure exchange economy.

The algorithms on S^n of both van der Laan and Talman [8] and Doup and Talman [1] were generalized for applications on the simplotope. The algorithm on S^n in [8] was generalized to a simplicial variable dimension algorithm on S with $\Sigma_{j=1}^{N}(n_j+1)$ rays to leave the arbitrary starting point. This sum-ray algorithm on S was introduced in [9] and was adapted in [11] for a more general applicability. The algorithm on S^n in [1] was generalized in the same paper to the product-ray algorithm on S with $\Pi_{j=1}^{N}(n_j+1)$ rays. The names of the algorithms are derived from the respective number of rays along which one can leave the starting point. The adjustment processes induced by the sum- and the product-ray algorithm on S were described in van den Elzen, van der Laan and Talman [6]. In that paper also a third process, which can be considered as the generalization of the exponent-process on S^n, was given. In this exponent-process on S there are $\Pi_{j=1}^{N}(2^{n_j+1}-2)$ rays to leave an arbitrarily chosen (interior) initial point. As argued in [4], the latter process has a very attractive interpretation as a price-adjustment process when applied to find equilibria in an economy.

In this paper, we present a new simplicial variable dimension restart algorithm whose sequence of adjacent simplices of varying dimension follows approximately the path of the exponent-process on S. Therefore, we call this algorithm the exponent-ray algorithm. The V-triangulation of S developed in [1] in order to underly the product-ray algorithm on S, will also underly the new algorithm. In this new algorithm there are an exponential number of rays to leave the starting point.

The paper is organized as follows. In Section 2 the piecewise linear path traced by the new algorithm, is described. This description gives insight in the relationship between the exponent-ray algorithm and the corresponding process. It appears that the algorithm can be interpreted as the exponent-process applied to the piecewise linear approximation of the continuous function z with respect to the V-triangulation. The steps of the algorithm are presented in Section 3. Finally, in Section 4 some computational results are given. The examples concern both international economies and noncooperative games. The results indicate that the exponent-ray algorithm is competitive with the product-ray algorithm and better than the sum-ray algorithm for the economic applications. For the noncooperative games the product-ray algorithm seems to be the most attractive algorithm.
We refer the reader to an earlier version of this paper [2] for a detailed description of the product-ray and the sum-ray algorithm.

2. THE PATH GENERATED BY THE EXPONENT-RAY ALGORITHM

The exponent-ray algorithm generates a piecewise linear (p.l.) path of points which can be seen as a piecewise linearization of the piecewise smooth path of the exponent-process. As described in [6], the exponent-process on S follows, when applied to an NLCP on S with respect to a function z, from an arbitrarily chosen starting point v in S, a path of points x in S satisfying for certain β, $0 \le \beta \le 1$, and certain numbers $\alpha_j \ge 0$, $j \in I_N$,

$$
\begin{aligned}
&x_{jk} = (1+\alpha_j)v_{jk} && \text{if } z_{jk}(x) > 0 \text{ and } v_{jk} > 0 \\
&x_{jk} = \alpha_j && \text{if } z_{jk}(x) > 0 \text{ and } v_{jk} = 0 \\
&\beta v_{jk} \le x_{jk} \le (1+\alpha_j)v_{jk} && \text{if } z_{jk}(x) = 0 \text{ and } v_{jk} > 0 \qquad (2.1) \\
&0 \le x_{jk} \le \alpha_j && \text{if } z_{jk}(x) = 0 \text{ and } v_{jk} = 0 \\
&x_{jk} = \beta v_{jk} && \text{if } z_{jk}(x) < 0.
\end{aligned}
$$

When the function z is continuously differentiable and some regularity condition is satisfied, then the set of points satisfying (2.1) consists of piecewise smooth paths and loops, one path connecting v with a solution of the NLCP w.r.t. z. The latter path, P, is the path followed by the exponent-process.

At a point x on the path P, x_{jk}/v_{jk} is equal to some number $1+\alpha_j$ larger than 1, for all those indices (j,k) for which $z_{jk}(x) > 0$ and $v_{jk} > 0$. When $z_{jk}(x) > 0$ but $v_{jk} = 0$, then x_{jk} is equal to α_j. Furthermore, x_{jk}/v_{jk} is equal to some number β smaller than 1 when $z_{jk}(x) < 0$ and $v_{jk} > 0$, while $x_{jk} = 0$ when $z_{jk}(x) < 0$ and $v_{jk} = 0$. Finally, when $z_{jk}(x) = 0$, x_{jk}/v_{jk} lies between β and $1+\alpha_j$ if $v_{jk} > 0$, and x_{jk} lies between 0 and α_j if $v_{jk} = 0$.

Observe that v satisfies (2.1) with $\beta=1$ and $\alpha_j=0$, j = 1,...,N. The path P leaves v by decreasing β from 1 and increasing the α_j's in order to keep the x_j's in S^{n_j}. So, the exponent-process which follows the path P from v, initially increases at x=v all the x_{jk}'s for which $z_{jk}(v) > 0$. For each j this increase is proportional if $v_{jk} > 0$ and absolute if $v_{jk} = 0$. On the other hand all the x_{jk}'s for which $z_{jk}(v) < 0$ are, at x = v, proportionally decreased. In an economic context, where x represents a price vector and z(x) the corresponding excess demand vector, such an (initial) adjustment is intuitively very appealing.

In order to follow the piecewise smooth path P of the exponent-process we propose a variable dimension (restart) algorithm which traces from v the piecewise linear path $\bar{P}$ of points x, in principle satisfying (2.1) with z replaced by its piecewise linear approximation (p.l.a.) $\bar{z}$. Therefore, we call this algorithm the exponent-ray algorithm. As will be shown

$\bar{P}$ exists in general and can be followed by alternating replacement steps in a triangulation and pivot steps in a linear system.

In order to describe the path $\bar{P}$ of the algorithm we need the notion of a sign vector. Let $I(j)$, $j \in I_N$, denote the index set $\{(j,1),\dots,(j,n_j+1)\}$ and let $I = \cup_{j=1}^{N} I(j)$. We call $s = (s_1,\dots,s_N)$ with $s_j = (s_{j1},\dots,s_{jn_j+1})^T$, $j \in I_N$, a sign vector in $\Pi_{j=1}^{N} \mathbb{R}^{n_j+1}$ if $s_{jk} \in \{-1,0,+1\}$ for all (j,k) in I. For a sign vector s we define the subsets $I_j^+(s)$, $I_j^0(s)$, and $I_j^-(s)$ of $I(j)$ by $I_j^+(s) = \{(j,h) \in I(j) \mid s_{jh} = +1\}$, $I_j^0(s) = \{(j,h) \in I(j) \mid s_{jh} = 0\}$, and $I_j^-(s) = \{(j,h) \in I(j) \mid s_{jh} = -1\}$, and accordingly $I^+(s)$, $I^0(s)$, and $I^-(s)$ as their respective union over all $j \in I_N$. The set Ω of feasible sign vectors is defined by

$$\Omega = \{s \in \Pi_{j=1}^{N} \mathbb{R}^{n_j+1} \mid s \text{ is a sign vector such that for all } j,\ I_j^+(s) \neq \emptyset \text{ or } V_j^c(v) \cap I_j^-(s) \neq \emptyset, \text{ while for at least one } k \in I_N \text{ both } I_k^+(s) \neq \emptyset \text{ and } I_k^-(s) \cap V_k^c(v) \neq \emptyset\},$$

where $V_j^c(v) = \{(j,h) \mid v_{jh} \neq 0\}$, $j \in I_N$.

For $s \in \Omega$ we define $A(s)$ and $\bar{C}(s)$ according to the left part and right part of (2.1) respectively, but related to the piecewise linear approximation $\bar{z}$ of z with respect to the underlying triangulation. More precisely, for $s \in \Omega$, we define

$$A(s) = \{x \in S \mid \begin{array}{ll} x_{jk} = (1+\alpha_j)v_{jk} & \text{if } s_{jk} = +1 \text{ and } v_{jk} > 0 \\ x_{jk} = \alpha_j & \text{if } s_{jk} = +1 \text{ and } v_{jk} = 0 \\ (\beta+\beta_j)v_{jk} \leq x_{jk} \leq (1+\alpha_j)v_{jk} & \text{if } s_{jk} = 0 \text{ and } v_{jk} > 0 \\ 0 \leq x_{jk} \leq \alpha_j & \text{if } s_{jk} = 0 \text{ and } v_{jk} = 0 \\ x_{jk} = (\beta+\beta_j)v_{jk} & \text{if } s_{jk} = -1, \end{array}$$

with for all $j \in I_N$, $0 \leq \beta \leq 1 \leq 1+\alpha_j$, $\beta_j \geq 0$, and $\beta_j = 0$ if $s_j \nleq 0\}$,

and

$$\bar{C}(s) = \text{cl}(\{x \in S \mid \text{sgn}\ \bar{z}_j(x) = s_j,\ j = 1,\ldots,N\})$$

where cl denotes the closure of a set and sgn is taken componentswise, i.e., $(\text{sgn}\ y)_i = \text{sign}\ y_i$ for all i.

Let $\bar{B}(s)$ be $A(s) \cap \bar{C}(s)$, $s \in \Omega$, and let $\bar{B}$ be the union of the $\bar{B}(s)$ over all sign vectors s in Ω. We prove that $\bar{B}$ consists of piecewise linear paths, one path being the path $\bar{P}$. More precisely, under some nondegeneracy assumption, each nonempty $\bar{B}(s)$, $s \in \Omega$, consists of piecewise linear loops and paths with two end points. The point v is the end point of exactly one p.l. path in $\bar{B}(s^0)$, where $s_j^0 = \text{sgn}\ z_j(v)$, $j \in I_N$, whereas each other end point of a path in $\bar{B}(s)$ is either an end point of a piecewise linear path in $\bar{B}(s')$ with s' different from s in one or two components or is an approximate solution of the NLCP. The path $\bar{P}$ consists of the sequence of linked piecewise linear paths in $\bar{B}(s)$ for varying s in Ω, starting in v with s equal to s^0. The exponent-ray algorithm describes how the path $\bar{P}$ can be followed by a sequence of adjacent simplices containing $\bar{P}$, through alternating replacement steps in a triangulation of A(s) and linear programming pivot steps in a linear system reflecting the fact that the points of the path also lie in $\bar{C}(s)$. Indeed, the underlying simplicial subdivision of S, i.e., the V-triangulation, is such that it triangulates each A(s), $s \in \Omega$.

The path $\bar{P}$ leads from v to a point $\bar{x}$ in S satisfying $\bar{z}_{jk}(\bar{x}) \le 0$ if $\bar{x}_{jk} = 0$, and for each j either $\bar{z}_{jk}(\bar{x}) \ge 0$ for all $\bar{x}_{jk} > 0$ or $\bar{z}_{jk}(\bar{x}) \le 0$ for all $\bar{x}_{jk} > 0$. Lemma 3.9 reveals that such a point $\bar{x}$ is indeed an approximate solution of the NLCP w.r.t. z. Notice that at the end point $\bar{x}$ of $\bar{P}$, $\bar{z}_{jk}(\bar{x})$ is in general not equal to zero for all (j,k) with $\bar{x}_{jk} > 0$, since $x_j^{\top}\bar{z}_j(x)$ might not be equal to zero, $j \in I_N$.

The description of the piecewise linear path $\bar{P}$ from v in terms of $\bar{z}$ is comparable to the description of P in terms of z. At x=v, the components x_{jk} for which $z_{jk}(v)$ is negative are relatively decreased with the same rate. The components x_{jk} at v with positive $z_{jk}(v)$ are increased. For each j these increases are relative if $v_{jk} > 0$ and absolute if $v_{jk} = 0$. Moreover, for each j the absolute increase is equal to the rate of the relative increase. If $v_{jk} = 1$ for some $(j,k) \in I(j)$, then x_j is initially not adapted when $z_j(v) \le 0$, whereas x_{jk} is decreased if $z_j(v) \nleq 0$.

In general $\bar{P}$ consists of points x in S such that the components x_{ih} of x for which $\bar{z}_{ih}(x) < 0$ and $\bar{z}_i(x) \nleq 0$, are relatively equal to each other and relatively smaller than all other components of x. If $\bar{z}_j(x) \leq 0$ for some j, then the components x_{jk} of x_j for which $\bar{z}_{jh}(x) < 0$ are also relatively equal to each other and relatively smaller than all other components of x_j. Furthermore, for each $j \in I_N$ the components x_{jk} of x_j with positive $z_{jk}(x)$ are relatively (or absolutely if $v_{jk} = 0$) equal to each other but relatively (absolutely) larger than the other components of x_j. The rate α_j with which these components x_{jk} of x_j with positive v_{jk} are larger than v_{jk} is equal to the value of those x_{jk}'s with v_{jk} equal to zero.

As soon as a point $\bar{x}$ is reached for which $\bar{z}_{jk}(\bar{x})$ is zero for some index (j,k) while $\bar{z}_{jk}(x)$ was negative, then $\bar{z}_{jk}(x)$ is kept equal to zero. Simultaneously, x_{jk} is relatively increased away from those x_{ih}'s with negative $z_{ih}(x)$ if $z_j(\bar{x}) \nleq 0$, while x_{jk} is relatively increased away from those x_{jh}'s with negative $\bar{z}_{jh}(x)$ if $\bar{z}_j(\bar{x}) \leq 0$ and for at least one index (j,h), $h \neq k$, $\bar{z}_{jh}(\bar{x}) < 0$ and $\bar{x}_{jh} > 0$. Finally, if $\bar{z}_{jh}(\bar{x}) = 0$ for all (j,h) with $\bar{x}_{jh} > 0$, then $\bar{z}_{j\ell}(x)$ is increased from zero for the index (j,ℓ) for which $x_{j\ell}$ is relatively (or absolutely if $v_{j\ell} = 0$) the largest component of $\bar{x}_j$. Observe that the latter two cases are different on the path P of the process because then $z_j(\bar{x}) \leq 0$ implies $z_{jh}(\bar{x}) = 0$ for all (j,h) with $x_{jh} > 0$. This is due to the fact that $x_j^{\top} z_j(x) = 0$ for all $x \in S$ and $j \in I_N$ whereas this property does not hold for $\bar{z}$.

When the path $\bar{P}$ reaches a point $\bar{x}$ for which $\bar{z}_{jk}(\bar{x})$ is zero for some index (j,k) while $\bar{z}_{jk}(x)$ was positive, then $\bar{z}_{jk}(x)$ is also kept equal to zero. Simultaneously, if $\bar{z}_j(\bar{x}) \nleq 0$ then x_{jk} is relatively (or absolutely if $v_{jk} = 0$) decreased away from the components x_{jh} of x_j having positive $\bar{z}_{jh}(x)$. If $\bar{z}_j(\bar{x}) \leq 0$ and $\bar{z}_{jh}(\bar{x}) < 0$ for at least one index (j,h) for which $\bar{x}_{jh} > 0$, then the x_{jh}'s for which $\bar{z}_{jh}(\bar{x}) < 0$ and $\bar{x}_{jh} > 0$ are relatively increased with the same rate. If, however, $\bar{z}_j(\bar{x}) \leq 0$ and $\bar{z}_{jh}(\bar{x}) = 0$ for all positive $\bar{x}_{jh}$, then the $\bar{z}_{jh}(x)$ is decreased from zero for the index (j,h) for which $\bar{x}_{jh}$ is the relatively smallest positive component of $\bar{x}_j$. The latter two cases are again due to the fact that $x_j^{\top}\bar{z}_j(x)$ is in general not equal to zero.

It can also occur that at a point $\bar{x}$ on the path $\bar{P}$ a component $\bar{x}_{jk}$ with $\bar{z}_{jk}(\bar{x}) = 0$ becomes relatively (or absolutely if $v_{jk} = 0$) equal to the $\bar{x}_{jh}$'s with positive $\bar{z}_{jh}(\bar{x})$. Then x_{jk} is kept relatively (absolutely) equal to the components x_{jh} of x_j with positive $\bar{z}_{jh}(x)$, and $\bar{z}_{jh}(x)$ is increased from zero. On the other hand, if $\bar{x}_{jk}$ with $\bar{z}_{jk}(\bar{x}) = 0$ becomes relatively equal to the $\bar{x}_{jh}$'s for which $\bar{z}_{jh}(\bar{x}) < 0$ and $\bar{x}_{jh} > 0$, then x_{jk} is kept relatively equal to these components of x_j, and $\bar{z}_{jk}(x)$ is decreased from zero. Finally, if $\bar{x}_{jk}$ with $\bar{z}_{jk}(\bar{x}) = 0$ becomes relatively equal to the $\bar{x}_{ih}$'s for which $\bar{z}_{ih}(\bar{x}) < 0$ and $\bar{x}_{ih} > 0$ and $\bar{z}_i(x) \nleq 0$, then x_{jk} is kept relatively equal to these components of x, and $\bar{z}_{jk}(x)$ is decreased from zero. Notice that in the latter two cases x_{jk} is (kept) equal to zero and $\bar{z}_{jk}(x)$ is made negative if $v_{jk} = 0$. This completes the description of the path $\bar{P}$ leading from v to an approximate solution.

3. THE EXPONENT-RAY ALGORITHM ON THE PRODUCT SPACE OF UNIT SIMPLICES

In this section we describe in detail how the piecewise linear path $\bar{P}$ can be followed by alternating linear programming pivot steps and replacement steps in the underlying simplicial subdivision of S. To describe this triangulation which will also triangulate each A(s), $s \in \Omega$, we need some more notation.

For $s \in \Omega$, let z(j) be the number of elements in $I_j^0(s)$, $j \in I_N$. A permutation of the elements of $I_j^0(s)$ is denoted by $\gamma_j(s) = ((j,k_1^j),\ldots,(j,k_{z(j)}^j))$, $j \in I_N$, while $\gamma(s)$ denotes the permutation vector $(\gamma_1(s),\ldots,\gamma_N(s))$. Let the sets $J^+(s)$, $J^0(s)$, and $J^-(s)$ be given by $J^+(s) = \{j \in I_N | I_j^+(s) \neq \emptyset\}$, $J^0(s) = \{j \in I_N | I_j^+(s) = \emptyset,\ I_j^0(s) \neq \emptyset\}$, and $J^-(s) = \{j \in I_N | I_j^+(s) = \emptyset,\ I_j^0(s) = \emptyset\}$. For each $\gamma(s)$, $s \in \Omega$, and $j \in I_N$, we define the index sets $Z_j^+(s)$, $Z_j^0(s)$, and $Z_j^-(s)$ as follows. When $j \in J^+(s)$ then $Z_j^+(s) = I_j^+(s)$, $Z_j^0(s) = I_j^0(s)$ and $Z_j^-(s) = \emptyset$. For all $j \in J^0(s)$, $Z_j^+(s) = \{(j,k_1^j)\}$, $Z_j^0(s) = I_j^0(s)\backslash\{(j,k_1^j)\}$ and $Z_j^-(s) = I_j^-(s)$, while if $j \in J^-(s)$ then $Z_j^+(s) = I_j^-(s)$ and $Z_j^0(s) = Z_j^-(s) = \emptyset$. Furthermore, let $Z_j(s) = Z_j^+(s) \cup Z_j^0(s) \cup Z_j^-(s)$ and accordingly let Z(s), $Z^+(s)$, $Z^0(s)$ and $Z^-(s)$ be the union of the corresponding sets over all $j \in I_N$. Now we can define sets $A(s,\gamma(s))$, $s \in \Omega$, forming a subdivision of S. Each subset $A(s,\gamma(s))$ is triangulated by the V-triangulation of S in the same way as the Q-triangulation of S^n triangulates S^n itself, see for example [2].

<u>Definition 3.1</u>. Let s be some sign vector in Ω and $\gamma(s)$ a permutation vector. The set $A(s,\gamma(s))$ is given by

$$A(s,\gamma(s)) = \{x \in S | x = v + \alpha(Z^+(s))q(Z^+(s)) + \sum_{(i,h)\in Z^0(s)} \alpha(i,h)q(i,h) + \sum_{j\in J^0(s)} \alpha(Z_j^-(s))q(Z_j^-(s))$$

with $0 \le \alpha(j,k^j_{z(j)}) \le \ldots \le \alpha(j,k^j_1) \le \alpha(Z^+(s)) \le 1,\ j \in J^+(s)$, and

$$0 \le \alpha(Z_j^-(s)) \le \alpha(j,k^j_{z(j)}) \le \ldots \le \alpha(j,k^j_2) \le \alpha(Z^+(s)) \le 1,\ j \in J^0(s)\},$$

where the vectors $q(Z^+(s))$, $q(j,k^j_i)$, $(j,k^j_i) \in Z^0(s)$, and $q(Z_j^-(s))$, $j \in J^0(s)$, are given by

$$q(Z^+(s)) = p(Z^+(s)) - v$$

$$q(j,k^j_i) = p(Z^+(s) \cup \{(j,k^j_1),\ldots,(j,k^j_i)\}) - p(Z^+(s) \cup \{(j,k^j_1),\ldots,(j,k^j_{i-1})\})$$

and

$$q(Z_j^-(s)) = p(Z^+(s) \cup Z_j^0(s) \cup Z_j^-(s)) - p(Z^+(s) \cup Z_j^0(s)).$$

Here the projection $p(K)$, $K \subset I$, of v on the face $S(K) = \{x \in S | x_{jh} = 0$ for all $(j,h) \notin K\}$ is defined as follows. Let $M_j(K)$ denote the number $\sum_{(j,h)\in K\cap I(j)} v_{jh}$ for all $j \in I_N$, let $K^0 = \{(i,h) \in K | v_{ih} = 0\}$, $K_j^0 = K^0 \cap I(j)$, $j \in I_N$, and let $|K_j^0|$ be the cardinality of K_j^0. Then the vector $p(K) = (p_1(K),\ldots,p_N(K))$ in $S(K)$ is defined by

$$p_{jh}(K) = \begin{cases} (1-M_j(K))/(M_j(K)+|K_j^0|) & , (j,h) \in K^0 \\ (v_{jh}(1+|K_j^0|))/(M_j(K)+|K_j^0|) & , (j,h) \in K\backslash K^0 \\ 0 & , (j,h) \notin K, \end{cases}$$

if $M_j(K) < 1$ and by

$$p_{jh}(K) = \begin{cases} 1/(|K_j^0|+M_j(K)) & ,\ (j,h) \in K^0 \\ v_{jh}/(|K_j^0|+M_j(K)) & ,\ (j,h) \in K\backslash K^0 \\ 0 & ,\ (j,h) \notin K, \end{cases}$$

if $M_j(K) = 1$. If $K \cap I(j) = \emptyset$, we define $p_j(K) = v_j$. In particular, $p(\emptyset) = v$.

The definition of the areas $A(s,\gamma(s))$, $s \in \Omega$, implies that some sets are represented by more than one sign vector. These cases are described in the following lemma, whose proof is a direct result of the definition of the $A(s,\gamma(s))$'s.

Lemma 3.2. Let s^1 be a sign vector in Ω with permutation vector $\gamma(s^1)$. If $I_j^-(s^1) = I(j)$ for some $j \in I_N$, then $A(s^1,\gamma(s^1)) = A(s^2,\gamma(s^2))$, where $s_{jk}^2 = 1$ for all $(j,k) \in I(j)$, $s_h^2 = s_h^1$ if $h \neq j$, and $\gamma(s^2) = \gamma(s^1)$. If $I_j^-(s^1) = \{(j,h)\}$ for some $j \in J^0(s^1)$, then $A(s^1,\gamma(s^1)) = A(s^2,\gamma(s^2))$, where $s_{jk}^2 = 1$ if $k = k_1^j$, $s_{jh}^2 = 0$, $s_{i\ell}^2 = s_{i\ell}^1$ if $(i,\ell) \notin \{(j,h),(j,k_1^j)\}$, $\gamma_j(s^2) = ((j,k_2^j), \ldots,(j,k_{z(j)}^j),(j,h))$, and $\gamma_i(s^2) = \gamma_i(s^1)$ if $i \neq j$.

Lemma 3.3. For each s, $s \in \Omega$, and $\gamma(s)$, the dimension of $A(s,\gamma(s))$ is equal to $t = 1 + \Sigma_{j=1}^N z(j)$.

The boundary of $A(s,\gamma(s))$, $s \in \Omega$, consists of a number of $(t-1)$-dimensional subsets with one of the inequalities for the α's in the definition of $A(s,\gamma(s))$ set to an equality. Thus, either $\alpha(Z^+(s)) = 1$ or, for some $j \in J^+(s)$, $\alpha(Z^+(s)) = \alpha(j,k_1^j)$, $\alpha(j,k_{i-1}^j) = \alpha(j,k_i^j)$ with $i \in \{2,\ldots, z(j)\}$ or $\alpha(j,k_{z(j)}^j) = 0$, or, for some $j \in J^0(s)$, $\alpha(Z^+(s)) = \alpha(j,k_2^j)$, $\alpha(j,k_{i-1}^j) = \alpha(j,k_i^j)$ with $i \in \{3,\ldots,z(j)\}$, $\alpha(j,k_{z(j)}^j) = \alpha(Z_j^-(s))$, or $\alpha(Z_j^-(s)) = 0$.

Clearly, $A(s)$, $s \in \Omega$, is the union of $A(s,\gamma(s))$ over all permutation vectors $\gamma(s)$ of $I^0(s)$. For the case $N = 2$, $n_1 = 2$, $n_2 = 1$ and the case $N = 3$, $n_1 = n_2 = n_3 = 1$ some areas are illustrated in Figure 1.a and 1.b, respectively.

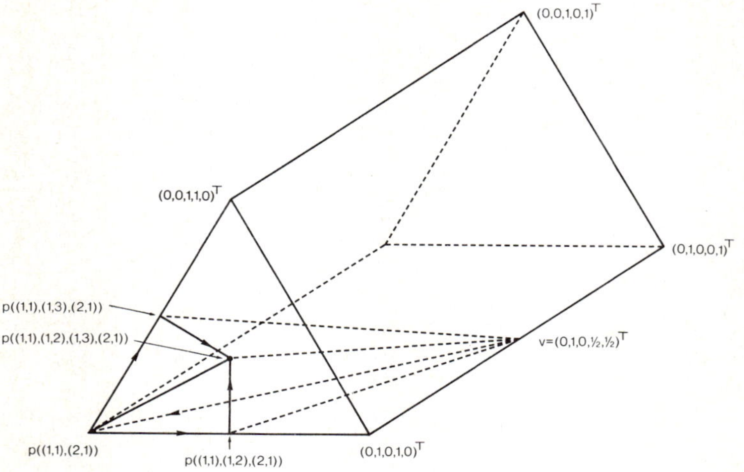

FIGURE 1.a

Illustration of A(s), s = $(+1,0,0,+1,-1)^T$, which is subdivided into A(s,((1,2),(1,3))) and A(s,((1,3),(1,2))).

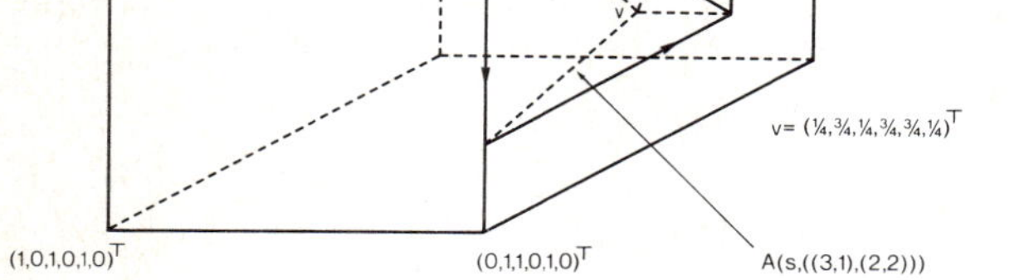

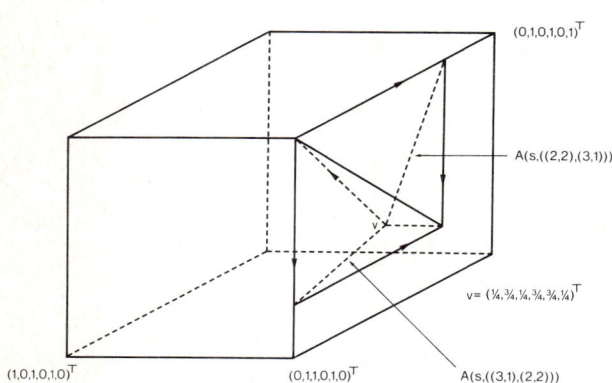

FIGURE 1.b

Illustration of A(s), s = $(-1,+1,0,-1,0,+1)^T$.

Let S be triangulated by the V-triangulation, with grid size m^{-1}, where m is some positive integer, then each region A(s), s ∈ Ω, is triangulated in t-simplices. In fact, each subset $A(s,\gamma(s))$ is triangulated by the set $G(s,\gamma(s))$ of t-simplices defined as follows.

Definition 3.4. Let s ∈ Ω and $\gamma(s)$ be a permutation vector of $I^0(s)$. The set $G(s,\gamma(s))$ is the collection of t-simplices $\sigma(y^1,\pi(s))$ with vertices $y^1,\ldots,y^{t+1}$ such that

i) $$y^1 = v + a(Z^+(s))m^{-1}q(Z^+(s)) + \sum_{(i,h)\in Z^0(s)} a(i,h)m^{-1}q(i,h) + \sum_{j\in J^0(s)} a(Z_j^-(s))m^{-1}q(Z_j^-(s)),$$

for integers $a(Z^+(s))$, $a(i,h)$, $(i,h) \in Z^0(s)$, and $a(Z_j^-(s))$, $j \in J^0(s)$, such that $0 \le a(j,k^j_{z(j)}) \le\ldots\le a(j,k^j_1) \le a(Z^+(s)) \le m-1$ for all $j \in J^+(s)$ and $0 \le a(Z_j^-(s)) \le a(j,k^j_{z(j)}) \le\ldots\le a(j,k^j_2) \le a(Z^+(s)) \le m-1$ if $j \in J^0(s)$

ii) $\pi(s) = (\pi_1,\ldots,\pi_t)$ is a permutation of the t elements consisting of the element $Z^+(s)$, the $(t-1) - |J^0(s)|$ elements of $Z^0(s)$, and the $|J^0(s)|$ elements $Z_j^-(s)$, $j \in J^0(s)$. Furthermore, if $a(j,k^j_1) = a(Z^+(s))$ or $a(j,k^j_i) = a(j,k^j_{i-1})$ for some i in {2,..., z(j)} and $j \in J^+(s)$, then p > p' with p and p' the indices for which $\pi_p = (j,k^j_1)$ and $\pi_{p'} = Z^+(s)$; $\pi_p = (j,k^j_i)$ and $\pi_{p'} = (j,k^j_{i-1})$, respectively. If for some $j \in J^0(s)$, $a(j,k^j_2) = a(Z^+(s))$ or $a(j,k^j_i) = a(j,k^j_{i-1})$ for some i in {3,...,z(j)} or $a(Z_j^-(s)) = a(j,k^j_{z(j)})$, this implies p > p' with $\pi_p = (j,k^j_2)$ and $\pi_{p'} = Z^+(s)$; $\pi_p = (j,k^j_i)$ and $\pi_{p'} = (j,k^j_{i-1})$; $\pi_p = Z_j^-(s)$ and $\pi_{p'} = (j,k^j_{z(j)})$, respectively

iii) $y^{i+1} = y^i + m^{-1}q(\pi_i)$, i = 1,...,t.

Now the union G(s) of $G(s,\gamma(s))$ over all $\gamma(s)$ triangulates A(s), whereas the union G of G(s) over all s in Ω triangulates S according to the V-triangulation with grid size m^{-1}. Since the exponent-ray algorithm moves from one simplex in G to an adjacent one, we describe in Table 1 how $\bar\sigma = \sigma(\bar y^1,\bar\pi(s))$ can be obtained from $\sigma(y^1,\pi(s))$ when σ and $\bar\sigma$ are two t-simplices in $G(s,\gamma(s))$ having a common facet opposite the vertex y^p of σ, 1 ≤

$p \le t+1$. In this table $e(Z^+(s))$, $e(i,h)$ for $(i,h) \in Z^0(s)$, and $e(Z_j^-(s))$ for $j \in J^0(s)$, are given by $e_{jk}(Z^+(s)) = 1$ if $(j,k) \in Z^+(s)$ and zero otherwise, $e_{jk}(i,h) = 1$ for $(j,k) = (i,h)$ and zero otherwise, while $e_{ih}(Z_j^-(s)) = 1$ if $(i,h) \in Z_j^-(s)$ and zero otherwise. Further, the $(N+n)$-vector a, $n = \Sigma_{j=1}^N n_j$, is defined by $a_{jk} = a(Z^+(s))$ if $(j,k) \in Z^+(s)$, $a_{jk} = a(j,k)$ if $(j,k) \in Z_j^0(s)$, $a_{jk} = a(Z_j^-(s))$ if $(j,k) \in Z_j^-(s)$, and $a_{jk} = 0$ for all $(j,k) \notin Z(s)$.

Table 1. Replacement rule for the vertex y^p.

	$\bar{y}^1$	$\bar{\pi}(s)$	$\bar{a}$
$p = 1$	$y^1 + m^{-1}q(\pi_1)$	$(\pi_2,\ldots,\pi_t,\pi_1)$	$a + e(\pi_1)$
$1 < p < t+1$	y^1	$(\pi_1,\ldots,\pi_{p-2},\pi_p,\pi_{p-1},\ldots,\pi_t)$	a
$p = t+1$	$y^1 - m^{-1}q(\pi_t)$	$(\pi_t,\pi_1,\ldots,\pi_{t-1})$	$a - e(\pi_t)$

We now consider the case that a facet τ of a t-simplex in $G(s,\gamma(s))$ lies in the boundary bd $A(s,\gamma(s))$ so that τ is not a facet of any other t-simplex in $G(s,\gamma(s))$.

Lemma 3.5. Let $\sigma(y^1,\pi(s))$ be a t-simplex in $G(s,\gamma(s))$ and τ the facet opposite vertex y^p for some p, $1 \le p \le t+1$. Then τ lies in the boundary of $A(s,\gamma(s))$ iff one of the following cases holds:

a) $p = 1$: $\pi_1 = Z^+(s)$ and $a(Z^+(s)) = m-1$

b) $1 < p < t+1$:
1. $\pi_{p-1} = Z^+(s)$, $\pi_p = (j,k_1^j)$ for certain $j \in J^+(s)$, and $a(\pi_{p-1}) = a(\pi_p)$
2. $\pi_{p-1} = (j,k_{i-1}^j)$, $\pi_p = (j,k_i^j)$ for certain $j \in J^+(s)$ and i, $1 < i \le z(j)$, and $a(\pi_{p-1}) = a(\pi_p)$
3. $\pi_{p-1} = Z^+(s)$, $\pi_p = (j,k_2^j)$ for certain $j \in J^0(s)$ and $a(\pi_{p-1}) = a(\pi_p)$
4. $\pi_{p-1} = (j,k_{i-1}^j)$, $\pi_p = (j,k_i^j)$ for certain $j \in J^0(s)$ and i, $2 < i \le z(j)$, and $a(\pi_{p-1}) = a(\pi_p)$
5. $\pi_{p-1} = (j,k_{z(j)}^j)$ if $z(j) > 1$ or $\pi_{p-1} = Z^+(s)$ if

$z(j) = 1$, $\pi_p = Z_j^-(s)$, and $a(\pi_{p-1}) = a(\pi_p)$ for certain $j \in J^0(s)$

c) $p = t+1$: 1. $\pi_t = (j,k^j_{z(j)})$ for certain $j \in J^+(s)$ and $a(\pi_t) = 0$
2. $\pi_t = Z_j^-(s)$ for certain $j \in J^0(s)$ and $a(\pi_t) = 0$.

The lemma follows immediately from the definitions of $G(s,\gamma(s))$ and $A(s,\gamma(s))$. In Lemma 3.6 the cases indicated in the foregoing lemma are considered in detail and it appears that a facet in bd $A(s,\gamma(s))$ lies either in bd S or is a facet of exactly one t-simplex in $G(s,\bar{\gamma}(s))$ with $\bar{\gamma}(s)$ different from $\gamma(s)$, or is a (t-1)-simplex in $A(\bar{s},\gamma(\bar{s}))$ for some $\bar{s}$ with $|I^0(\bar{s})| = |I^0(s)| - 1$.

Lemma 3.6. In case a of Lemma 3.5 τ lies in $S(Z(s))$, i.e., τ lies in the face $\{x \in S|x_{jk} = 0$ for all $(j,k) \in I_j^-(s)$, $j \in J^+(s)\}$ of S. For the cases b1 - b5 of Lemma 3.5 we have

b1) $\tau = \sigma(y^1,\pi(\bar{s}))$ is a (t-1)-simplex in $G(\bar{s},\gamma(\bar{s}))$, where $\bar{s}_{ih} = 1$ if $(i,h) = (j,k^j_1)$, $\bar{s}_{ih} = s_{ih}$ if $(i,h) \neq (j,k^j_1)$, $\gamma_j(\bar{s}) = ((j,k^j_2),\ldots,(j,k^j_{z(j)}))$, $\gamma_h(\bar{s}) = \gamma_h(s)$ if $h \neq j$, and $\pi(\bar{s}) = (\pi_1,\ldots,\pi_{p-2},Z^+(\bar{s}),\pi_{p+1},\ldots,\pi_t)$

b2) τ is a facet of the t-simplex $\sigma(y^1,\bar{\pi}(s))$ in $G(s,\bar{\gamma}(s))$, where $\bar{\gamma}_j(s) = ((j,k^j_1),\ldots,(j,k^j_{i-2}),(j,k^j_i),(j,k^j_{i-1}),\ldots,(j,k^j_{z(j)}))$, $\bar{\gamma}_h(s) = \gamma_h(s)$ if $h \neq j$, and $\bar{\pi}(s) = (\pi_1,\ldots,\pi_{p-2},\pi_p,\pi_{p-1},\pi_{p+1},\ldots,\pi_t)$

b3) τ is a facet of the t-simplex $\sigma(y^1,\bar{\pi}(s))$ in $G(s,\bar{\gamma}(s))$, where $\bar{\gamma}_j(s) = ((j,k^j_2),(j,k^j_1),\ldots,(j,k^j_{z(j)}))$, $\bar{\gamma}_h(s) = \gamma_h(s)$ if $h \neq j$, and $\bar{\pi}(s) = (\pi_1,\ldots,\pi_{p-2},Z^+(s),(j,k^j_1),\pi_{p+1},\ldots,\pi_t)$

b4) this case has already been described in b2)

b5) τ is the (t-1)-simplex $\sigma(y^1,\pi(\bar{s}))$ in $G(\bar{s},\gamma(\bar{s}))$, where $\bar{s}_{ih} = -1$ if $(i,h) = (j,k^j_{z(j)})$, $\bar{s}_{ih} = s_{ih}$ if $(i,h) \neq (j,k^j_{z(j)})$, $\gamma_j(\bar{s}) = ((j,k^j_1,\ldots,(j,k^j_{z(j)-1}))$, $\gamma_h(\bar{s}) = \gamma_h(s)$ if $h \neq j$, $\pi(\bar{s}) = (\pi_1,\ldots,\pi_{p-2},Z_j^-(\bar{s}),\pi_{p+1},\ldots,\pi_t)$ if $z(j) > 1$, and $\pi(\bar{s}) = (\pi_1,\ldots,\pi_{p-2},Z^+(\bar{s}),\pi_{p+1},\ldots,\pi_t)$ if $z(j) = 1$.

Finally, for the cases c1) and c2) of Lemma 3.5 holds

c1) τ is the (t-1)-simplex $\sigma(y^1,\pi(\bar{s}))$ in $G(\bar{s},\gamma(\bar{s}))$, where $\bar{s}_{ih} = -1$ if $(i,h) = (j,k^j_{z(j)})$, $\bar{s}_{ih} = s_{ih}$ if $(i,h) \neq (j,k^j_{z(j)})$, $\gamma_j(\bar{s}) = ((j,k^j_1), \ldots,(j,k^j_{z(j)-1}))$, $\gamma_h(\bar{s}) = \gamma_h(s)$ if $h \neq j$, and $\pi(\bar{s}) = (\pi_1,\ldots,\pi_{t-1})$

c2) τ is the (t-1)-simplex $\sigma(y^1,\pi(\bar{s}))$ in $G(\bar{s},\gamma(\bar{s}))$, where $\bar{s}_{ih} = 1$ if $(i,h) = (j,k^j_1)$, $\bar{s}_{ih} = s_{ih}$ if $(i,h) \neq (j,k^j_1)$, $\gamma_j(\bar{s}) = ((j,k^j_2),\ldots,(j,k^j_{z(j)}))$, $\gamma_h(\bar{s}) = \gamma_h(s)$ if $h \neq j$, and $\pi(\bar{s}) = (\pi_1,\ldots,\pi_{t-1})$.

The algorithm now generates a sequence of adjacent t-simplices of the triangulation $G(s,\gamma(s))$ in $A(s,\gamma(s))$ for varying s, $s \in \Omega$, and $\gamma(s)$. This sequence of simplices of varying dimension contains the path $\bar{P}$. Moving from one simplex to an adjacent one has been described in Table 1 and Lemma 3.6. Inside a given t-simplex σ in A(s) the path $\bar{P}$ is linear and can therefore be followed by making a linear programming pivot step in a linear system which reflects that the points x on the path $\bar{P}$ in σ must satisfy sgn $\bar{z}_j(x) = s_j$, $j = 1,\ldots,N$. Therefore such a t-simplex σ is called s-complete. In the next definition $\underline{0}$ denotes the zero-vector while e(j,k), $(j,k) \in I$, is the (j,k)-th unit vector in $\prod_{j=1}^{N} \mathbb{R}^{n_j+1}$.

<u>Definition 3.7</u>. For an arbitrary sign vector s, a g-simplex $\sigma(y^1,\ldots, y^{g+1})$, g = t-1 or t with $t = 1 + |I^0(s)|$, is s-complete if the system of linear equations

$$\sum_{i=1}^{g+1} \lambda_i \binom{z(y^i)}{1} - \sum_{(j,k)\notin I^0(s)} \mu_{jk} s_{jk} \binom{e(j,k)}{0} = \binom{\underline{0}}{1} \tag{3.1}$$

has a nonnegative solution λ^*_i, $i = 1,\ldots,g+1$, and μ^*_{jk}, $(j,k) \notin I^0(s)$. A solution of (3.1) is denoted by (λ^*,μ^*).

In the system (3.1) the vector $z(y^i)$, $i = 1,\ldots,g+1$, denotes the column vector with the $\Sigma^N_{j=1}(n_j+1)$ components, $z_{jk}(y^i)$, $(j,k) \in I$. The linear programming pivot steps are made in system (3.1). Clearly, if $\sigma(y^1,\ldots, y^{g+1})$ is an s-complete g-simplex in A(s) with solution (λ^*,μ^*), then the point $x^* = \Sigma^{g+1}_{i=1} \lambda^*_i y^i$ lies in $\bar{B}(s)$. On the other hand, if a point x^* lies in $\bar{B}$, then there is an s-complete g-simplex σ in A(s) with s equal to sgn $\bar{z}(x^*)$ containing x^* and with solution (λ^*,μ^*) for which $x^* = \Sigma_{i=1}^{g+1} \lambda_i^* y^i$ and $\mu_{jk}^* = |\bar{z}_{jk}(x^*)|$, $(j,k) \notin I_j^0(s)$, $j = 1,\ldots,N$.

Nondegeneracy assumption. For $g = t-1$ the system (3.1) has a unique solution (λ^*,μ^*) with $\lambda_i^* > 0$, $i = 1,\ldots,t$, and $\mu_{jk}^* > 0$, $(j,k) \notin I^0(s)$. For $g = t$, at most one variable of λ_i^*, $i = 1,\ldots,t+1$, and μ_{jk}^*, $(j,k) \notin I^0(s)$, is equal to zero.

If for all x in an s-complete g-simplex $\sigma(y^1,\ldots,y^{g+1})$, $g = t-1$ or t, $x_{jk} = 1$ for some $(j,k) \notin I^0(s)$, then according to the condition that $x_j^T z_j(x) = 0$, we have $z_{jk}(x) = 0$ so that $\mu_{jk} = 0$. In order to obtain a nondegenerate solution (λ^*,μ^*) we perturb $z_{jk}(x)$ slightly as follows. For all vectors y in S having one or more components equal to one we define $z_{jk}(y) = +\alpha$ if both $y_{jk} = 1$ and $z_j(y) \leq 0$, and $z_{jk}(y) = -\alpha$ if $y_{jk} = 1$ and $z_{jh}(y)$ is positive for at least one $(j,h) \in I(j)$, where α is some small positive number. Without loss of generality we assume that v does not solve the NLCP on S with respect to z.

For varying $s \in \Omega$ the exponent-ray algorithm generates from v a sequence of adjacent t-simplices with s-complete common facets in A(s). The algorithm stops whenever it reaches a complete simplex as defined below. In Lemma 3.9 it is shown that such a simplex yields an approximate solution to the NLCP.

Definition 3.8. For an arbitrary sign vector s with $1 \leq t \leq n+1$ an s-complete (t-1)-simplex $\sigma(y^1,\ldots,y^t)$ is complete if $s_{jk} \leq 0$ when $\bar{x}_{jk} = 0$ and for each $j \in I_N$ either

$$s_{jh} \leq 0 \qquad \text{for all } (j,h) \in I(j) \text{ for which } \bar{x}_{jh} > 0$$

or

$$s_{jh} \geq 0 \qquad \text{for all } (j,h) \in I(j) \text{ for which } \bar{x}_{jh} > 0,$$

where $\bar{x} = \Sigma_{i=1}^{t} \lambda_i^* y^i$.

Notice that s does not necessarily lie in Ω. If a (t-1)-simplex is complete and $\bar{x} = \Sigma_{i=1}^{t} \lambda_i^* y^i$, then according to (3.1) $\bar{z}_{jk}(\bar{x}) \leq 0$ if $\bar{x}_{jk} = 0$ and for each $j \in I_N$ either $\bar{z}_{jh}(\bar{x}) \leq 0$ for all $(j,h) \in I(j)$ for which $\bar{x}_{jh} > 0$, or $\bar{z}_{jh}(\bar{x}) \geq 0$ for all $(j,h) \in I(j)$ for which $\bar{x}_{jh} > 0$. Recall that $\bar{x}_j^T \bar{z}_j(\bar{x})$ is in general not equal to zero although $\bar{x}_j^T z_j(\bar{x}) = 0$, $j \in I_N$.

Lemma 3.9. Let $\varepsilon > 0$ and let the grid size of the V-triangulation be such that $\max_{(j,h)\in I} |z_{jh}(x) - z_{jh}(y)| < \varepsilon$ for all x and y in any simplex σ, and let $\sigma^*(y^1,\ldots,y^t)$ be a complete simplex with solution (λ^*,μ^*). Then $\bar{x} = \Sigma_{i=1}^t \lambda_i^* y^i$ lies in σ^* and satisfies

$$-\varepsilon < z_{jh}(\bar{x}) < \varepsilon \qquad \text{if } (j,h) \in I^0(s)$$

$$z_{jh}(\bar{x}) < \varepsilon \qquad \text{if } (j,h) \in I^-(s)$$

$$\bar{z}_{jh}(\bar{x}) - \varepsilon < z_{jh}(\bar{x}) < \bar{z}_{jh}(\bar{x}) + \varepsilon \qquad \text{if } (j,h) \in I^+(s)$$

and for all j

$$\sum_{(j,\ell)\in I_j^+(s)} \bar{x}_{j\ell}\, \bar{z}_{j\ell}(\bar{x}) < \varepsilon.$$

Now we describe when an s-complete simplex in A(s) is complete. Let $V_j(x) = \{(j,h) \in I(j) | x_{jh} = 0\}$ and $V_j^c(x) = I(j)\backslash V_j(x)$, $j \in I_N$ and $x \in S$. Furthermore, for $j \in I_N$, let $c_j(s) = \min\{|I_j^+(s)|, |I_j^-(s) \cap V_j^c(v)|\}$ and $c(s) = \sum_{j\in J^+(s)} c_j(s)$.

Theorem 3.10. Let $\sigma(y^1,\pi(s))$, $s \in \Omega$, be an s-complete t-simplex in $G(s,\gamma(s))$. Then σ is complete iff at a solution (λ^*,μ^*) for some (j,k) not in $I_j^0(s)$, $j \in J^+(s)$, holds that $\mu_{jk}^* = 0$, $c(s) = 1$, and either $I_j^+(s) = \{(j,k)\}$ or $I_j^-(s) \cap V_j^c(v) = \{(j,k)\}$.
A facet of σ is complete iff $\lambda_1^* = 0$, $\pi_1 = Z^+(s)$ and $a(Z^+(s)) = m-1$.

Proof. We first prove that $I_j^+(s) \cap V_j(x) = \emptyset$, $j \in I_N$, for all x in $\sigma(y^1,\pi(s))$ with x not equal to v. Since σ lies in $G(s,\gamma(s))$ we have for all $(j,k) \in I_j^+(s)$

$$y_{jk}^1 = v_{jk} + a(Z^+(s))m^{-1}q_{jk}(Z^+(s)) + \sum_{(j,h)\in I_j^0(s)} a(j,h)m^{-1}q_{jk}(j,h).$$

Suppose that $a(Z^+(s)) = 0$. Then, according to Definition 3.4, $a(j,h) = 0$ for all $(j,h) \in I_j^0(s)$, $j \in J^+(s) \cup J^0(s)$. Hence, the vertex y^1 is equal to v and π_1 must be equal to $Z^+(s)$. Since for $(j,k) \in I_j^+(s)$, $i = 2,\ldots,t+1$,

$$y^i_{jk} = v_{jk} + (\Sigma^{i-1}_{p=1} q_{jk}(\pi_p))/m$$

$$= (1 - \frac{1}{m})v_{jk} + \frac{1}{m} p_{jk}(Z^+(s) \cup \{\pi_2,\ldots,\pi_{i-1}\})$$

we obtain that $y^i_{jk} > 0$. Consequently, $x_{jk} > 0$ for all $x \neq y^1 = v$. When $a(Z^+(s)) > 0$ it follows immmediately that $y^i_{jk} > 0$ for all $i = 1,\ldots,t+1$ so that $x_{jk} > 0$ for all x in σ and $(j,k) \in I^+_j(s)$.

On the other hand, for all $j \in J^+(s)$ we have that for x in σ, $I^-_j(s) \cap V^c_j(x) = I^-_j(s) \cap V^c_j(v)$, because $Z^-_j(s) = \emptyset$ and $x_{jk} = (1-\alpha(Z^+(s)))v_{jk}$, $0 < \alpha(Z^+(s)) < 1$, for all $(j,k) \in I^-_j(s)$.

If σ is an s-complete t-simplex with $c(s) = 1$, $\mu^*_{jk} = 0$ for some $(j,k) \notin I^0_j(s)$ and either $I^+_j(s) = \{(j,k)\}$ or $I^-_j(s) \cap V^c_j(v) = \{(j,k)\}$, where $j \in J^+(s)$, then σ is also an $\bar{s}$-complete simplex. For $\bar{s}$ holds that $\bar{s}_{jk} = 0$, $\bar{s}_{ih} = s_{ih}$ for all $(i,h) \neq (j,k)$ whereas $I^+_j(\bar{s}) \cap V_j(x) = \emptyset$ as shown above and either $I^+_j(\bar{s}) \cap V^c_j(x) = \emptyset$ or $I^-_j(\bar{s}) \cap V^c_j(x) = \emptyset$ for all x in σ and $j \in J^+(\bar{s})$. Hence, σ is a complete simplex according to Definition 3.8. The reverse implication is now straightforward to derive.

When $\lambda^*_1 = 0$, $\pi_1 = Z^+(s)$ and $a(Z^+(s)) = m-1$, then according to Lemma 3.6, the facet τ of σ opposite vertex y^1 lies in the set $\{x \in S|x_{jk} = 0, (j,k) \in I^-_j(s) \text{ and } j \in J^+(s)\}$. Consequently, $I^-_j(s) \cap V^c_j(x) = \emptyset$ for all x in τ and $j \in J^+(s)$, so that τ is complete. The reverse implication follows along the same lines.

□

We remark that if $z(v) \leq 0$ then v solves the nonlinear complementarity problem. If not $z(v) \leq 0$, then the 0-dimensional simplex $\sigma(v)$ is an s^0-complete facet of the 1-dimensional simplex $\sigma(v,(Z^+(s^0)))$ in $A(s^0)$, where $s^0 = \text{sgn}\, z(v)$. Recall that $s^0_{jk} = +1$ if $v_{jk} = 1$ and $z_j(v) \leq 0$ while $s^0_{jk} = -1$ if $v_{jk} = 1$ and $z_{jh}(v) > 0$ for at least one index $(j,h) \in I(j)$ unequal to (j,k). From the nondegeneracy assumption it follows that there is no other sign vector s in Ω for which $\sigma(v)$ is an s-complete facet of a 1-simplex $\sigma(v,\pi(s))$ in $A(s)$. For given $s \in \Omega$, the s-complete t-simplices in $A(s)$ form sequences of adjacent t-simplices with common s-complete facets. A sequence which is not a loop has two end simplices. An end simplex is either an s-complete t-simplex σ in $G(s,\gamma(s))$ with a solution (λ^*,μ^*) such that $\mu^*_{jk} = 0$ for some (j,k) in $I^+(s) \cup I^-(s)$ or is an s-complete t-simplex with an s-complete facet τ in de boundary of $A(s)$. In the latter case the facet τ is either, according to Theorem 3.10, a complete (t-1)-simplex or is, according to Lemma 3.6, an $\bar{s}$-complete (t-1)-simplex in $A(\bar{s})$ for some $\bar{s} \neq s$. This simplex in $A(\bar{s})$ is again an end simplex of a sequence of adjacent (t-1)-simplices in $A(\bar{s})$ with common $\bar{s}$-complete facets, where $\bar{s}$ differs from s in only one component which is 0 in s. In the first case, the s-complete t-simplex σ is complete iff the conditions of Theorem 3.10 hold. The case in which σ is not complete is described in the next two lemmas. Lemma 3.11 describes the case when $\mu^*_{jk} = 0$ for some (j,k) in $I^+(s)$ and Lemma 3.12 describes the case when $\mu^*_{jk} = 0$ for some (j,k) in $I^-(s)$.

Lemma 3.11. If $\mu^*_{jk} = 0$ for some (j,k) in $I^+_j(s)$ and σ is not complete, then the s-complete t-simplex $\sigma(y^1,\pi(s))$ is either 1) a facet of an $\bar{s}$-complete (t+1)-simplex $\bar{\sigma}$ in $G(\bar{s})$ with $\bar{s}_{jk} = 0$ or 2) an $\bar{s}$-complete t-simplex $\bar{\sigma}$ in $G(\bar{s})$ with $\bar{s}_{jk} = 0$, $\bar{s}_{jh} = -1$ with $(j,h) = (j,k^j_{z(j)})$, and $\bar{s}_{ih} = s_{ih}$ otherwise. More precisely, the following possibilities can occur.

1. i) $|I^+_j(s)| = 1$ and $I^-_j(s) \neq \emptyset$: $\sigma(y^1,\pi(s))$ is a facet of the (t+1)-simplex $\sigma(y^1,\pi(\bar{s}))$ in $G(\bar{s},\gamma(\bar{s}))$, where $\bar{s}_{jk} = 0$, $\bar{s}_{ih} = s_{ih}$, $(i,h) \neq (j,k)$, $\gamma_j(\bar{s}) = ((j,k),(j,k^j_1),\ldots,(j,k^j_{z(j)}))$, $\gamma_h(\bar{s}) = \gamma_h(s)$ for all $h \neq j$, and $\pi(\bar{s}) = (\pi_1,\ldots,\pi_t,Z^-_j(\bar{s}))$

   ii) $|I^+_j(s)| > 1$: $\sigma(y^1,\pi(s))$ is a facet of the (t+1)-simplex $\sigma(y^1,\pi(\bar{s}))$ in $G(\bar{s},\gamma(\bar{s}))$, where $\bar{s}_{jk} = 0$, $\bar{s}_{ih} = s_{ih}$, $(i,h) \neq (j,k)$, $\gamma_j(\bar{s}) = ((j,k),(j,k^j_1),\ldots,(j,k^j_{z(j)}))$, $\gamma_h(\bar{s}) = \gamma_h(s)$ for all $h \neq j$, and $\pi(\bar{s}) = (\pi_1,\ldots,\pi_{p-1},Z^+(\bar{s}),(j,k),\pi_{p+1},\ldots,\pi_t)$ where $\pi_p = Z^+(s)$.

2) $|I^+_j(s)| = 1$ and $I^-_j(s) = \emptyset$: $\sigma(y^1,\pi(s))$ is also the t-simplex $\sigma(y^1,\pi(\bar{s}))$ in $G(\bar{s},\gamma(\bar{s}))$, where $\bar{s}_{jk} = 0$, $\bar{s}_{ih} = -1$ if $(i,h) = (j,k^j_{z(j)})$, $\bar{s}_{ih} = s_{ih}$ for all other (i,h), $\gamma_j(\bar{s}) = ((j,k),(j,k^j_1),\ldots,(j,k^j_{z(j)-1}))$, $\gamma_h(\bar{s}) = \gamma_h(s)$ for all $h \neq j$, and $\pi(\bar{s}) = (\pi_1,\ldots,\pi_{p-1}, Z^-_j(\bar{s}),\pi_{p+1},\ldots,\pi_t)$ where $\pi_p = (j,k^j_{z(j)})$.

In case 1 of Lemma 3.11, σ is an $\bar{s}$-complete facet of the uniquely determined (t+1)-simplex $\sigma(y^1,\pi(\bar{s}))$ in $A(\bar{s})$. In case 2 of Lemma 3.11, the t-simplex σ is also an $\bar{s}$-complete simplex in the area $A(\bar{s},\gamma(\bar{s}))$ which is equal to $A(s,\gamma(s))$ (see Lemma 3.2). We illustrate this case in Figure 2 where $N = 2$ and $n_1 = n_2 = 1$.

In this figure the starting point v lies in the interior of $S^1 \times S^1$. The grid size of the triangulation is $\frac{1}{2}$. Concerning the sign pattern of z we have that $\text{sgn}\ z(y^3) = \text{sgn}\ z(y^1) = (-1,+1,-1,+1)^T$ and $\text{sgn}\ z(y^2) = (+1,-1,-1,+1)^T$. Further, $\text{sgn}\ \bar{z}(a) = (0,+1,-1,+1)^T$, $\text{sgn}\ \bar{z}(b) = (0,0,-1,+1)^T$, $\text{sgn}\ \bar{z}(c) = (-1,0,-1,+1)^T$, $\text{sgn}\ \bar{z}(d) = (0,-1,-1,+1)^T$ and $\text{sgn}\ \bar{z}(e) = (+1,0,-1,+1)^T$. The algorithm follows the heavily drawn line $x = \Sigma_i \lambda_i y^i$ and goes from $\bar{B}((-1,+1,-1,+1)^T)$ via $\bar{B}((0,+1,-1,+1)^T)$ into $\bar{B}((-1,0,-1,+1)^T)$.

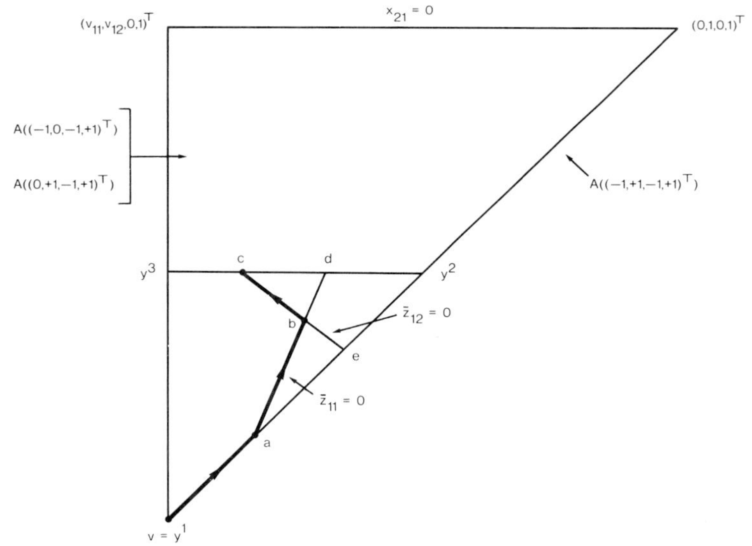

FIGURE 2
Illustration of case 2 of Lemma 3.11.

Lemma 3.12. If $\mu^*_{jk} = 0$ for some (j,k) in $I^-_j(s)$ and σ is not complete, then the s-complete t-simplex $\sigma(y^1,\pi(s))$ is either 1) a facet of an $\bar{s}$-complete (t+1)-simplex $\bar{\sigma}$ in $G(\bar{s})$ with $\bar{s}_{jk} = 0$ or 2) an $\bar{s}$-complete t-simplex in $G(\bar{s})$ with $\bar{s}_{jk} = 0$ and $\bar{s}_{jh} = 1$ with $(j,h) = (j,k^j_1)$. More precisely, the following possibilities can occur.

1. i) $|I^-_j(s)| > 1$, $I^+_j(s) = \emptyset$ and $I^0_j(s) \neq \emptyset$: $\sigma(y^1,\pi(s))$ is a facet of the (t+1)-simplex $\sigma(y^1,\pi(\bar{s}))$ in $G(\bar{s},\gamma(\bar{s}))$, where $\bar{s}_{jk} = 0$, $\bar{s}_{ih} = s_{ih}$, $(i,h) \neq (j,k)$, $\gamma_j(\bar{s}) = ((j,k^j_1),\ldots,(j,k^j_{z(j)}),(j,k))$, $\gamma_h(\bar{s}) = \gamma_h(s)$

for all $h \neq j$, and $\pi(\bar{s}) = (\pi_1,\ldots,\pi_{p-1},(j,k),Z_j^-(\bar{s}),\pi_{p+1},\ldots,\pi_t)$ where $\pi_p = Z_j^-(s)$

ii) $|I_j^-(s)| > 1$, $I_j^+(s) = \emptyset$ and $I_j^0(s) = \emptyset$: $\sigma(y^1,\pi(s))$ is a facet of the (t+1)-simplex $\sigma(y^1,\pi(\bar{s}))$ in $G(\bar{s},\gamma(\bar{s}))$, where $\bar{s}_{jk} = 0$, $\bar{s}_{ih} = s_{ih}$, $(i,h) \neq (j,k)$, $\gamma_j(\bar{s}) = ((j,k))$, $\gamma_h(\bar{s}) = \gamma_h(s)$ for all $h \neq j$, and $\pi(\bar{s}) = (\pi_1,\ldots,\pi_{p-1},Z^+(\bar{s}),Z_j^-(\bar{s}),\pi_{p+1},\ldots,\pi_t)$ where $\pi_p = Z^+(s)$

iii) $|I_j^-(s)| \geq 1$ and $I_j^+(s) \neq \emptyset$: $\sigma(y^1,\pi(s))$ is a facet of the (t+1)-simplex $\sigma(y^1,\pi(\bar{s}))$ in $G(\bar{s},\gamma(\bar{s}))$, where $\bar{s}_{jk} = 0$, $\bar{s}_{ih} = s_{ih}$, $(i,h) \neq (j,k)$, $\gamma_j(\bar{s}) = ((j,k_1^j),\ldots,(j,k_{z(j)}^j),(j,k))$, $\gamma_h(\bar{s}) = \gamma_h(s)$ for all $h \neq j$, and $\pi(\bar{s}) = (\pi_1,\ldots,\pi_t,(j,k))$.

2) $|I_j^-(s)| = 1$ and $I_j^+(s) = \emptyset$: $\sigma(y^1,\pi(s))$ is also the t-simplex $\sigma(y^1,\pi(\bar{s}))$ in $G(\bar{s},\gamma(\bar{s}))$, where $\bar{s}_{jk} = 0$, $\bar{s}_{jh} = 1$ with $(j,h) = (j,k_1^j)$, $\bar{s}_{ih} = s_{ih}$ otherwise, $\gamma_j(\bar{s}) = ((j,k_2^j),\ldots,(j,k_{z(j)}^j),(j,k))$, $\gamma_h(\bar{s}) = \gamma_h(s)$ for all $h \neq j$, and $\pi(\bar{s}) = (\pi_1,\ldots,\pi_{p-1},(j,k),\pi_{p+1},\ldots,\pi_t)$ where $\pi_p = Z_j^-(s)$.

Case 2 of Lemma 3.12 is comparable to case 2 of Lemma 3.11. Observe that each simplex defined in the two lemmas indeed exists since σ is not complete. So, the end simplex of each sequence of adjacent s-complete t-simplices in A(s) with s-complete common facets, not being a loop, can be linked with a sequence in another area $A(\bar{s})$ unless the end simplex is complete or equal to $\sigma(v)$. The latter sequence can be a sequence of adjacent $\bar{s}$-complete (t-1)-simplices with common $\bar{s}$-complete facets in $A(\bar{s})$, where for some $(j,k) \in I$, $\bar{s}_{jk} = \pm 1$ and $s_{jk} = 0$, while $\bar{s}_{\ell p} = s_{\ell p}$ for all $(\ell,p) \neq (j,k)$ (see Lemma 3.6). Another possibility is that an end simplex in A(s) is an $\bar{s}$-complete facet of a (t+1)-simplex $\bar{\sigma}$ in $A(\bar{s})$, with $\bar{s}_{jk} = 0$ and $s_{jk} = \pm 1$ for some $(j,k) \in I$, and $\bar{s}_{\ell p} = s_{\ell p}$ for all $(\ell,p) \neq (j,k)$ (see Lemma 3.11.1 and 3.12.1). The simplex $\bar{\sigma}$ is then an end simplex of a path of adjacent $\bar{s}$-complete (t+1)-simplices in $A(\bar{s})$ with common $\bar{s}$-complete facets. The last possibility concerns the case in which an s-complete end simplex σ in A(s) is also an $\bar{s}$-complete t-simplex in $A(\bar{s})$ for some $\bar{s} \in \Omega$ (see Lemma 3.11.2 and 3.12.2). The simplex σ is then also an end simplex of a sequence of adjacent $\bar{s}$-complete t-simplices in $A(\bar{s})$.

In this way all paths can be linked. As a result there exists a path of adjacent s-complete simplices in regions A(s), $s \in \Omega$, connecting $\sigma(v)$ with a complete simplex. The number of simplices along this path is finite because the total number of simplices in S is finite. The exponent-ray algorithm generates this sequence of simplices starting with $\sigma(v)$ and follows the piecewise linear path $\bar{P}$ from v to an approximate solution x^*. The successive steps of the algorithm result from linear programming pivot steps in system (3.1) combined with corresponding replacement steps in the triangulation. A decrease in dimension of the current simplex is followed by reintroducing a unit vector column in system (3.1). On the other hand, the dimension is increased when such a column is eliminated by a linear programming pivot step. We remark that the p.l. path followed by the algorithm might have more than one linear piece in a simplex (see Lemma 3.11.2, 3.12.2, and Figure 2). This is caused by the fact that $\bar{x}_j^T\bar{z}_j(\bar{x})$ is in general unequal to zero, $j \in I_N$. We conclude this section with a formal presentation of the steps of the algorithm.

<u>Step 0</u>. [Initialization] Set $s_{jk} = \text{sgn } z_{jk}(v)$ for all $(j,k) \in I$. If $s_{jk} \leq 0$ for all $(j,k) \in I$ then the algorithm stops with the solution v. Otherwise, set $t = 1$, $y^1 = v$, $\pi(s) = (Z^+(s))$, $\sigma = \sigma(y^1,\pi(s))$, $\gamma_j(s) = \emptyset$ for all $j \in I_N$, $\bar{p} = 2$, $a_{jk} = 0$ for all $(j,k) \in I$, $\mu_{jk} = |z_{jk}(v)|$ for all $(j,k) \in I$, $\lambda_1 = 1$, $c_j(s) = \min\{|I_j^+(s)|\ ,\ |I_j^-(s) \cap V_j^c(v)|\}$ for all $j \in I_N$.

<u>Step 1</u>. Calculate $z(y^{\bar{p}})$ and perform an l.p pivot step by bringing $(z^T(y^{\bar{p}}),1)^T$ in the linear system

$$\sum_{\substack{i=1\\ i\neq\bar{p}}}^{t+1} \lambda_i \binom{z(y^i)}{1} - \sum_{(j,k)\notin I^0(s)} \mu_{jk}s_{jk}\binom{e(j,k)}{0} = \binom{0}{1}.$$

If for some $(j,k) \notin I^0(s)$, μ_{jk} becomes zero, then go to Step 3. Otherwise λ_p becomes zero for exactly one $p \neq \bar{p}$ and the facet $\tau(y^1,\ldots,y^{p-1},y^{p+1},\ldots,y^{t+1})$ is s-complete.

<u>Step 2</u>. If $p = 1$, $\pi_1 = Z^+(s)$, and $a(Z^+(s)) = m-1$, then τ is complete and the algorithm stops.

In the case $1 < p < t+1$ and if

i) $\pi_{p-1} = Z^+(s)$, $\pi_p = (j,k^j_1)$ for some $j \in J^+(s)$, and $a(\pi_{p-1}) = a(\pi_p)$, then s, $\gamma(s)$ and $\sigma(y^1,\pi(s))$ are adapted according to Lemma 3.6, case b1; set $t = t-1$ and $(i,h) = (j,k^j_1)$ and adapt $c_j(s)$; go to Step 4

ii) $\pi_{p-1} = (j,k^j_{i-1})$, $\pi_p = (j,k^j_i)$ for some $j \in J^+(s)$, $1 < i \le z(j)$, and $a(\pi_{p-1}) = a(\pi_p)$, then $\gamma(s)$ and $\sigma(y^1,\pi(s))$ are adapted according to Lemma 3.6, case b2; return to Step 1 with $\bar{p}$ the index of the new vertex of σ

iii) $\pi_{p-1} = Z^+(s)$, $\pi_p = (j,k^j_2)$ for certain $j \in J^0(s)$ and $a(\pi_{p-1}) = a(\pi_p)$, then $\gamma(s)$ and $\sigma(y^1,\pi(s))$ are adapted according to lemma 3.6, case b3; return to Step 1 with $\bar{p}$ the index of the new vertex of σ

iv) $\pi_{p-1} = (j,k^j_{i-1})$, $\pi_p = (j,k^j_i)$ for certain $j \in J^0(s)$, $2 < i \le z(j)$, and $a(\pi_{p-1}) = a(\pi_p)$, then $\gamma(s)$ and $\sigma(y^1,\pi(s))$ are adapted according to case b4 of Lemma 3.6; return to Step 1 with $\bar{p}$ the index of the new vertex of σ

v) $\pi_{p-1} = (j,k^j_{z(j)})$ if $z(j) > 1$ or $\pi_{p-1} = Z^+(s)$ if $z(j) = 1$, $\pi_p = Z^-_j(s)$ and $a(\pi_{p-1}) = a(\pi_p)$ for certain $j \in J^0(s)$, then s, $\gamma(s)$ and $\sigma(y^1,\pi(s))$ are adapted according to Lemma 3.6, case b5; set $t = t-1$, $(i,h) = (j,k^j_{z(j)})$, and adapt $c_j(s)$; go to Step 4.

In the case $p = t+1$ and if

i) $\pi_t = (j,k^j_{z(j)})$ for certain $j \in J^+(s)$ and $a(\pi_t) = 0$, then s, $\gamma(s)$ and $\sigma(y^1,\pi(s))$ are adapted according to Lemma 3.6, case c1; set $t = t-1$, $(i,h) = (j,k^j_{z(j)})$, and adapt $c_j(s)$; go to Step 4

ii) $\pi_t = Z^-_j(s)$ for some $j \in J^0(s)$ and $a(\pi_t) = 0$, then s, $\gamma(s)$ and $\sigma(y^1,\pi(s))$ are adapted according to Lemma 3.6, case c2; set $t = t-1$, $(i,h) = (j,k^j_1)$, and adapt $c_j(s)$; go to Step 4.

In all other cases $\sigma(y^1,\pi(s))$ and a are adapted according to Table 1 and return to Step 1 with $\bar{p}$ the index of the new vertex of σ.

Step 3. [Increase dimension] If $c(s) = 1$ and either $I_j^+(s) = \{(j,k)\}$ or both $j \in J^+(s)$ and $I_j^-(s) \cap V_j^c(v) = \{(j,k)\}$, then σ is complete and the algorithm stops.

If σ is not complete, $(j,k) \in I_j^+(s)$, and if $|I_j^+(s)| = 1$ and $I_j^-(s) = \emptyset$, then s, $\gamma(s)$ and $\sigma(y^1,\pi(s))$ are adapted according to Lemma 3.11, case 2; set $(i,h) = (j,k^j_{z(j)})$ and adapt $c_j(s)$; go to Step 4.

If σ is not complete, $(j,k) \in I_j^-(s)$, and if $|I_j^-(s)| = 1$ and $I_j^+(s) = \emptyset$, then s, $\gamma(s)$ and $\sigma(y^1,\pi(s))$ are adapted according to Lemma 3.12, case 2; set $(i,h) = (j,k^j_1)$ and adapt $c_j(s)$; go to Step 4.

In all other cases adapt s, $\gamma(s)$, and $\sigma(y^1,\pi(s))$ according to Lemma 3.11, case 1, if $(j,k) \in I_j^+(s)$ and according to Lemma 3.12, case 1, if $(j,k) \in I_j^-(s)$; set $t = t+1$ and adapt $c_j(s)$; return to Step 1 with $\bar{p}$ the index of the new vertex of σ.

Step 4. [Decrease dimension] Perform an l.p. pivot step by bringing $-s_{ih}(e^\top(i,h),0)^\top$ in the system

$$\sum_{i=1}^{t+1} \lambda_i \binom{z(y^i)}{1} - \sum_{\substack{(j,k)\notin I^0(s)\\(j,k)\neq(i,h)}} \mu_{jk} s_{jk} \binom{e(j,k)}{0} = \binom{0}{1}.$$

If μ_{jk}, $(j,k) \notin I^0(s)$ and $(j,k) \neq (i,h)$, becomes zero then return to Step 3. If λ_p becomes zero then go to Step 2.

4. COMPUTATIONAL RESULTS

The three algorithms on S mentioned in this paper have been applied to some examples of noncooperative N-person games and international trade economies. In both applications we start the algorithms in the barycenter of S. For the first application the starting grid size equals 1 while the grid size is ½ for the second application. When a complete simplex is found the grid is refined with a factor of two and we restart in the approximate solution. In a game it can occur that such an approximate solution lies close to a boundary face of S. Then the solution is projected on that boundary face. The restarting is stopped when the accuracy of the approximate solution is sufficient. We measure the accuracy by $\max_I z_{jk}(x^\nu)$ where x^ν is the approximate solution in round ν, $\nu = 1,2,\ldots$. In the first application the algorithms are stopped when we obtain an accuracy of 10^{-8} and in the second application if we obtain an accuracy of 10^{-7}. Throughout this section we use the following notation:

FE: accumulated number of function evaluations

LP: accumulated number of linear programming steps

ν: the number of rounds necessary to obtain the required accuracy.

We applied the algorithms to three games whose data can be found in [1]. Game 1 has three players with each player having two strategies. In Game 2 there are also three players but each having three strategies. Game 3 concerns a game in which there are four players with each player having two strategies. The performance of the algorithms, when applied to these games, is summarized in Table 2. We remark that all algorithms converged to the same Nash equilibrium solution. The second application concerns the international trade economy described in van der Laan [7]. The computational results presented in Table 3, concern the same examples as described in [1] and [7]. Each country has two non-common goods, the number of common goods varies between 2 and 6, whereas the number of countries varies between 2 and 5. For each run the number of rounds necessary to obtain the required accuracy is equal to the difference between the number of function evaluations and linear programming steps.

Table 2. The computational results for the three games.

	sum-ray algorithm			product-ray algorithm			exponent-ray algorithm		
Game	FE	LP	ν	FE	LP	ν	FE	LP	ν
1	54	51	7	33	35	4	59	82	7
2	21	18	3	15	14	1	21	23	2
3	18	14	3	18	16	2	41	56	8

Table 3. The computational results for the international trade economies.

number of common goods	number of countries	sum-ray alg.		product-ray alg.		exponent-ray alg.	
		FE	LP	FE	LP	FE	LP
2	2	60	53	54	47	60	53
	3	125	117	85	78	81	74
	4	178	170	97	90	116	109
	5	225	217	128	121	148	142
3	2	97	90	56	49	60	52
	3	127	119	87	80	91	84
	4	182	174	95	88	123	116
	5	261	253	109	102	151	144
4	2	113	105	67	60	68	60
	3	132	124	107	100	104	97
	4	212	204	118	111	133	126
	5	309	301	145	138	163	155
5	2	134	126	79	72	76	68
	3	157	149	97	90	120	112
	4	257	249	145	138	167	161
	5	354	346	182	175	170	162
6	2	166	158	89	82	95	87
	3	176	168	147	139	115	107
	4	346	338	195	188	188	183
	5	458	450	221	214	212	206

The computational results show that both the exponent-ray and the product-ray algorithm are significantly better than the sum-ray algorithm in case of the international trade economies, whereas the product-ray algorithm is superior to the other two algorithms in case of a noncooperative game.

The sum-ray algorithm on S leaves x=v by increasing the component x_{jk} of x for which $z_{jk}(v) = \max_I z_{ih}(v)$. In general, the algorithm generates points x for which for each j, $j \in I_N$, the components x_{jk} of x_j having

$z_{jk}(x) < \max_I z_{ih}(x)$ are relatively equal to each other and smaller than the other components of x_j. The product-ray algorithm on S leaves x=v by increasing for each j, $j \in I_N$, the component x_{jk} of x_j for which $z_{jk}(v) = \max_{I(j)} z_{jh}(v)$. In general, this algorithm generates points x for which the components x_{jk} of x having $z_{jk}(x) < \max_{I(j)} z_{jh}(x)$ are relatively equal to each other and smaller than the other components of x.

Concerning the accuracy of the three algorithms, the product-ray algorithm yields a better approximation for a given grid size than the other two algorithms (see [1] for the accuracy of the product-ray algorithm). So, to obtain the same accuracy, the product-ray algorithm might need less restarts. This feature happened in all three games. In the economic application the sum-ray algorithm always needed more restarts than the other two algorithms.

A second difference among the three algorithms is the number of rays to leave the starting point. This number is exponential for the exponent-ray algorithm. This could be disadvantageous in case of the noncooperative games. A change in the probability x_{jk} of a player j with which he plays his k-th pure strategy does not influence the marginal payoff of this strategy. Therefore in this application the algorithms in general leave the starting point v along a ray which does not lead in the direction of the approximate solution which will be found. This might lead to a larger number of iterations when there are more rays.

More tests and research could clarify the different results for the two applications given above.

REFERENCES

[1] T.M. Doup and A.J.J. Talman, "A new variable dimension simplicial algorithm to find equilibria on the product space of unit simplices", Research Memorandum FEW 146, Tilburg University, Tilburg, The Netherlands, 1984, to appear in Mathematical Programming.

[2] T.M. Doup, A.H. van den Elzen and A.J.J. Talman, "Simplicial algorithms for solving the nonlinear complementarity problem on the simplotope", Research Memorandum FEW 213, Tilburg University, Tilburg, The Netherlands, 1986.

[3] T.M. Doup, G. van der Laan and A.J.J. Talman, "The $(2^{n+1}-2)$-ray algorithm: a new simplicial algorithm to compute economic equilibria", Research Memorandum FEW 151, Tilburg University, Tilburg, The Netherlands, 1984, to appear in Mathematical Programming.

[4] A.H. van den Elzen and G. van der Laan, "A price adjustment process for an economy with a block-diagonal pattern", Research Memorandum FEW 229, Tilburg University, Tilburg, The Netherlands, 1986.

[5] A.H. van den Elzen and A.J.J. Talman, "A new strategy-adjustment process for computing a Nash equilibrium in a noncooperative more-person game", *Methods of Operations Research* 54, Verlag Anton Hain, Frankfurt, 1986, pp. 469-481.

[6] A.H. van den Elzen, G. van der Laan and A.J.J. Talman, "Adjustment processes for finding equilibria on the simplotope", Research Memorandum FEW 196, Tilburg University, Tilburg, The Netherlands, 1985.
[7] G. van der Laan, "The computation of general equilibrium in economies with a block diagonal pattern", *Econometrica* 53 (1985) 659-665.
[8] G. van der Laan and A.J.J. Talman, "A restart algorithm for computing fixed points without an extra dimension", *Mathematical Programming* 17 (1979) 74-84.
[9] G. van der Laan and A.J.J. Talman, "On the computation of fixed points in the product space of unit simplices and an application to non-cooperative N-person games", *Mathematics of Operations Research* 7 (1982) 1-13.
[10] G. van der Laan and A.J.J. Talman, "Adjustment processes for finding economic equilibria", Research Memorandum FEW 174, Tilburg University, Tilburg, The Netherlands, 1985, to appear in this volume.
[11] G. van der Laan, A.J.J. Talman and L. Van der Heyden, "Variable dimension algorithms for unproper labellings", Research Memorandum FEW 147, Tilburg University, Tilburg, The Netherlands, 1984, to appear in Mathematics of Operations Research.
[12] A.J.J. Talman, *Variable dimension fixed point algorithms and triangulations,* Mathematical Centre Tracts 128, Mathematisch Centrum, Amsterdam, The Netherlands, 1980.

The Computation and Modelling of Economic Equilibria
A.J.J. Talman, G. van der Laan (Editors)
Elsevier Science Publishers B.V. (North-Holland), 1987

GENERALIZED PIVOTING AND COALITIONS

Hans van MAAREN

Econometric Institute, Erasmus University, P.O. Box 1738, 3000 DR Rotterdam, The Netherlands

1. INTRODUCTION

In the last decade the computation of economic equilibria has grown into an adult mathematical discipline. After Scarf [2] this computation became more and more related to other branches of mathematics such as homotopy theory, triangulation theory and functional analysis. Some people even think that its development has reached its end stage, at least from a theoretic-algorithmic point of view. Without advocating this opinion we believe that a search for mathematical structures which can be related to the underlying ideas of the known algorithms may be useful, at least interesting. Especially the involved *Lemke-Howson* argument seems to be too valuable to be forgotten. In this paper we leave Euclidean space and formulate the essence of the early algorithms in a new setting.

In [1] Gould and Tolle presented a unifying mathematical structure, a *pseudo manifold* to be precise, to which this Lemke-Howson argument still applies. In [4] Tuy develops an algorithm, going back to the early versions of Scarf, in a more general setting. Tuy chooses *orderings* as entities, an approach that we shall follow too. The main goal of this paper even is to emphasize the role of these orderings involved. In fact, we shall study *multiply ordered spaces*. These spaces consist of a set of possible choices for a finite set P of persons, each with his specific preference relation $\precsim_s$ on the set of choices. We shall formulate an algorithm which is concerned with general feasibility. That is, for multiply ordered spaces X and Y and mappings F and G from X to Y, we investigate the system of inequalities

$$F(x) \precsim_s G(x) \text{ for all } s \in P$$

on *feasibility* (with respect to the preferences on Y) and, at the same time, on *optimality* (with respect to the preferences on X). We also present a point to set version of this general feasibility problem. The above formulation ranges from *fixed point* problems to *surjectivity* problems, depending on the actual structures involved. The choice of multiply ordered spaces as our entities makes it possible to relate the general feasibility problem directly to problems in economics, incentive theory, game theory or any other theory concerned with preference relations. It also seems the most friendly context for those who are interested in modeling their particular (economic) problems into a mathematical equilibrium problem, especially in cases where an embedding in Euclidean setting is not natural at first sight. Since we want to avoid topological spaces in first instance, our results are primarily concerned with a *discrete* version of the general feasibility problem. As our emphasis is on the mutual relationships of the preference relations we present a start of a *coalition theory*. This theory investigates which of these relationships makes a solution to the general feasibility problem possible, at least plausible. To this end a number of associated combinatorial invariants are defined. These invariants, the *dimension, coalition number, preference number* and *exchange number,* try to characterize the impact of the algorithm on the feasibility problem, also in cases where a continuous, rather than a discrete, variant is aimed at.

In this paper we sometimes use a terminology which suggests the underlying objects to be supplied with a topology. This will not always be the case. We make use of topological terms rather loosely, as is motivated by Section 2, see also Section 5.3.

The algorithm consists of maximization and minimization procedures, which are performed with respect to the preference relations on X and are steered by feasibility checks (labeling) of the outputs of F and G in Y. These maximization and minimization steps are carried out over a finite grid of X and are thus *combinatorial* in nature. One should notice however that these optimization procedures in X may behave far from "linear", depending on the preferences involved. Globally, the algorithm follows the lines of Scarf's version, which uses primitive sets. This approach is needed because in a non-Euclidean setting triangulation methods are not available, at least not directly related to the entities chosen. In [4] Tuy gives a similar (integer labeling) algorithm which uses dummy-orderings in order to comprehend its description. However, from a coalition theoretic point of view, it is more natural to do without as we shall explain the steps of the algorithm in terms of our entities. These steps may be considered as a policy for a number of persons who want to establish a desired decision, that is, a feasible solution satisfying some optimality properties. According to this policy, *coalitions* are formed and *agreements* are made, leading finally to the solution.

We have chosen to present our study informally. Only a few theorems are included, the proofs of which are not profoundly stated. In these cases the reader easily may fill in any gap, since the lines along which this can be performed are indicated or simply known from the literature. This informal approach is justified by our main purpose: to lay the foundations of a study of interesting features which are associated to a general constructive equilibrium theory rather than to specify the details of such a theory, the latter being an impossible task without an actual substitution of our entities.

2. MULTIPLY ORDERED SPACES, COALITIONS AND AGREEMENTS

We consider a set X, a finite set P, and for each $p \in P$ a relation $\lesssim_p$ on X satisfying

1) $x \lesssim_p x$ (reflexivity)

2) $x \lesssim_p y$ and $y \lesssim_p z$ imply $x \lesssim_p z$ (transitivity)

3) $x \lesssim_p y$ or $y \lesssim_p x$ (completeness)

for all $x,y,z \in X$. Such a system is called a *multiply ordered space*. One may think of X as a set of, for instance, alternatives, goods or strategies, where the $\lesssim_p$ can be the preference relations of the members of P, who can be decision makers, consumers or players. Also, X might be a subset of the Euclidean space, like a polytope, or more specific a (price) simplex. In this case $\lesssim_p$ can be thought of a relation induced by a real valued (utility) function, or some pay-off function, or $\lesssim_p$ simply may represent the pth barycentric coordinate.

A finite subset A of X is called a *random grid* if each $\lesssim_p$ becomes *anti symmetric* on A, that is

4) $a \lesssim_p b$ and $b \lesssim_p a$ imply $a = b$.

As we can imagine, the actual selection of such a grid may be troublesome. Indeed this fact made the simplicial subdivision approach for calculating approximate fixed points of (upper-semi) continuous (multi) functions a more favorite method than Scarf's original idea of using primitive sets. However, in a general context we cannot do without the notion of random grids. We come to this matter again in Section 5.5. Let us think of A as a set of possible alternatives for the persons of P, while each person p has his particular preference relation $\lesssim_p$ on A.

A nonempty subset Q of P is called a *coalition*. Now there are some subsets of A of special interest. Suppose that in a coalition Q each q chooses an alternative a_q. If $a_q \lesssim_q a_r$ for all $r \in Q$, $r \neq q$, each person certainly agrees with the choice of any other coalition member, which is seemingly even more favorite to him than his own alternative. If moreover no alternative a exists which is favorite to all members of Q, compared to their own decision, one says that the coalition agrees.

Definition 2.1. A coalition Q is said to *agree* on $\{a_q | q \in Q\}$ if (i) $a_q \lesssim_q a_r$ for all $q, r \in Q$, $q \neq r$, and (ii) for no $a \in A$ we have $a_q \lesssim_q a$ for all $q \in Q$.

Notice that the set of *agreement* $\{a_q | q \in Q\}$ can be viewed upon as a Pareto-optimal set, relative to Q and A. From a mathematical standpoint it makes sense to use also more neutral terms for the above: a *crystal* is an agreement (as a generalization of Scarf's primitive set), the a_q's are the *points* of the crystal and the $\lesssim_q$'s the corresponding *sides*.

It is sometimes useful to picture crystals as subsets of Euclidean space, the sides being curves of indifference of linear functionals, for example see Figure 1. One must realize, however, that this linearity is only assumed to make the drawings more easily to interpret, not because of essential reasons. In fact, in general cases any attempt to geometrize the situation may fail.

There is one particular aspect related to the above notions which we want to discuss at this stage. As we know from Scarf [2], the points of a primitive set are close if the grid involved is sufficiently fine. Since in our context topological concepts are not present yet we cannot state such things formally. We shall do so in Section 5.3. Here we want to deal with topological notions rather loosely. If we indeed think of A as possible alternatives for the persons of P we must realize that these persons

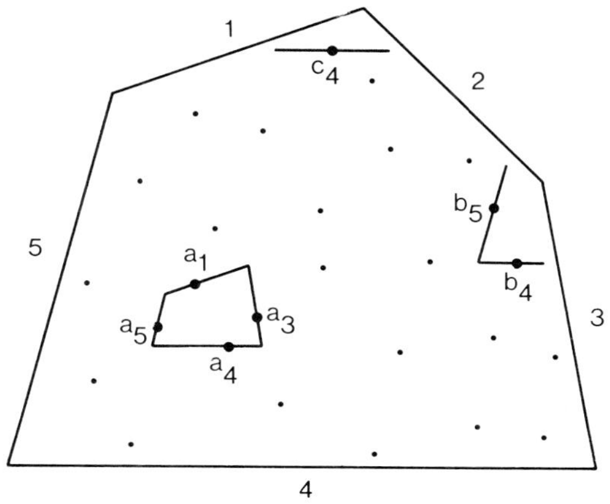

FIGURE 1
The points of A are dotted. Coalition {1,3,4,5} agrees on $\{a_1,a_3,a_4,a_5\}$; coalition {4,5} on $\{b_4,b_5\}$; coalition {4} on $\{c_4\}$.

together rule their world A rather than Euclid does: two alternatives a and b are *close* in the eyes of $p \in P$ if the set $\{c \in A | a <_p c <_p b\}$ (in case $a <_p b$) is small, relative to the size of A. Hence, if a coalition Q agrees on a set $\{a_q | q \in Q\}$ the fact that no alternative is more satisfactory for the whole of the coalition simply means that in the eyes of the coalition as a whole their a_q's are close, although persons outside the coalition may have another opinion. Figure 2 illustrates the above.

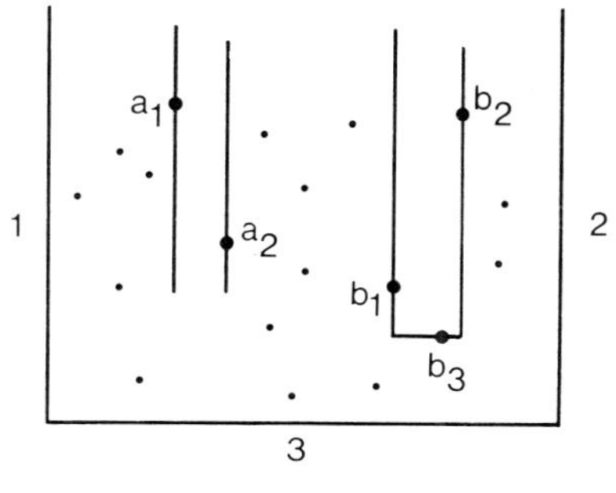

FIGURE 2
a_1 and a_2 are close in the eyes of 1 and 2, not in the eyes of 3. The same holds for b_1, b_2 and b_3.

In Figure 2 the agreement $\{b_1,b_2,b_3\}$ of coalition $\{1,2,3\}$ shows a *degenerated* case: the three points are close for 1 and 2 but not so for 3. Still it remains that any unilateral change in alternative makes the situation worse. In Section 5.2 we return to this matter and shall relate it to an important invariant for multiply ordered spaces.

3. THE GENERAL FEASIBILITY PROBLEM

The context of the following discussion is that of two multiply ordered spaces X and Y with associated sets of persons P and $\bar{P}$, respectively. Also, two mappings F and G from X to Y are considered. The general feasibility problem is concerned with approximating an $x^* \in X$ which solves the system of inequalities

$$F(x^*) \lesssim_s G(x^*) \qquad \text{for all } s \in \bar{P}.$$

Notice that the above covers a wide range of interesting mathematical problems. For instance,

a) choosing G to be constant and $\bar{P}$ an *exhausting* set of orderings (that is: $a \lesssim_s b$ for all $s \in \bar{P}$ implies $a = b$), we obtain the *surjectivity* problem $F(x) = G$

b) choosing $X = Y$, G to be the identity mapping and again $\bar{P}$ exhausting, we obtain the *fixed point* problem $F(x) = x$

c) letting $Y = \mathbb{R}^n$, $\lesssim_s$ the ordering on the sth coordinate, and $F_i, G_i : X \to \mathbb{R}$, we read the feasibility problem $F_i(x) \le G_i(x)$ for $i = 1,\dots,n$.

In fact, $\mathbb{R}^n$ may be replaced in this example by any product of n ordered spaces. This example shows that in the general feasibility problem we may as well replace the condition $F(x) \lesssim_s G(x)$ for all $s \in \bar{P}$ by the seemingly more general one $F_s(x) \lesssim_s G_s(x)$ for all $s \in \bar{P}$, where it is assumed that the mappings F_s and G_s from X to Y are given for each $s \in \bar{P}$.

We assume for the moment that P and $\bar{P}$ have the same number of members. It is possible that P and $\bar{P}$ consists of the same persons, each with a preference relation on X as well as on Y. One may even think of "true" preference relations on X and "lied" preference relations on Y = X in a sort of *Clarke-Groves mechanism*. We shall use an interpretation which is rather flexible and also provides the algorithm to be presented in Section 4 with some conceptual background. Imagine that X consists of alternatives for a set of persons P. Each of these persons has his preference relation on X which should be looked upon as a preference "at first glance": he is not able to calculate all consequences of his possible choices but simply makes a comparison with respect to some easily established aspects of them. Now we imagine Y as a space of possible consequences (a pay-off space for instance) and the members of $\bar{P}$ as representatives of the members of P. These representatives compare the consequences of the alternatives chosen by the members of P, again also each in his characteristic manner. A pay-off space therefore should not be seen as a set of real numbers in this context, but as a set of points with different aspects. Further, the mappings F and G are considered to express some sort of cost and profit mechanisms, respectively. Now clearly, an alternative x^* with $F(x^*) \underset{\sim s}{<} G(x^*)$ for all $s \in \bar{P}$, is certainly a good one. It is sometimes useful to think of F(x) as a budget vector needed for alternative x and G(x) = c as a global budget limitation. Conversely, G(x) can be thought of a pay-off while F(x) = c expresses a global minimal desire.

It is our intention to present an algorithm which partly solves the general feasibility problem.

Theorem 3.1. If A is a random grid of X and if the system $F(x) >_s G(x)$, $s \in \bar{P}$, is unsolvable, then there exists a coalition $Q \subset P$, a permutation σ of Q and an agreement $\{a_q | q \in Q\}$ of Q with

$$F(a_{\sigma(q)}) \underset{\sim\bar{q}}{<-} G(a_{\sigma(q)}) \tag{3.1}$$

for all $q \in Q$, $\bar{q}$ denoting the representative of q.

The proof of Theorem 3.1 is given in Section 4.

If we think of the alternatives a_q being close together we may select any of them, say a, and substitute a in expression (3.1), obtaining *approximately*

$$F(a) \underset{\sim\bar{q}}{<-} G(a) \qquad \text{for all } q \in Q.$$

Of course, it is understood that F and G behave "continuously" with respect to the multiply ordered spaces X and Y, see also Section 5.3.

If Q is a proper subset of P the above does not cover our wishes fully. However, recalling our interpretations of our entities we conclude that a coalition is established which succeeded in making a decision which is profitable for all of its members. Moreover, *and this is important for the correct interpretation of our theorem, this decision is such that no other decision is more preferred at first glance by the whole of the coalition.*

A lot of questions arise. What is the role of the condition that $F(x) >_s G(x)$, $s \in \bar{P}$, is unsolvable? What really happens if we obtain a proper subcoalition of P? Can we force the coalition to be equal P? How relevant is the assumption that P and $\bar{P}$ have the same number of members? These questions cannot be answered in a global way. Their answers depend on the actual structures involved. For instance, how does the shape of X looks like with respect to (w.r.t.) the preference relations? Are there boundary conditions on F and G? Do the orderings have any mutual relationships? In Section 5 we present a start of a theory on coalitions which provides the context in which these kind of questions are to be discussed.

4. THE ALGORITHM, AN INTEGER-VERSION

In this section we are concerned with the determination of agreements of a special kind. We consider a multiply ordered space X with set of persons P and a random grid A.

A *labeling* is a function $\ell : A \to P$. For instance, in the context of Theorem 3.1 a labeling ℓ might be any function with $\ell(a) \in \{p | F(a) \underset{\sim p}{<} G(a)\}$. For a given labeling ℓ and $B \subset A$ we set $\ell(B) = \{\ell(b) | b \in B\}$.

Theorem 4.1. There exists an agreement, consisting of a coalition Q which agrees on $A_Q = \{a_q | q \in Q\}$, satisfying $\ell(A_Q) = Q$.

It is easily seen that Theorem 4.1 proves Theorem 3.1. As mentioned before, the algorithm providing such Q and A_Q is essentially already in Scarf [2] and Tuy [4]. Therefore we present no detailed proof, but merely investigate the steps of the algorithm on their possible interpretations.

The algorithm constructs a sequence of agreements satisfying the condition $\ell(A_Q) = Q$ possibly except for one element. This sequence can be shown to be free of cycling, which means that it must be finite. Since the algorithm can perform another step as long as $\ell(A_Q) \neq Q$ it must end with a desired agreement.

We first introduce some terminology. Consider a coalition $Q = \{q_1, \ldots, q_k\}$ which agrees on $\{a_1, \ldots, a_k\}$. If $p \notin Q$, p is called a *passive* label of the agreement (p is not a member of the coalition involved). If $p \in$

$\ell(\{a_1,\ldots,a_k\})$, p is called an *active* label (p contributes to the pay-off). The agreement is *completely* labeled (or *complete)* if its active label set is just Q, or equivalently, if its whole label set equals P. The agreement is *almost* completely labeled if its whole label set misses at most one element of P.

Let us assume that some person p_1 takes the initiative. He chooses his best alternative at first glance, a_1, which is $\max_{p_1} A$ (the maximum over A of $\lesssim_{p_1}$), thus forming the first almost completely labeled agreement, in which all other persons act as passive labels.

If $\ell(a_1) = p_1$ he finds himself in the very happy circumstances that his most suitable alternative already has a positive balance: $F(a_1) \lesssim^{-}_{p_1} G(a_1)$. In terms of labels solely: the agreement is even complete.

If $\ell(a_1) = p_2 \neq p_1$ he notices that his most suitable alternative is attractive to p_2 (since $F(a_1) \lesssim^{-}_{p_2} G(a_1)$) and hence p_2 is invited by him to constitute a coalition. Now there is little conflict: p_1 wants a decision a_1, letting p_2 pay the bill. Of course p_2 has his wishes too and perhaps a_1 is not so favorite to him. Therefore, a decision a_2 is determined in such a way that

i) $a_2 \in \{a \in A \mid a >_{p_2} a_1\}$

ii) a_2 is the best alternative for p_1 satisfying i).

Now we are in the situation of a new agreement. The coalition involved is $Q = \{p_1,p_2\}$, where p_1 takes standpoint a_2 (forced by p_2) and p_2 takes standpoint a_1. This new agreement is again almost completely labeled, and the algorithm performs with calculating $\ell(a_2)$. If in the above situation such a_2 does not exist, it is easily seen that p_2 is the happy person: $a_1 = \max_{p_2} A$ and $F(a_1) \lesssim^{-}_{p_2} G(a_1)$. Person p_1 is dropped from the coalition. If a_2 exists and $\ell(a_2) = p_1$, the algorithm reaches a complete agreement,

$$F(a_1) \lesssim^{-}_{p_2} G(a_1)$$

and

$$F(a_2) \lesssim^{-}_{p_1} G(a_2).$$

By choosing an $\bar{a}$ close to a_1 and a_2 the two persons p_1 and p_2 may share cost and profit in a convenient way. If $\ell(a_2) \neq p_1$ the algorithm performs a new step.

We now give a general description of the algorithm. At each stage, which is not an end stage, exactly one label is missing, or equivalently, exactly one label appears twice. We remove the appearance of this double appearing label which was *not* introduced in the just preceeding stage. There are four cases to consider,

RPA: replacement of a passive label by an active one
RPP: replacement of a passive label by a passive one
RAA: replacement of an active label by an active one
RAP: replacement of an active label by a passive one.

In the RPA-case some person p is asked to join an existing coalition since p has been introduced as an active label in the previous stage, which means that for the existing coalition the inequality $F(a) \leq_{\sim p} G(a)$ holds for some possible alternative a. He is offered the most humble position w.r.t. his preference, say a_r. At his turn, person r shall have to play a less decisive role in the coalition. An alternative b is determined, see Figure 3, satisfying

i) $b >_q a_q$ for all coalition members $q \neq r$
ii) $b >_p a_r$
iii) among the alternatives satisfying i) and ii) b is the most preferred by r.

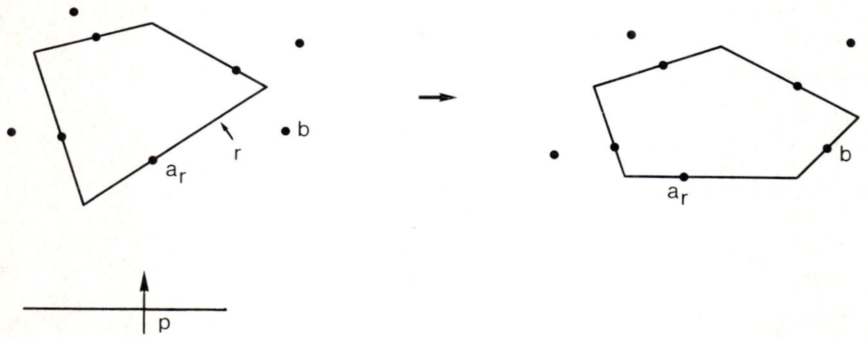

FIGURE 3
Replacing passive p by active $\ell(b)$, the RPA-case.

Since decision b is considered now by the new coalition they compute its balance: for which $s \in P$ is $F(b) \underset{\sim s}{<} G(b)$. That is, $\ell(b)$ is introduced.

In the RPA-case a decision b may not exist. This means that the new coalition partner p makes active contribution of r to form an agreement unnecessary. Hence r is excluded from the coalition and is introduced as a passive label, which is just the RPP-case.

In the RAA-case an active label $\ell(a_p) = s$ should be replaced. This means that either s was introduced as an active label in the previous stage, associated to a point a_q, or s has just been introduced as a passive label. In the first case the condition $F(x) \underset{\sim s}{<} G(x)$ is met by both a_q and a_p. Of these two persons q changed his position in the previous step, so now p is offered a promotion within the coalition. To promote q would lead to the previous stage again. To promote s also. Let a_r be the first preferable alternative of the agreement with respect to $\underset{\sim p}{<}$. Now person r has to pay for the promotion of p and an alternative b is determined, see Figure 4, satisfying

i) $b >_q a_q$ for $q \in Q$, $q \notin \{p,r\}$

ii) $b >_p a_r$

iii) b is the most suitable to r satisfying i) and ii).

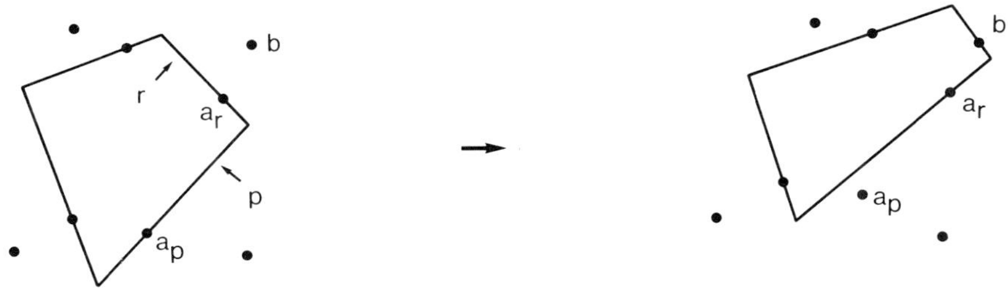

FIGURE 4
Replacing active $\ell(a_p)$ by active $\ell(b)$, the RAA-case.

If in the above such an alternative b does not exist, person r is excluded and he is introduced as a passive label, yielding the RAP-case.

Apart from the applicability in a general context, Theorem 4.1 is also interesting when considered in Euclidean setting. First, it shows that in $\mathbb{R}^n$ an integer labeling procedure can be carried out with as many labels as one wants. For instance, if one considers a random polytope X in $\mathbb{R}^n$ (that is a polytope without coincidences on the sets of its faces) one can use the facets of X to induce the orderings (by translation). After selecting a grid the algorithm provides a completely labeled crystal. This can be seen as a *generalized Sperner's lemma*. Passivity of a label in a complete crystal means that the corresponding facet is not needed to keep the crystal small. Figure 5 illustrates the above.

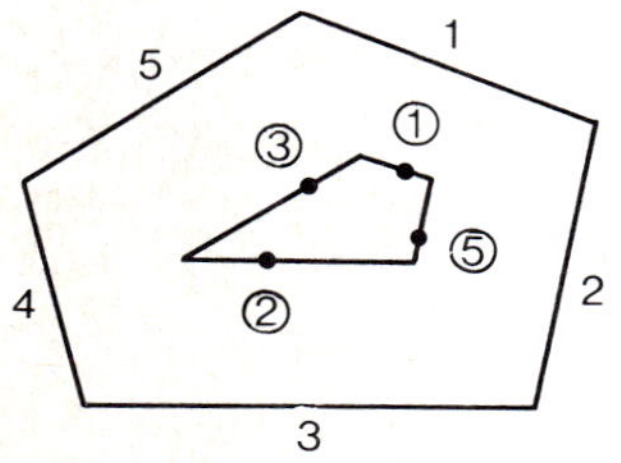

FIGURE 5a
A random polytope, the labels are circumferenced.

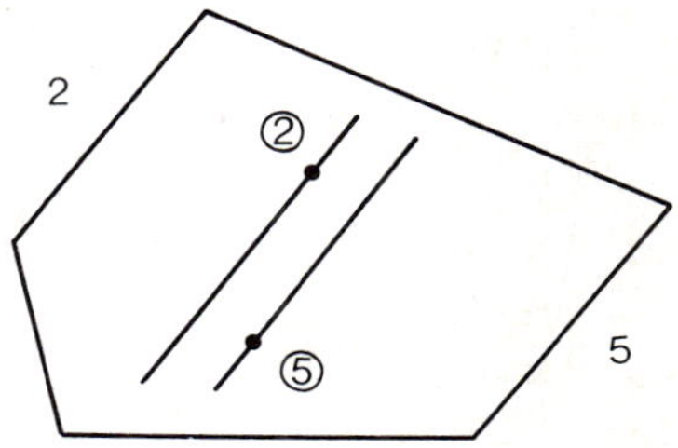

FIGURE 5b
Not a random polytope; the facets 2 and 5 are parallel.

Theorem 4.1 also indicates that the shape of the set $X \subset \mathbb{R}^n$ and the structure of the set of orderings need not to be correlated such as is the case in the current applications of fixed point algorithms, see Figure 6.

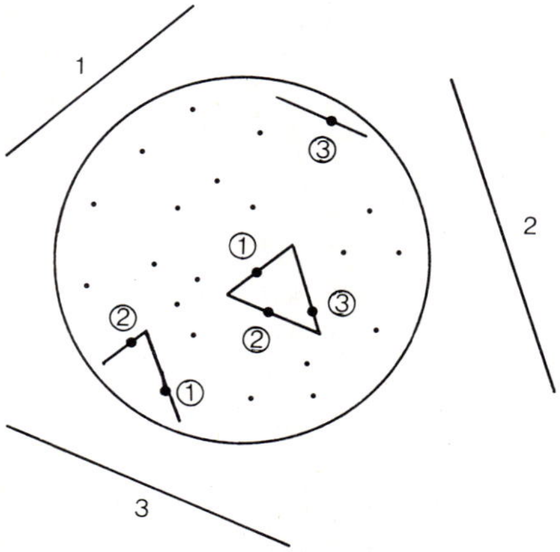

FIGURE 6

If $f : C \to \mathbb{R}^2$ is continuous and satisfies the inwardness condition at the boundary and if ℓ is the labeling associated to f in the canonical way, the completely labeled crystals drawn approximate fixed points of f on C.

5. TOWARDS A THEORY ON COALITIONS

In the previous sections we presented Theorem 3.1 as a discrete version of the general feasibility theorem. Going from this version to the continuous case generally shall require extra assumptions. We want to indicate here which concepts may play an important role in the formulation of these assumptions. Moreover, these concepts also have their meaning from a coalition-theoretic point of view.

5.1. Independency, Dimension, and Parasitism

In solving systems of inequalities a first need is a notion of dependency. For a coalition $Q \subset P$ and an element $a \in X$ we define the *Q-cone at a* as the set $\{x \in X | x \succsim_q a$ for all $q \in Q\}$. We denote this set by $C_Q(a)$. The *open* Q-cone at a is the set $C_Q(a) = \{x \in X | x >_q a$ for all $q \in Q\}$. Now a coalition Q is called *dependent* at a if for some proper subset S of Q we have $C_S(a) = C_Q(a)$. A coalition is *independent* at a if it is not dependent at a. A coaliton $Q \subset P$ is a *basis* at a if it is independent at a and $C_Q(a) = C_P(a)$. The *dimension* of X at a is the minimal cardinality of a basis at a.

The above notions are locally defined. A coalition is (globally) dependent if it is dependent at all $a \in X$. Global versions of independency, basis and dimension are defined accordingly. A little carefulness is needed in handling with these notions. For instance, it is not by all means true that in general two bases have the same cardinality, see for example Figure 7.

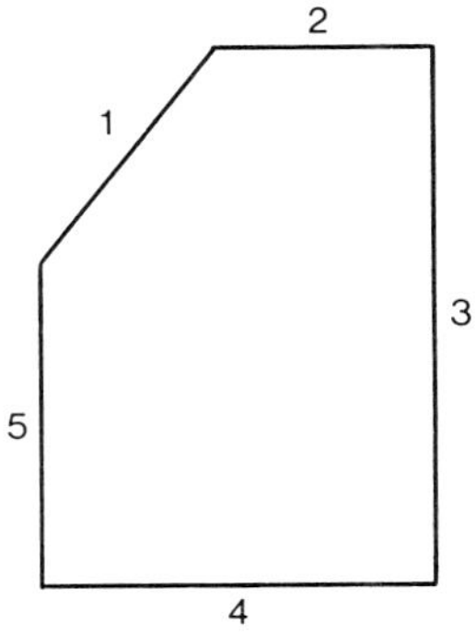

FIGURE 7

Coalitions {1,3,4} and {2,3,4,5} are both bases. The dimension of X is 3.

In terms of the algorithm of Section 4 dependency of a coalition $\bar{Q} \subset \bar{P}$ means that some members of the coalition Q play the role of a *parasite*, although they may be needed to constitute an agreement in case Q is independent.

By an accurate labeling device (such as label r can always be replaced by label p or by label q in the example of Figure 8) parasites can always be excluded in the final agreement. If one wishes to do so one should realize that possible solutions to the system, located in the "middle" of X, have no chance to show up.

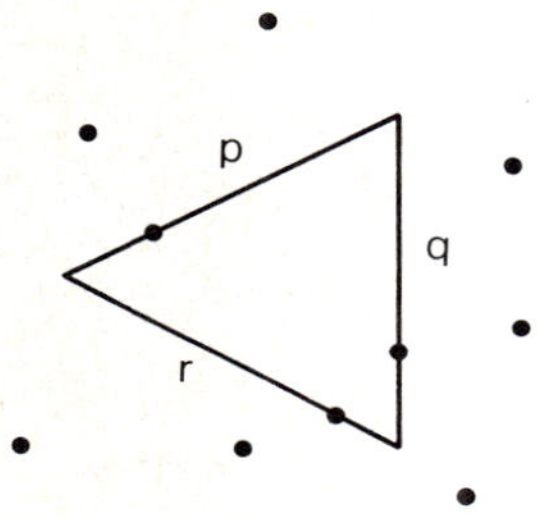

FIGURE 8a
Coalition {p,q,r} agrees.

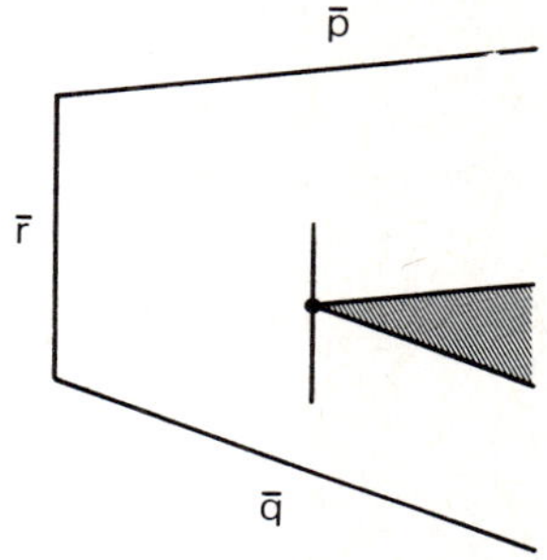

FIGURE 8b
r is a parasite.

5.2. The Coalition number, Domination, Boundaries, and Exhaustive coalitions

As we have seen from the example of Figure 2 some coalitions may constitute agreements whose alternatives are not close at all, not even in the eyes of some of their members. This is the case when some coalition members have more or less opposite interests, while still not being a basis. A coalition $Q \subset P$ is called *dominant* at $a \in X$ if $\mathring{C}_Q(a) = \emptyset$ and dominant if it is globally dominant. We call Q *strongly* dominant (at a) if no proper subcoalition of Q is dominant (at a). In Figure 2, {1,2,3} is dominant and {1,2} strongly dominant. Intuitively, an agreement of a non-dominant coalition is expected only to occur somewhere at the boundary of X, at least if the grid is taken sufficiently fine. Since, however, no topology is assumed, we define a notion of boundary in a combinatorial manner. For a coalition $Q \subset P$ the *Q-boundary* of X is the set $\partial_Q(X) = \{a \in X | Q \text{ is dominant at } a\}$.

The *coalition number* of a multiply ordered space X (at $a \in X$) is the smallest cardinality of a strongly dominant coalition (at a), if it exists. Equivalently, it is the smallest cardinality of a coalition Q with $X = \partial_Q(X)$ ($a \in \partial_Q(X)$). In Figure 9, 1 and 3 have opposite interests and {1,3} is strongly dominant but not a basis. Further, $\partial_{\{5\}}(X) = A$, $\partial_{\{1,2\}}(X) = AB \cup BC$ and $\partial_{\{4,5\}}(X) = AD$. The coalition number is equal to 2. If $\lesssim_3$ is slightly perturbed the coalition number becomes 3.

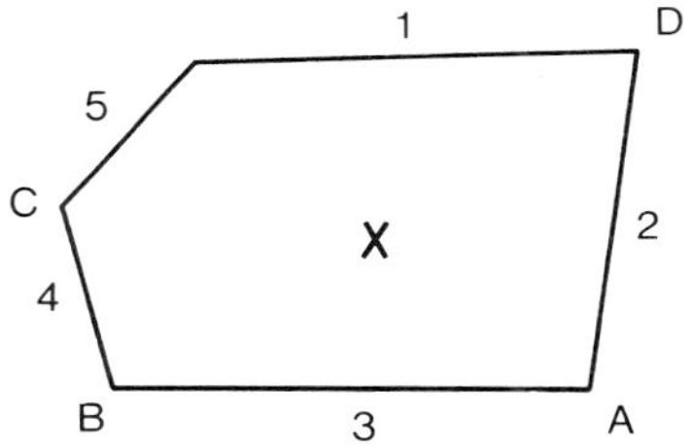

FIGURE 9

A coalition Q is called *exhaustive* at $a \in X$ iff $C_Q(a) = \{a\}$. In Figure 9, {1,3} is not exhaustive, but {2,4,5} is. Clearly, an exhaustive coalition is dominant, but not conversely. As we have seen, exhaustive coalitions are used in surjectivity and fixed point problems. Thusfar, topology is not assumed in advance. If X is a topological space it is natural to restrict the class of preference relations to be considered. We do so in Section 5.3.

5.3. Topological multiply ordered spaces, Preference-topologies and Preference numbers

The notions defined in the previous section may still lack the possibility of describing converging processes accurately. Consider for instance some topological space X. It is clear that X can be supplied with some total linear ordering $\lesssim$. This ordering, together with its converse, $\lesssim^*$, defined by $a \lesssim^* b$ iff $b \lesssim a$, constitutes an independent, dominant, and exhaustive coalition. However, it may fail to give any valuable information on feasibility problems. If X is both topological and multiply ordered we call X *upper-continuous* if the sets $\overset{\circ}{C}_p(a)$ are open for each $p \in$

P. X is called *continuous* if, besides, the sets $C_p(a)$ are closed. Thus, in a continuous, multiply ordered space, the sets $\{x|x \lesssim_p a\}$, $\{x|x \gtrsim_p a\}$ and $\{x|x \approx_p a\}$ are closed and the sets $\{x|x <_p a\}$ and $\{x|x >_p a\}$ are open.

We present two different concepts of topological multiply ordered spaces here because it seems that limit procedures in the image space Y (in the notation of Theorem 3.1) requires closedness of the sets $\{x|x \lesssim_p a\}$ and $\{x|x \gtrsim_p a\}$, while such limit procedures in X seem to require only that the sets $\{x|x >_p a\}$ are open.

For a multiply ordered space X the *upper-preference topology* is the topology generated by the $\mathring{C}_p(a)$, $a \in X$, $p \in P$, as open sets. The *preference topology* on X is the topology generated by the $\mathring{C}_p(a)$ as open sets and the $C_p(a)$ as closed sets. The (*upper-) preference number* of a topological space X is the smallest cardinality of a set of preference relations on X for which the (upper-) preference topology equals the given topology on X. The (upper-) preference number of a multiply ordered space is the (upper-) preference number of X supplied with the (upper-) preference topology. As an example consider the n-dimensional cube, the orderings being induced by the facets as in Figure 1. Both the preference topologies are Euclidean, so that X is a continuous, multiply ordered space. The dimension of X equals 2n, the coalition number is 2, and the preference number is at most n (in fact it equals n as we know from topological dimension theory). The upper-preference number is at most n+1 and probably equals n+1 (which is an open question). We see that the cube is highly degenerated from the view point of coalition theory, for instance compared to the n-dimensional simplex, which is also continuous, with dimension n+1, coalition number n+1, and upper-preference number (probably) n+1.

5.4. Boundary conditions

As emphasized earlier, the interpretation of Theorem 3.1 heavily depends on the actual structures. First there are topological requirements as compactness, connectedness and (local) contractability which are involved in the majority of feasibility problems. Second, boundary conditions are always included, at least if one wants to avoid proper subcoalitions. We only want to indicate here which kind of boundary conditions are natural, in view of the notions defined before.

First, of course, an investigation on the Q-boundaries of X, $Q \subset P$, justifies boundary conditions (in terms of labels) as

$$a \in \partial_Q(X) \Rightarrow \ell(a) \text{ can be each label not in } \bar{Q}.$$

The condition is motivated by the expectation that an agreement involving Q is situated near $\partial_Q(X)$. It is assumed that $\bar{P}$ is a basis in which case the condition considered is not too restrictive. Also, one may relate the boundary conditions more directly to the preference relations, for example

$$a \text{ is minimal w.r.t. } \underset{\sim p}{<} \Rightarrow \ell(a) = p.$$

This condition seems to be a natural one in simplex-like structures, which are spaces X satisfying that a is maximal w.r.t. $\underset{\sim p}{<}$ iff a is minimal w.r.t all other $\underset{\sim q}{<}$, $q \neq p$. In a topological setting, finally, restrictions may be required which relate the combinatorial boundaries to the topological boundaries.

5.5. Random and regular grids

If one wants to use grids which are not random a tie breaking rule is available in case coalition P is exhaustive. Suppose the relations considered are $\underset{\sim 1}{<}, \underset{\sim 2}{<}, \ldots, \underset{\sim n}{<}$. Now a set of new relations $\underset{\sim 1}{\tilde{<}}, \ldots, \underset{\sim n}{\tilde{<}}$ is defined in such a way that

1) $\underset{\sim i}{\tilde{<}}$ is a total (linear) order relation
2) $x \underset{\sim i}{\tilde{<}} y$ implies $x \underset{\sim i}{<} y$.

Because of 1) each grid becomes automatically random. Moreover, any agreement (in the new sense) yields alternatives which are still close together (in the old sense) because of 2). One should realize however that the new set of relations defines other preference topologies and may give a different coalition number or dimension. There are many ways to select the orderings $\underset{\sim i}{\tilde{<}}$. One way is suggested in Scarf [2]. Another possible way is

$$x \underset{\sim i}{\tilde{<}} y \Leftrightarrow x = y \text{ or } x <_i y \text{ or } (x \approx_i y \text{ and for the least number } k \text{ for which } x \not\approx_k y \text{ we have } x <_k y).$$

Notice that, because of the exhaustiveness of P, the above relations are defined properly.

6. VECTOR LABELING AND THE EXCHANGE NUMBER

In this section we discuss a variant of the algorithm which is based on vector labeling. This variant is used to study feasibility (or fixed point) properties of multifunctions.

We consider a set Y, the set B of subsets of Y having n elements, and a mapping $H : B \to \mathbb{P}(Y)$. We write $H(y_1,\dots,y_n)$ for $H(\{y_1,\dots,y_n\})$. It is assumed that H satisfies the (local) *exchange property* at $e \in Y$, that is $(y_1,\dots,y_n) \in B$ and $e \in H(y_1,\dots,y_n)$ imply that there is an i such that

$$(y_1,\dots,y_{i-1},y,y_{i+1},\dots,y_n) \in B$$

and

$$e \in H(y_1,\dots,y_{i-1},y,y_{i+1},\dots,y_n).$$

The most famous example of such an exchange procedure is undoubtedly the one from the simplex method. Here, B is taken as the set of bases of $Y = \mathbb{R}^n$ and $H(y_1,\dots,y_n)$ is the positive cone generated by the y_i's. Another example, which serves a heuristic purpose in view of our algorithm, is the exchange procedure w.r.t. the convex hull operator. That is, $Y = \mathbb{R}^k$, $k < n$, $B = Y^n$, and $H(y_1,\dots,y_n)$ is the convex hull of the set $\{y_1,\dots,y_n\}$, see for example Figure 10.

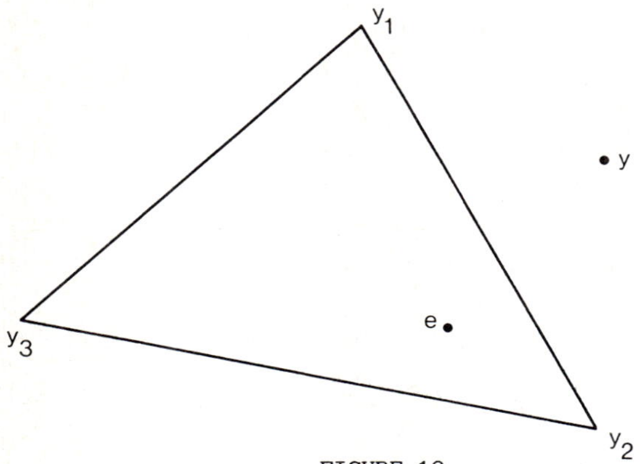

FIGURE 10
y_1 is exchangable with y; y_2 and y_3 are not.

The *exchange number* of a system <Y,B,H> (at e) is the least number n for which the exchange property is valid (at e). In [3] the exchange number was first introduced in connection with a set of hull systems. In various studies afterwards this invariant is related to the invariants of Carathéodory, Helly and Radon. It became a key concept in abstract hull theory and is also used to characterize the topological dimension of topological hull spaces. Thusfar, however, this invariant was never directly related to fixed point theory.

Now we define the context of our algorithm. It is assumed that a system $\langle Y,B,H\rangle$ is given with exchange number $k \leq n$ at $e \in Y$. Also we assume the presence of a multiply ordered space X, a set P with n members and associated preference relations $\lesssim_1,\ldots,\lesssim_n$ on X. Further a multifunction $F: X \to Y$ is considered and a selection f of F (which means $f(x) \in F(x)$ for $x \in X$) is taken. The relation $e \in H(D_1,\ldots,D_n)$ is supposed to be satisfied for some choice of $(D_1,\ldots,D_n) \in B$. An element of B is called a basis. For an agreement of a coalition Q on $\{a_q | q \in Q\}$, where A is a random grid of X, $f(a_q)$ is called an *active* label. If $p \notin Q$, D_p is a *passive* label of the agreement.

The algorithm will provide an agreement in such a way, that the following relations are satisfied

i) $e \in H(y_1,\ldots,y_n)$ and $(y_1,\ldots,y_n) \in B$
ii) each y_i is precisely one of the labels of the agreement.

Let us try to describe the algorithm in a manner analogously to Section 4. Again, X is considered as a set of possible investments for the persons of P. For $x \in X$, $F(x)$ is the set of possible profits of the investment x. The result of the algorithm makes more sense if we think of $F(x)$ as a set which is closed under the operation H. For $y_1,\ldots,y_n \in F(x)$ we have $H(y_1,\ldots,y_n) \subset F(x)$. This is the case when H represents some mixture operation on Y. If $y_1,\ldots,y_n$ are possible profits of an investment x, each mixture is also such a profit. Further, let us think of D_i as a guaranteed contribution of person i to a coalition in which his role is not active. Thus, the desired profit e can be assured by passivity of all persons if they just pay their "tax". We assume that paying tax is less attractive than any active contribution, for all persons involved. Now some person, say the first one, takes the initiative. The label of $a = \max_1 A$ is calculated.

If D_1 is exchangeable with $f(a)$ the algorithm terminates already, since $e \in H(f(a),D_2,\ldots,D_n)$ and the coalition $\{1\}$, which agrees on $\{a\}$, satisfies our requirements.

If D_1 is not exchangeable with f(a) some other D_i is. We exchange D_i with f(a) if i is the *least* index for which this is possible.

The next step in the algorithm is to "promote" person i, who is invited to join person 1 to constitute an agreement, that is, an RPA or RPP replacement (see Section 4) is carried out.

Now a uniquely determined new label shows up. If this label is active, say f(b), we proceed the algorithm with exchanging some element of the new basis

$$(D_1,\dots,D_{i-1},f(a),D_{i+1},\dots,D_n) \in B$$

with f(b). If a passive label D_k has shown up we exchange some element of the above basis with D_k. We shall *always* exchange the first possible y_i in $(y_1,\dots,y_n) \in B$ if more choices can be made!

The element exchanged in $(D_1,\dots,D_{i-1}, f(a),D_{i+1},\dots,D_n)$ now determines our next step. If this element is some D_j, person j is asked to join the coalition and an RPA or RPP step is made. If the element is f(a), the person with investment a is promoted, and an RAA or RAP step is executed. Schematically the algorithm proceeds as follows

→	Exchangement of the previously introduced new label with the first possible element of the current basis. A new basis is established.	→	The previously removed label of the current agreement is replaced by a new label, according to an RAA,RAP,RPA or RPP step. A new agreement is established.	→

The arguments which prove that the algorithm will provide a desired agreement, after a finite number of steps, are already in [2]. We are only concerned with the tie breaking rule that is put in to avoid cycling. The exchangement of an element of a basis may not be uniquely determined, see Figure 11.

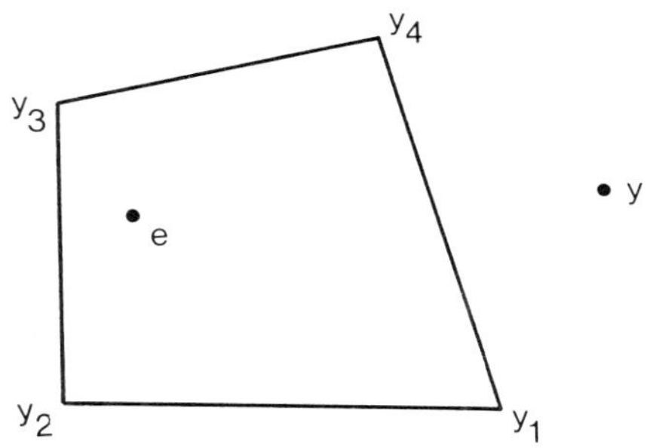

FIGURE 11
The point y is exchangeable with both y_1 and y_4.

The rule that an exchangement is carried out with the first possible input of H will, however, avoid cycling. To see this, suppose that we have obtained $(y_1,\ldots,y_{i-1},y,y_{i+1},\ldots,y_n) \in B$ by exchanging some $y \in Y$ with y_i, according to the tie breaking rule. If we exchange y_i again according to this rule and this can be done with, say, y_k with $k < i$, we obtain

$$e \in H(y_1,\ldots,y_{k-1},y_i,y_{k+1},\ldots,y_{i-1},y,y_{i+1},\ldots,y_n)$$

but also

$$e \notin H(y_1,\ldots,y_{k-1},y,y_{k+1},\ldots,y_{i-1},y_i,y_{i+1},\ldots,y_n).$$

This contradicts the symmetry of H w.r.t. its variables. We conclude that exchanging y_i again will bring us in the previous basis. Therefore, no basis and no agreement will show up more than once during the execution of the algorithm, so that cycling is not possible and termination is assured. Termination only can happen in an agreement of the desired form, that is, we obtain a coalition Q which agrees on $\{a_q | q \in Q\}$ and, moreover, the desired profit e appears to be a mixture of the profits $\{f(a_q) | q \in Q\}$ and the taxes $\{D_p | p \notin Q\}$.

We conclude with the remark that a continuous variant of the above results generates a point $a \in A$ with $e \in F(a)$. Of course this presupposes for instance the possibilities of removing the slack elements D_i, an upper-semicontinuity property of F, closedness of the sets F(a) under H, compactness of X, and, finally, continuity properties of H w.r.t. a suitable topology on $\mathbf{P}(Y)$ or Y^n. As far as approximations are concerned, however, we believe that our discrete version is interesting in its own right.

REFERENCES

[1] F.J. Gould and J.W. Tolle, *Complementary pivoting on a pseudomanifold structure with applications in the decision sciences,* Sigma Series in Applied Mathematics, Heldermann Verlag, Berlin, 1983.

[2] H.E. Scarf, *The computation of economic equilibria,* Yale University Press, New Haven, 1973.

[3] G. Sierksma, Axiomatic convexity theory and the convex product space, Ph.D. Dissertation, Rijksuniversiteit Groningen, Groningen, The Netherlands, 1976.

[4] H. Tuy, "Pivotal methods for computing equilibrium points: unified approach and new restart algorithm", *Mathematical Programming* 16 (1979) 210-227.

The Computation and Modelling of Economic Equilibria
A.J.J. Talman, G. van der Laan (Editors)

ON A THEOREM OF SCARF

Ludo VAN DER HEYDEN*

School of Organization and Management, Yale University, P.O. Box 1A, New Haven, CT 06520, USA

Scarf's *The Computation of Economic Equilibria* is a fundamental contribution to the area of fixed point computations. Its main theorem and algorithm were originally stated in terms of combinatorial objects called primitive sets. In this paper the Scarf theorem is given an alternative formulation as an intersection theorem for labelled polyhedra. This polyhedral framework offers a more natural geometry for the Scarf theorem and for its associated algorithm than that of primitive sets. It also clearly links the theorem with the linear complementarity problem, which is a central problem in mathematical programming. In the polyhedral framework the linear complementarity problem becomes an intersection problem among labelled halfspaces. Finally, the paper presents other instances of the polyhedral Scarf theorem, including generalizations of the linear complementarity problem and the problem of finding a point in the core of a balanced finitely polyhedral game.

1. INTRODUCTION

Scarf's *The Computation of Economic Equilibria* is a fundamental contribution to the area of fixed point computations. Its main theorem, Scarf [11, Theorem 4.2.3], originally stated in terms of combinatorial objects called primitive sets, is here formulated as an intersection theorem for labelled polyhedral sets.

One goal of the paper is to present a geometry for the Scarf theorem that is more standard, and possibly more accessible, than that traditionally associated with primitive sets. We show that primitive sets can be defined in terms of particular intersections of polyhedra. Movements among

---

* The paper was first written while the author was visiting the Center for Econometrics and Mathematical Economics at the Université Libre de Bruxelles, Belgium. We thank its members for their cordial hospitality.

primitive sets give way to the more familiar notion of piecewise linear path following. A path following aspect of the Scarf algorithm appears that is not transparent in its original combinatorial form.

Our polyhedral framework also provides a clear link between the Scarf theorem and the linear complementarity problem (LCP). The LCP is a central problem in mathematical programming. Its instances include quadratic programming and bimatrix games, for example see Cottle and Dantzig [2]. In our polyhedral framework, the LCP becomes an intersection problem among labelled halfspaces. The constructive procedure used to prove the polyhedral Scarf theorem, when applied to the LCP, reduces to the path following procedure proposed by Lemke [8]. Conversely, our intersection theorem for labelled polyhedra can be formulated as an LCP in a higher dimensional space. However, this LCP formulation of the polyhedral intersection problem hides the lower dimensional nature of the polyhedral intersection problem.

The paper concludes by indicating how three other problems have natural formulations as intersection problems among labelled polyhedra. Two of these problems are generalizations of the LCP due to Scarf [10] and to Cottle and Dantzig [2]. The third problem concerns the computation of a point in the core of a balanced finitely polyhedral game.

2. A POLYHEDRAL VERSION OF SCARF'S THEOREM

For a given positive integer k, let I^k denote the set $\{1,2,...,k\}$. Let $\{P^j | j \in I^k\}$ be a finite collection of polyhedral sets in $\mathbb{R}^n$, where, for each $j \in I^k$, $P^j = \{x \in \mathbb{R}^n | A^j x \leq b^j\}$ with $A^j \in \mathbb{R}^{mj\times n}$ and $b^j \in \mathbb{R}^{mj}$, mj denoting a positive integer. Let $m = \Sigma_{j=1}^k mj$. Let $A = [A^j] \in \mathbb{R}^{m\times n}$ be the matrix containing the k submatrices A^j, $j \in I^k$, each matrix A^{j+1} being positioned in A below matrix A^j. Similarly, let $b = [b^j] \in \mathbb{R}^m$ be the vector containing the k subvectors b^j, $j \in I^k$. Throughout the paper subscripts will refer to row indices. Hence, the i-th row of A^j is denoted A_i^j, $i \in I^{mj}$. The identity matrix will be denoted U; its i-th row, a unit vector, will be denoted U_i. Finally, given vector $y \in \mathbb{R}^p$, its transpose will be denoted y^T.

With this collection of polyhedra is associated a linear system,

$$Ly = d, \; y \geq 0, \tag{2.1}$$

with $L \in \mathbb{R}^{nxk}$, $y \in \mathbb{R}^k$, and $d \in \mathbb{R}^n$. The j-th column of L, $L^j \in \mathbb{R}^n$, is an n-dimensional vector called the *label* of P^j. Let $J = \{j_1, j_2, \ldots, j_p\} \subset I^k$. The labels $\{L^j | j \in J\}$ are said to be *complete* if they correspond to a feasible solution for linear system (2.1), i.e. if there exists a solution $y \in \mathbb{R}^k$ for (2.1) such that $y_j > 0$ only if $j \in J$. The polyhedra associated with a complete set of labels are said to be *completely* labelled.

The polyhedral Scarf theorem presents sufficient conditions for n completely labelled polyhedra, $\{P^j | j \in J\}$ with $J = \{j_1, j_2, \ldots, j_n\} \subset I^k$, to meet in a point which is not interior to any of them. Such a point, say x, satisfies

$$\begin{aligned} \max(A^j x - b^j) &\geq 0, \; j \in I^k, \\ &= 0, \; j \in J, \end{aligned}$$

where $\{L^j | j \in J\}$ is complete and where, for any $z = (z_1, z_2 \ldots, z_p)^T \in \mathbb{R}^p$, $\max(z) = \max(z_1, z_2, \ldots, z_p)$. The problem of determining such a point x will be referred to as a *polyhedral intersection problem* and will be denoted $P(A,b;L,d)$.

In this paper we restrict ourselves to polyhedral intersection problems *in standard form,* that is:

(i) the first n polyhedra are assumed to be coordinate halfspaces, i.e., $P^j = \{x \in \mathbb{R}^n | x_j \leq 0\}$ for $j \in I^n$,

(ii) the label of P^j, $j \in I^n$, is the j-th unit vector in $\mathbb{R}^n$, $(U_j)^T$,

(iii) the right-hand side d of linear system (2.1) is strictly positive.

Notice that an intersection problem in standard form verifies, for $j \in I^n$, $mj = 1$, $A^j = U_j$, and $b^j = 0$. In addition, $L = (U,M)$ with $U \in \mathbb{R}^{nxn}$ the identity matrix of order n and with $M \in \mathbb{R}^{nx(k-n)}$. The standard form assumption is met in the applications considered in this paper. It allows a convenient initialization of the constructive procedure used in the proof of the polyhedral Scarf theorem. The reader will observe the similarity with the standard form assumption of linear programming.

Sufficient conditions for a polyhedral intersection problem in standard form to have a solution are now stated. They require boundedness and ensure that the operations in our constructive proof are well defined.

Assumption 2.1. The label system $Ly = d$, $y \geq 0$, is bounded.

Assumption 2.2. (i) The homogeneous polyhedral intersection problem $P(A,c;L,d)$, where $c^j = 0$ for $j \in I^k$, admits the unique solution $x = 0$. (ii) There exists a nonnegative vector $f = [f^j] \in \mathbb{R}^m_+$ with $f^j = 0$ for $j \in I^n$ and $f^j \neq 0$ for $j \notin I^n$ such that the polyhedral intersection problem $P(A,-f;L,d)$ admits the unique solution $x = 0$.

Having developed terminology and presented assumptions, we now state the main theorem.

Theorem 2.3. (Polyhedral Scarf Theorem). A polyhedral intersection problem in standard form satisfying Assumptions 2.1 and 2.2 has a solution.

The case where all labels are unit vectors and where the right-hand side d of equation (2.1) is strictly positive has an equivalent interpretation in terms of *integer labels*, the j-th unit vector corresponding to integer label j. A collection of integer labels is complete if it contains I^n. Let ℓ^j denote the integer label of polyhedron P^j, $j \in I^k$. A polyhedral intersection problem with integer labels is denoted $P(A,b;\ell)$. Observe that the standard form assumption requires that $\ell^i = i$ for $i \in I^n$. A polyhedral intersection problem with integer labels clearly satisfies Assumption 2.1. A condition which is easily shown to imply Assumption 2.2 is the following.

Assumption 2.4. Let $P(A,b;\ell)$ be a polyhedral intersection problem with integer labels. Let $J = \{j_1,j_2,\dots,j_n\}$ be the indices of a complete set of labels $\{\ell^j | j \in J\}$. Then $x \geq 0$ and $\max(A^j x) \leq 0$ for $j \in J$ implies $x = 0$.

The reader will notice that, for an intersection problem in standard form, the conditions $x_j \geq 0$ and $\max(A^j x) \leq 0$ with $j \in I^n$ imply $x_j = 0$. In Section 4.3 it will be shown that an intersection problem involving k vector labelled polyhedra in $\mathbb{R}^n$ $(k > n)$ can be formulated as an intersection problem involving integer labelled polyhedra in $\mathbb{R}^k$. This transformation establishes the conceptual generality of polyhedral intersection problems with integer labels, but its computational interest is limited. It does not recognize the privileged role of the linear system of labels and thus fails to recognize the lower dimensional nature of the computation.

Finally, we observe that a different version of the polyhedral Scarf theorem can be obtained by eliminating the first n polyhedra and their labels.

3. A CONSTRUCTIVE PROOF

Following Lemke [8] we consider the parametrized family of polyhedral intersection problems $P(A,b(\vartheta);L,d)$ obtained by perturbing the vector of right-hand sides $b = [b^j] \in \mathbb{R}^m$. For each $\vartheta \in \mathbb{R}$, $b(\vartheta) = b - f\vartheta = [b^j - f^j\vartheta]$, where $f = [f^j] \in \mathbb{R}^m$ is the vector introduced in Assumption 2.2. Furthermore, let $\bar{P}^j = \{(x,\vartheta) | A^j x \leq b^j(\vartheta)\} \subset \mathbb{R}^{n+1}$ and let x^ϑ denote a solution of $P(A,b(\vartheta);L,d)$. We recall that each polyhedral intersection problem is assumed to be in standard form. In particular this implies that $b^j = f^j = 0$ for $j \in I^n$.

The procedure used to prove Theorem 2.3 consists in describing a piecewise linear path of points $[x^{\vartheta(t)},\vartheta(t)]$ until $\vartheta(t) = 0$. Each point on this path satisfies

$$\max(A^j x + f^j\vartheta - b^j) \geq 0, \; j \in I^k, \qquad (3.1)$$

$$= 0, \; j \in J,$$

with $J = \{j_1, j_2, \ldots, j_n\}$ the index set of a complete set of labels, $\{L^j | j \in J\}$. As will be shown shortly, different line segments along the path may be associated with different complete sets of labels.

Some technical assumptions need to be satisfied for these points to form a path.

Assumption 3.1. The label system $Ly = d$, $y \geq 0$ is nondegenerate, i.e., any solution y has at least n nonzero components.

Assumption 3.2. The hyperplanes defining the faces of the polyhedra $\bar{P}^j = \{(x,\vartheta) | A^j x + f^j\vartheta \leq b^j\}$ meet nondegenerately in $\mathbb{R}^{n+1}$, i.e., no point (x,ϑ) satisfies more than n+1 among the m equations $A^j x + f^j\vartheta = b^j$, $j \in I^k$.

These assumptions involve no loss of generality. They can always be satisfied by applying lexicographic tie-breaking techniques to the right-hand sides of the equations (2.1) and of the inequalities (3.1), see for example Dantzig [3].

Assumption 3.1, when considered jointly with Assumption 2.1, implies that a complete set of n+1 labels contains precisely two complete subsets of n labels each. When an arbitrary (n+1)-st label is added to a complete set of n labels, precisely one among the latter n labels can be replaced with the (n+1)-st label so as to yield a new complete set of n labels. The identification of the departing label involves a standard linear programming pivot step, see Dantzig [3], and is one of the two operations central to our constructive proof. The second operation consists in following a piecewise linear path of solutions for (3.1). Consider a line segment of solutions as defined in (3.1), with $J = \{j_1, j_2, \ldots, j_n\}$ denoting the index set of a complete set of labels, $\{L^j | j \in J\}$. Such a line segment is part of the intersection of particular faces of the polyhedra $\bar{P}^j$, $j \in J$. These faces identify indices $i_j \in I^{mj}$, $j \in J$, such that points (x, ϑ) on the line segment satisfy, for each $j \in J$,

$$A_i^j x + f_i^j \vartheta - b_i^j = 0 \text{ when } i = i_j, \qquad (3.2)$$

$$\leq 0 \qquad i \neq i_j,$$

while, for each $j \in I^k \backslash J$,

$$\max(A^j x + f^j \vartheta - b^j) \geq 0. \qquad (3.3)$$

The procedure follows the line segment to one of its end points, where one of the above inequalities becomes an equality. By nondegeneracy Assumption 3.2 precisely one inequality becomes an equality at the end point. The fact that it is an inequality in (3.2) that becomes an equality signals that another face of a polyhedron $\bar{P}^j$ with $j \in J$ has been reached. If an inequality in (3.3) becomes satisfied with equality, then the boundary of a polyhedron $\bar{P}^j$ with $j \notin J$ has been reached. The first possibility leads to a *position of type* 1, the second to a *position of type* 2. At a position of type 1 the path changes direction without leaving the boundary of any of the polyhedra it was travelling on; at a position of type 2 the path changes direction so as not to move into the interior of a polyhedron whose boundary was just reached.

The examination of both types of position will reveal that there are precisely two line segments of solutions for (3.1) incident to every position.

A position of type 1, (x,ϑ), is associated with n complete labels, $\{L^j | j \in J\}$ with $J = \{j_1, j_2, \ldots, j_n\}$, and n+1 indices, $\{i_j | j \in J\} \cup \{i'_j | j = j_n\}$, such that

$$A^j_i x + f^j_i \vartheta - b^j_i = 0, \ i = i_j \text{ with } j \in J,$$

$$= 0, \ i = i'_j \text{ with } j = j_n,$$

all other inequalities being strict by Assumption 3.2. It is easily seen that the only two line segments of solutions for (3.1) incident to this position are obtained by turning one of the last two equations, $A^j_i x + f^j_i \vartheta - b^j_i = 0$ with $i = i_j, i'_j$ and $j = j_n$, into an inequality (<0).

A position of type 2, (x,ϑ), is associated with n+1 complete labels, $\{L^j | j \in J\}$ with $J = \{j_1, j_2, \ldots, j_{n+1}\}$, and n+1 indices, $\{i_j | j \in J\}$, such that

$$A^j_i x + f^j_i \vartheta - b^j_i = 0, \ i = i_j \text{ with } j \in J,$$

all other inequalities being strict. If $\{L^j | j = j_1, j_2, \ldots, j_n\}$ and $\{L^j | j = j_2, j_3, \ldots, j_{n+1}\}$ are the two complete subsets of labels of cardinality n, then the only two line segments of solutions for (3.1) incident to this position consist of points satisfying n among the above equations, and

$$A^j_i x + f^j_i \vartheta - b^j_i > 0, \ i = i_j,$$

with $j = j_1$ for the first line segment and $j = j_{n+1}$ for the second line segment. Every position of type 2 is thus also incident to precisely two line segments of solutions for (3.1).

The procedure is now easily described. One particular line segment of solutions for (3.1) serves to initialize the procedure. For all sufficiently large ϑ the points $(x,\vartheta) = (0,\vartheta)$ satisfy (3.1) with $j_i = i$, $i \in I^n$. This initial line segment is followed in the direction of decreasing values of ϑ. Generally, a line segment of solutions for (3.1) is followed until either $\vartheta = 0$ or until a new position is reached. In the latter case, the procedure leaves the position along the other line segment incident to it.

The argument establishing the finiteness of this path following procedure is due to Lemke [8]. We repeat it here for completeness. Every position is incident to two line segments. Since the procedure never moves backward along the path, the first position that could be visited twice is the initial one. However, this position was initially reached via an unbounded line segment and therefore cannot be revisited either. The finiteness of the number of positions, which follows from Assumption 3.2, implies that the procedure either terminates with a solution for P(A,b;L,d) - when $\vartheta = 0$ - or finds a second unbounded line segment for (3.1). We now argue that the latter possibility is ruled out by boundedness Assumption 2.2. The direction $(\bar{x},\bar{\vartheta})$ of an unbounded line segment of solutions for (3.1) would satisfy $\bar{\vartheta} \geq 0$ and

$$\max(A^j\bar{x} + f^j\bar{\vartheta}) \geq 0 \text{ for } j \in I^k,$$

$$= 0 \text{ for } j \in J = \{j_1, j_2, \ldots, j_n\},$$

the label set $\{L^j | j \in J\}$ being complete. Without loss of generality we may assume $\bar{\vartheta} = 0$ or 1. Assumption 2.2 implies $\bar{\vartheta} = 1$ and thus $\bar{x} = 0$. The fact that $f^j \neq 0$ for $j \notin I^n$ then requires $J = I^n$. The initial line segment is thus the only unbounded line segment of solutions for (3.1).

The procedure thus always terminates with a solution for P(A,b;L,d). This proves Scarf's theorem constructively. All steps in the procedure are standard operations involving linear equality or inequality systems. They are easily implemented.

4. APPLICATIONS

4.1. The Scarf theorem for primitive sets

Consider a sequence $P = \{p^j | j \in I^k\}$ of k vectors in $\mathbb{R}^n_+$ $(k > n)$. The vectors are all assumed to have strictly positive coordinates, except for the first n which verify $p^j_i = 0$ for $i = j$ and $p^j_i = +\infty$ for $i \neq j$, $j \in I^n$. The first n vectors are called *slack* vectors. It is furthermore assumed that, for each $i \in I^n$, the i-th coordinates of the nonslack vectors all differ.

The Scarf theorem for primitive sets corresponds to a polyhedral intersection problem involving the polyhedra $P^j = \{x \in \mathbb{R}^n | x \leq p^j\}$. Each vector (and corresponding polyhedron) is associated with a label $L^j \in \mathbb{R}^n$. Slack vector p^j, $j \in I^n$, is given the unit label $(U_j)^T$. Since the polyhedron corresponding to slack p^j can be written $P^j = \{x \in \mathbb{R}^n | x_j \le 0\}$, the polyhedral intersection problem is in standard form. Furthermore, $A^j = U$ for $j \notin I^n$. This is easily seen to imply that boundedness Assumption 2.2 is satisfied.

Theorem 2.3 asserts the existence of a point $x \in \mathbb{R}^n$ such that $\max(x-p^j) \ge 0$ for $j \in I^k$ and $\max(x-p^j) = 0$ for $j \in J = \{j_1, j_2, \ldots, j_n\}$, with $\{L^j | j \in J\}$ being a complete set of labels. Observe that $\max(x-p^j) = 0$ if and only if $x \le p^j$ with equality in at least one coordinate. Since the i-th coordinates of the vectors in P all differ when they are finite, x shares a different coordinate with each vector p^j, $j \in J$, and also is the coordinate-wise minimum of the vectors p^j, $j \in J$. In addition, no vector p^j, $j \in I^k \setminus J$, has all its coordinates larger than the corresponding coordinates of x, i.e., no p^j strictly dominates x. The set of n vectors in P thus identified, $\{p^j | j \in J\}$, is called *primitive* in Scarf [11]. Theorem 2.3 asserts the existence in a list of labelled vectors of a completely labelled primitive set.

The Scarf primitive set theorem and its constructive proof have numerous applications in mathematical programming, well described by Scarf [11]. More recently, this theorem has been applied to the solution of integer programming problems, see Scarf [12].

4.2. The linear complementarity problem (LCP)

The linear complementarity problem with data $M \in \mathbb{R}^{n \times n}$ and $q \in \mathbb{R}^n$, denoted LCP(M,q), consists in finding a vector $x \in \mathbb{R}^n_+$ satisfying

$$Mx \ge q \tag{4.1}$$

and

$$M_j x = q_j \text{ if } x_j > 0, \ j \in I^n. \tag{4.2}$$

This problem corresponds to an intersection problem in standard form involving 2n integer labelled polyhedra, with $P^{n+j} = \{x | M_j x \le q_j\}$ for $j \in I^n$. Both P^j and P^{n+j} receive integer label j. A completely labelled set of n polyhedra, $\{P^j | j \in J\}$, contains, for each $j \in I^n$, either P^j or P^{n+j}. A solution of this polyhedral intersection problem satisfies inequalities (4.1) and complementarity conditions (4.2). Boundedness Assumption 2.2 requires that both LCP(M,0) and LCP(M,-f), with f being a certain strictly positive vector in $\mathbb{R}^n$, admit the unique solution x = 0. This condition is standard in LCP theory (Garcia [7]).

4.3. Two piecewise linear generalizations of the LCP

The first generalization of the LCP is due to Cottle and Dantzig [2]. For each $j \in I^n$ let mj denote a positive integer. Given matrices $M^j \in \mathbb{R}^{mj \times n}$ and vectors $q^j \in \mathbb{R}^{mj}$, $j \in I^n$, the Cottle and Dantzig generalization of the LCP consists in finding a vector $x \in \mathbb{R}^n_+$ such that

$$\begin{aligned} \min(M^j x - q^j) &\geq 0 \text{ for } j \in I^n, \\ &= 0 \text{ if } x_j > 0. \end{aligned} \tag{4.3}$$

The notation adopted in the above statement is, for $y \in \mathbb{R}^p$, $\min(y) = -\max(-y)$. This problem can be interpreted as a polyhedral intersection problem in standard form by associating with each system $\min(M^j x - q^j) \geq 0$ the mj polyhedra $P^{n+j,k} = \{x \in \mathbb{R}^n | M^j_k x \leq q^j_k\}$, $k \in I^{mj}$, each polyhedron $P^{n+j,k}$ receiving integer label j. Assumption 2.2 includes the condition given by Cottle and Dantzig sufficient for existence of a solution. This condition extends to certain rectangular matrices the notion of strict semi-monotonicity defined by Cottle and Dantzig [1] for square matrices.

A second generalization of the LCP is due to Scarf [10]. Its mathematical statement is obtained by substituting min with max in (4.3). More precisely, it consists in finding a vector $x \in \mathbb{R}^n_+$ such that

$$\begin{aligned} \max(M^j x - q^j) &\geq 0 \text{ for } j \in I^n, \\ &= 0 \text{ if } x_j > 0. \end{aligned}$$

This problem is easily seen to be a polyhedral intersection problem among $2n$ integer labelled polyhedra, $P^j = \{x \in \mathbb{R}^n | x_j \leq 0\}$ and $P^{n+j} = \{x \in \mathbb{R}^n | M^j x \leq q^j\}$, $j \in I^n$. Both P^j and P^{n+j} carry integer label j.

A slight extension of the condition imposed by Scarf for convergence of his procedure is, that for every nonempty subset J of I^n, the inequalities $x_J \geq 0$ and $(M^j)^J x_J \leq 0$ for $j \in J$ imply $x_J = 0$, where $(M^j)^J$ is obtained from M^j by deleting all columns with indices not in J and where x_J is obtained from x by deleting all elements with indices not in J. This condition, which is easily seen to imply Assumption 2.2, also extends to a collection of rectangular matrices the property of strict semi-monotonicity of Cottle and Dantzig [1] mentioned above. This extension differs from the Cottle and Dantzig [2] extension.

There is a converse to the relationship between the polyhedral intersection problem and the complementarity problem considered by Scarf. Consider the polyhedral intersection problem $P(A,b;L,d)$. Let $L = (U,M)$ with $U \in \mathbb{R}^{n\times n}$ and $M \in \mathbb{R}^{n\times(k-n)}$, see Assumption 2.1. Let $x \in \mathbb{R}^n$ denote a solution for the polyhedral intersection problem and let $y \in \mathbb{R}^k$ denote the vector of weights associated with this solution, with $y^\top = (v^\top,w^\top)$ and $v \in \mathbb{R}^n$, $w \in \mathbb{R}^{k-n}$. Linear system (2.1) can be written $Uv + Mw = d$, $v \geq 0$, $w \geq 0$. Elimination of v yields the inequality $Mw \leq d$, $w \geq 0$. Observe that x and v are complementary, i.e., $x_jv_j = 0$ for $j \in I^n$. This implies that $(x^\top,w^\top)^\top \in \mathbb{R}^k$ satisfies

$$x_j \geq 0, \qquad -M_jw + d_j \geq 0, \qquad j \in I^n$$

$$w_{j-n} \geq 0, \qquad \max(A^jx - b^j) \geq 0, \qquad j \in I^k\backslash I^n$$

with

$$-M_jw + d_j = 0 \qquad \text{if } x_j > 0, \qquad j \in I^n$$

$$\max(A^jx - b^j) = 0 \qquad \text{if } w_{j-n} > 0, \qquad j \in I^k\backslash I^n.$$

This shows that an intersection problem in standard form involving k vector labelled polyhedra in $\mathbb{R}^n$ $(k > n)$ can be formulated as a piecewise linear complementarity problem in $\mathbb{R}^k$. In the beginning of this subsection, we showed that the latter problem is a special case of an intersection problem in standard form involving 2k integer labelled polyhedra in $\mathbb{R}^k$. Hence, any intersection problem in standard form involving k vector labelled polyhedra in $\mathbb{R}^n$ can be formulated as an intersection problem in standard form involving 2k integer labelled polyhedra in $\mathbb{R}^k$.

4.4. Finding a point in the core of a balanced finitely polyhedral game

We first introduce additional notation. Given a set X, let S(X) denote the collection of nonempty subsets of X. Given $C \in S(I^n)$ and $x = (x_1,x_2,\ldots,x_n)^\top \in \mathbb{R}^n$, let x_C denote the vector $(x_i|i \in C)$.

We now define an n-person cooperative game. The index set I^n identifies the *players* of the game. A set $C \in S(I^n)$ represents a *coalition* of players. The *characteristic function* $V : S(I^n) \to S(\mathbb{R}^n)$ of an n-person cooperative game is a mapping defining the utility vectors members of C can ensure for themselves (by acting jointly). The characteristic function is assumed to obey the following properties:

a) $V(C)$ is a nonempty closed subset of $\mathbb{R}^n$
b) $x \in V(C)$, $y \in \mathbb{R}^n$, and $y_C = x_C$ imply $y \in V(C)$
c) $x \in V(C)$, $y \in \mathbb{R}^n$, and $y \leq x$ imply $y \in V(C)$ (4.4)
d) $V(C) \cap \{x \in \mathbb{R}^n | x_i = 0 \text{ for } i \notin C\}$ is bounded from above
e) $V(\{i\}) = \{x \in \mathbb{R}^n | x_i \leq 0\}$ for each $i \in I^n$.

These assumptions are standard. They are discussed, for example, in Scarf [11]. An *n-person cooperative game* consists of a set of players, I^n, and of a characteristic function, V, defined on the coalitions of players and satisfying properties (4.4). Such a game is said to be *finitely polyhedral* if each characteristic set, $V(C)$, is a finite union of n_C polyhedra, $V^k(C)$ with $k \in I^{n_C}$, each polyhedron $V^k(C)$ satisfying (4.4). Observe that $n_C = 1$ when $C = \{i\}$, $i \in I^n$. Let $V^k(C) = \{x \in \mathbb{R}^n | A^{C,k} x_C \leq b^{C,k}\}$. The properties (4.4) imply $A^{C,k} \geq 0$ and

$$x_C \geq 0 \text{ and } A^{C,k} x_C \leq 0 \Rightarrow x_C = 0. \tag{4.5}$$

An important solution concept in cooperative game theory is the core. The *core* of an n-person cooperative game consists of the utility vectors that can be achieved by the coalition of all players and that have the property that no coalition disposes of a utility vector that is strictly preferred by all its members. Mathematically the core is the set $\{x \in V(I^n) | x \notin \text{int}(V(C)) \text{ for any } C \in S(I^n)\}$, where int(X) denotes the interior of a given set X.

A fundamental result in cooperative game theory is the assertion that every balanced game has a nonempty core (Scarf [11]). To define balanced games, we introduce the notion of a balanced collection of coalitions. A collection of coalitions, $\{C_j \in S(I^n) | j \in J\}$, is *balanced* if there exist nonnegative weights, $\{y_j \in \mathbb{R}_+ | j \in J\}$, satisfying for all $i \in I^n$

$$\textstyle\sum_{j \in J_i} y_j = 1$$

where $J_i = \{j \in J | i \in C_j\}$. A game is *balanced* if for every balanced collection $\{C_j \in S(I^n) | j \in J\}$, $\cap_{j \in J} V(C_j) \subset V(I^n)$.

We now specify how the polyhedral Scarf theorem and associated algorithm can be applied to the computation of a point in the core of a balanced finitely polyhedral game. The polyhedra considered in this application of the polyhedral Scarf theorem are the polyhedra $V^k(C)$ defining the characteristic sets of all coalitions C with $C \neq I^n$. The label associated with polyhedron $V^k(C)$, $L^{C,k}$, is the indicator of coalition C:

$$(L^{C,k})_j = 1 \text{ if } j \in C$$

$$= 0 \text{ otherwise.}$$

The right-hand side of label system (2.1) is equal to a vector of ones, $d = (1,1,\ldots,1)^T \in \mathbb{R}^n$. With the label system thus defined, a collection of polyhedral sets is completely labelled if the associated coalitions are balanced. The labels are nonnegative and nonzero. Boundedness Assumption 2.1 is thus satisfied. Finally, it easily follows from property (4.4) that boundedness Assumption 2.2 is satisfied as well.

The stage is set for an application of Theorem 2.3. The constructive procedure used in the proof of the theorem determines a point $x \in \mathbb{R}^n$ and a balanced collection of coalitions $\{C_j \in S(I^n) | j \in J\}$ such that $x \in \cap_{j\in J}V(C_j)$ and $x \notin \text{int}(V(C))$ for any $C \in S(I^n)\backslash\{I^n\}$. The balancedness of the game then yields $x \in V(I^n)$. Observe that $x \notin V(I^n)$ would indicate that the game is not balanced. Any point $x' \in V(I^n)\backslash\text{int}(V(I^n))$ satisfying $x' \geq x$ lies in the core of the game. Such a point can be obtained by increasing any coordinate of x until the boundary of $V(I^n)$ is reached.

5. CONCLUSION

This paper proposes a polyhedral framework for Scarf's fundamental fixed point theorem. Primitive sets, which appear in the original statement of the theorem, are replaced with intersections of polyhedra. The constructive proof of the theorem then involves the familiar concept of piecewise linear path following.

Our polyhedral version of the Scarf theorem clearly establishes the intimate relationship between the theorem and the linear complementarity problem. Lemke [9], in arguing the generality of the LCP, already showed that both Scarf problems, the problem of determining a completely labelled primitive set and Scarf's piecewise linear complementarity problem, could be formulated as LCP's. Lemke's approach is purely algebraic. Our approach is more geometric. In our framework, the LCP is an intersection problem involving halfspaces, the primitive set problem is an intersection problem involving sets that are translations of the nonpositive orthant, and the piecewise linear complementarity problem is an intersection problem involving more general polyhedra. It is clear that this geometric framework can easily be extended to sets that are more general than polyhedra (Van der Heyden [13]).

Another generalization of our polyhedral intersection theorem is suggested by LCP theory (Lemke [8]). We could relax boundedness Assumption 2.2 and determine conditions under which the nonconvergence of the constructive procedure - caused by the existence of a second unbounded line of solutions for (3.1) - signals the infeasibility of the polyhedral intersection problem. In particular, this infeasibility could be due to the fact that the interiors of the polyhedra cover $\mathbb{R}^n$.

We conclude the paper by mentioning other work that is related to this paper. As was already stated in Section 4, the paper by Scarf [10] is particularly close to ours. It might be worth to point out some differences between the papers. Scarf's paper discusses a particular intersection problem involving 2n integer labelled polyhedra in standard form. No link is made in that paper with primitive sets. The problem of computing a point in the core of a balanced polyhedral game is discussed. The convergence condition mentioned in the paper is, however, not met in the core problem, though Scarf observes that the procedure successfully processes the problem.

The work on fixed point computations that followed Scarf [11] replaced the concept of primitive set with the more familiar and computationally more tractable notion of triangulation. An elegant framework for presenting fixed point methods based on triangulations is given by Eaves and Scarf [6]. The problem considered in that paper consists in solving a system of n piecewise linear equations in as many unknowns. The system is solved by a homotopic transformation that is similar to the introduction of the artifical parameter, ϑ, in our constructive proof of Theorem 2.3. A system of n piecewise linear equations in n+1 unknowns is generated. Under suitable nondegeneracy conditions, the solution set consists of a collection of disjoint piecewise linear paths. The procedure selects one of these paths and follows it to a solution. The piecewise linear framework of Eaves and Scarf encompasses the nonlinear complementarity problem of

Scarf [10]. The latter problem was shown in Section 4 to subsume the polyhedral intersection problem. The polyhedral intersection problem can thus be cast in the Eaves and Scarf framework. The path following that arises in the procedure of Secticn 3 is conceptually similar to that which arises in the Eaves and Scarf framework. To complete our round of equivalences, we further mention that Eaves and Lemke [5] established the problem of solving a system of piecewise linear equations to be conceptually equivalent with the LCP. This then establishes that the polyhedral intersection problem also is conceptually equivalent with the LCP and with the piecewise linear system of equations problem. One point made in this paper, however, is that these problems are geometrically not equivalent, as the dimensions of the geometrical spaces in which these problems are stated differ. These differences in dimension are typically reflected in the algorithms that are associated with each of these problems.

Finally, we mention that Eaves [4] has proposed a method for computing a point in the core of a balanced game that is based on triangulations.

REFERENCES

[1] R.W. Cottle and G.B. Dantzig, "Complementary pivot theory of mathematical programming", *Linear Algebra and its Applications* 1 (1968) 103-125.

[2] R.W. Cottle and G.B. Dantzig, "A generalization of the linear complementarity problem", *Journal of Combinatorial Theory* 8 (1970) 79-90.

[3] G.B. Dantzig, *Linear programming and extensions*, Princeton University Press, Princeton, 1963.

[4] B.C. Eaves, "Properly labelled simplices", in: *Studies in Mathematics 10: Studies in Optimization*, G.B. Dantzig and B.C. Eaves, eds., Mathematical Association of America, 1974, pp. 71-93.

[5] B.C. Eaves and C.E. Lemke, "Equivalence of LCP and PLS", Technical Report, Department of Operations Research, Stanford University, Stanford, CA, USA, 1979.

[6] B.C. Eaves and H.E. Scarf, "The solution of systems of piecewise linear equations", *Mathematics of Operations Research* 1 (1976) 1-27.

[7] C.B. Garcia, "Some classes of matrices in linear complementarity theory", *Mathematical Programming* 5 (1973) 299-310.

[8] C.E. Lemke, "Bimatrix equilibrium points and mathematical programming", *Management Science* 11 (1965) 681-689.

[9] C.E. Lemke, "Recent results on complementarity problems", in: *Nonlinear programming*, J.B. Rosen et al., eds., Academic Press, New York, 1970, pp. 349-384.

[10] H.E. Scarf, "An algorithm for a class of nonconvex programming problems", Cowles Foundation Discussion Paper No. 211, Yale University, New Haven, CT, USA, 1966.

[11] H.E. Scarf, *The computation of economic equilibria*, Yale University Press, New Haven, 1973.

[12] H.E. Scarf, "Production sets with indivisibilities. Part I. Generalities", *Econometrica* 49 (1981) 1-32.

[13] L. Van der Heyden, "A path following procedure for finding a point in the core of a balanced n-person game", Cowles Foundation Discussion Paper No. 575, Yale University, New Haven, CT, USA, 1980.

The Computation and Modelling of Economic Equilibria
A.J.J. Talman, G. van der Laan (Editors)

COMPETITIVE EQUILIBRIA IN THE MARKET WITH INDIVISIBILITY

Yoshitsugu YAMAMOTO

Institute of Socio-Economic Planning, University of Tsukuba,
Sakura, Ibaraki 305, Japan

This paper considers a market model with two commodities, one is a perfectly divisible commodity and the other is an indivisible commodity subject to quality differentiation. Each agent is initially endowed with several units of the indivisible commodity but has no use for more than one unit of it. We prove that there is a competitive equilibrium in this market under some mild assumptions on the utility functions of the agents.

1. INTRODUCTION

Since the pioneering work of Gale and Shapley [2] market models with indivisible commodities have been intensively investigated by several researchers, e.g. Shapley and Shubik [11], Shapley and Scarf [10], Kaneko [4,5], Kaneko and Wooders [6], Quinzii [9], Gale [1], and Svensson [12]. There are two commodities in the models of Shapley and Shubik [11] and Kaneko [4]. One is a perfectly divisible commodity called money and the other is an indivisible commodity subject to quality differentiation. The crucial assumption of these models is that each agent has no use for more than one unit of the indivisible commodity. Therefore this commodity could be regarded as houses. Their models are not symmetric in the sense that agents are partitioned into two groups with different roles, e.g. seller and buyer. The model of Shapley and Scarf [10] is symmetric in this sense but does not permit the presence of money. Quinzii [9] proposed a symmetric market model which permits the presence of money and unified these different models. She proves that the associated game is balanced and that the market has a nonempty core. She further shows that the market has a competitive equilibrium under several additional assumptions on the utility functions of the agents. Gale [1] directly makes assumptions on demand rather than on the utility function and presents an elegant proof of the existence of a competitive equilibrium. In these and Svensson's models it is assumed that each agent is initially endowed with at most one unit of the indivisible commodity.

In this paper we will remove some assumptions of Quinzii's and Svensson's models and prove the existence of a competitive equilibrium based on the fixed point argument.

In Section 2 we will introduce the market model considered and describe the difference from the models of Quinzii and Svensson. The main theorem of this paper will be found in this section. In Section 3 we will give the proofs of the theorem and its corollaries.

2. THE MARKET WITH AN INDIVISIBLE COMMODITY

Let $N = \{1,2,\ldots,n\}$ be the set of all agents in the market and let $(w^i, I_i) \in \mathbb{R}^{s+1}$ be agent i's initial endowment, where $\mathbb{R}^{s+1}$ is the (s+1)-dimensional Euclidean space. We assume that

$$w^i = \kappa_i e^i \text{ for some positive integer } \kappa_i \text{ for } 1 \leqq i \leqq s$$
$$w^i = 0 \quad \text{for } s+1 \leqq i \leqq n$$
$$I_i > 0 \quad \text{for all } i \in N,$$

where e^i is the i-th unit vector of $\mathbb{R}^s$. Namely, agent i is endowed with κ_i units of the indivisible commodity of type i for $1 \leqq i \leqq s$ and the others are endowed with no indivisible commodity. This means for example that agent i has a building with κ_i apartments of a certain quality for $1 \leqq i \leqq s$. The set of the first s agents or the index set of buildings will be denoted by M, i.e., $M = \{1,2,\ldots,s\}$. Let $\kappa = (\kappa_1,\ldots,\kappa_s)^T \in \mathbb{R}^s$, $X = \{x \mid 0 \leqq x \leqq \kappa$, x is an integer vector of $\mathbb{R}^s\}$ and let $\mathbb{R}_+$ be the set of all nonnegative real numbers. We assume that each agent i has a utility function u_i defined on $X \times \mathbb{R}_+$ satisfying the following three assumptions.

<u>Assumption A</u>. $u_i(x,.)$ is a continuous and monotonically nondecreasing function for each $x \in X$.

<u>Assumption B</u>. $u_i(x,0) \leqq u_i(w^i, I_i)$ for all $x \in X$.

<u>Assumption C</u>. $u_i(x,m) = \max\{u_i(y,m) \mid y \in \{0,e^1,\ldots,e^s\},\ y \leqq x\}$ for each $x \in X$ and for each $m \in \mathbb{R}_+$.

Assumption B means that the initial endowment is preferred to any state without consumption, and Assumption C means that each agent has no use for more than one unit of the indivisible commodity.

A *competitive equilibrium* is a pair $(p,x) = (p,x^1,x^2,\ldots,x^n) \in \mathbb{R}^S \times X^n$ satisfying the following three conditions:

(i) $0 \leqq p \in \mathbb{R}^S$

(ii) $x^i \in X$, $px^i \leqq pw^i + I_i$, and
$u_i(x^i, pw^i+I_i-px^i) = \max\{u_i(y,m) \mid y \in X,\ m \geqq 0,\ py + m \leqq pw^i + I_i\}$
for all $i \in N$

(iii) $\sum_{i\in N} x^i = \sum_{i\in N} w^i \ (=\kappa)$.

The main theorem of this paper is as follows.

Theorem. Under Assumptions A-C, there exists a competitive equilibrium in the market.

The following corollary shows that each agent has at most one unit of the indivisible commodity at an equilibrium when there are not more apartments than agents in the market.

Corollary 2.1. If $\Sigma_{j\in M} \kappa_j \leqq n$, then under Assumptions A-C, there is a competitive equilibrium $(p,x^1,\ldots,x^n) \in \mathbb{R}^S \times X^n$ such that $x^i \in \{0,e^1,\ldots,e^S\}$ for all $i \in N$.

In Quinzii's model each agent has at most one unit of the indivisible commodity as his initial endowment. She also assumes the Archimedian property, i.e., $u_i(x,m) \to \infty$ as $m \to \infty$ (Assumption A.1 of Theorem 3 in [9]), and proves the existence of a competitive equilibrium in her market model by showing that the set of core allocations coincides with the set of competitive equilibrium allocations. Svensson makes a similar assumption on the preference of agents, Assumption C.2 in [12]. It should be noted that we permit each agent to have more than one unit of the indivisible commodity as his initial endowment and do not require such an assumption as the Archimedian property.

The model introduced above is symmetric in the sense that there is no difference between the roles of agents except whether he is initially endowed with the indivisible commodity or not. In contrast to such a symmetric model, the models in Shapley and Shubik [11], Kaneko [4], and Kaneko and Yamamoto [7] are not symmetric and have two types of agents called seller and buyer. The sellers are endowed with an indivisible commodity of a certain type and are interested in the indivisible commodity of their own type as well as in the divisible commodity. To explain such asymmetric models we introduce an additional assumption.

Assumption D. For each $i \in N$ let $M_i = \{j \in M | u_i(e^j,m) \leqq u_i(0,m)$ for any $m \in \mathbb{R}_+\}$. Then

i) $\bigcap_{i \in N} M_i = \emptyset$

ii) if $M_i \neq \emptyset$, then $u_i(x,.)$ is an increasing function at each $x \in X$.

Remark. Assumption C implies $u_i(y,m) \leqq u_i(x,m)$ for all $x,y \in X$ with $y \leqq x$, and in particular $u_i(0,m) \leqq u_i(x,m)$ for all $x \in X$. Therefore $u_i(e^j,m) = u_i(0,m)$ for $j \in M_i$.

Corollary 2.2. Under Assumptions A-D there is a competitive equilibrium $(p,x^1,\ldots,x^n) \in \mathbb{R}^s \times X^n$ such that $x_j^i = 0$ for $j \in M_i$ and $i \in N$.

Remark. Let $M_i = M\backslash\{i\}$ for $i \in M$. Then the competitive equilibrium in Corollary 2.2 satisfies that $x^i \in \{0,e^i,2e^i,\ldots,\kappa_i e^i\}$ for $i \in M$, that is agent $i \in M$ behaves as a seller. Therefore a seller could be characterized as an agent who is interested in money and the indivisible commodity of his own type.

3. PROOF OF THE THEOREM AND COROLLARIES

We begin with a fixed point lemma.

Lemma 3.1. Let $\bar{p}$ be a positive vector of $\mathbb{R}^s$ and let $P = \{p \in \mathbb{R}^s | \ 0 \leqq p \leqq \bar{p}\}$. Let F be a nonempty convex-valued and upper semi-continuous point-to-set mapping from P into the power set of some compact subset C of $\mathbb{R}^s$. Then there is a $\tilde{p} \in P$ such that $F(\tilde{p})$ has a vector $\tilde{z}$ satisfying

$$\begin{aligned} \tilde{z}_j &\leqq 0 && \text{if } \tilde{p}_j = 0 \\ &= 0 && \text{if } 0 < \tilde{p}_j < \bar{p}_j \qquad (3.1) \\ &\geqq 0 && \text{if } \tilde{p}_j = \bar{p}_j . \end{aligned}$$

Proof. Let $r : \mathbb{R}^s \to P$ be a mapping defined by

$$r_j(q) = 0 \qquad \text{if } q_j \leqq 0$$
$$= q_j \qquad \text{if } 0 < q_j < \bar{p}_j \tag{3.2}$$
$$= \bar{p}_j \qquad \text{if } q_j \geqq \bar{p}_j.$$

Then r is continuous, and hence a retraction from $\mathbb{R}^s$ to P (see for example Kojima and Saigal [8]). Let

$$H(q) = r(q) + F(r(q)) \text{ for each } q \in \mathbb{R}^s.$$

Since $F(p) \subseteq C$ for any $p \in P$, $H(q)$ is included in the compact subset $P+C$ for any $q \in \mathbb{R}^s$. By the assumption on F and the continuity of r, H is non-empty, convex-valued and upper semi-continuous on $\mathbb{R}^s$. Therefore applying Kakutani's fixed point theorem to H, we have a fixed point $\tilde{q} \in \mathbb{R}^s$ of H, i.e., $\tilde{q} \in H(\tilde{q})$. Let $\tilde{p} = r(\tilde{q}) \in P$ and $\tilde{z} = \tilde{q} - \tilde{p}$. Then $\tilde{z} \in F(\tilde{p})$ and $\tilde{z} = \tilde{q} - r(\tilde{q})$ satisfies (3.1) by (3.2).

□

Let $\bar{m}$ be a real number with $\bar{m} > \Sigma_{i \in N} I_i$ and let

$$P = \{p \in \mathbb{R}^s | 0 \leqq p_j \leqq \bar{m} \text{ for } j \in M\}.$$

For $i \in N$ define the *demand correspondence* D_i by

$$D_i(p) = \{x| \quad \text{i) } x \in X$$
$$\text{ii) } px \leqq pw^i + I_i$$
$$\text{iii) } u_i(x, pw^i + I_i - px) = \max\{u_i(y,m) | y \in X,\ m \geqq 0,\ py + m \leqq pw^i + I_i\}\}$$

and let

$$D_i'(p) = D_i(p) \cap \{0, e^1, \ldots, e^s\}.$$

In the following we denote the δ-neighborhood of a point p by $B(p,\delta)$.

Lemma 3.2. For all $i \in N$, the point-to-set mapping D'_i is nonempty-valued and upper semi-continuous on P.

Proof. For simplicity of notation we omit the suffix i. Let $\hat{p}$ be an arbitrary point of P. Suppose $y \in D(\hat{p})$, then by Assumptions A and C there is an $x \in \{0,e^1,\ldots,e^s\}$ such that $\hat{p}x \leqq \hat{p}y$ and $u(x,\hat{p}w+I-\hat{p}x) \geqq u(y,\hat{p}w+I-\hat{p}y)$. Therefore $D'(\hat{p})$ is nonempty for each $\hat{p} \in P$. To show the upper semi-continuity of D' we prove that there exists a $\delta > 0$ such that $p \in B(\hat{p},\delta)$ implies $D'(p) \subseteq D'(\hat{p})$. This together with the closedness of $D'(\hat{p})$ implies the upper semi-continuity of D' at $\hat{p}$. Suppose $y \notin D'(\hat{p})$, then either

$$\hat{p}y > \hat{p}w + I \tag{3.3}$$

or

$$u(y,\hat{p}w+I-\hat{p}y) < u(x,\hat{p}w+I-\hat{p}x) \text{ for some } x \in D'(\hat{p}). \tag{3.4}$$

If (3.3) occurs, there is a $\delta > 0$ such that $p \in B(\hat{p},\delta)$ implies $py > pw+I$, consequently $y \notin D'(p)$. If (3.4) occurs, we can choose an $x \in D'(\hat{p})$ such that $\hat{p}x < \hat{p}w+I$ and it also satisfies (3.4) by Assumptions B and C and $I > 0$. Then there is a $\delta > 0$ such that $p \in B(\hat{p},\delta)$ implies $px < pw+I$ and $u(y,pw+I-py) < u(x,pw+I-px)$, consequently $y \notin D'(p)$. Thus for each $y \notin D'(\hat{p})$ we can find a positive real number $\delta(y)$. Then $\delta = \min\{\delta(y) \mid y \in \{0,e^1,\ldots,e^s\}\backslash D'(\hat{p})\}$ is the desired real number.

□

Define the *excess demand correspondence* E by

$$E(p) = \sum_{i\in N} D_i(p) - \{\kappa\} \qquad \text{for each } p \in P$$

and define also

$$E'(p) = \sum_{i\in N} D'_i(p) - \{\kappa\} \qquad \text{for each } p \in P.$$

Then by Lemma 3.2, the point-to-set mapping E' is nonempty-valued and upper semi-continuous on P. Let F be a point-to-set mapping defined on P such that F(p) is the convex hull of E'(p) for each $p \in P$.

Lemma 3.3. The point-to-set mapping F is nonempty, convex-valued and upper semi-continuous on P.

Proof. We prove only the upper semi-continuity. First note that $F(p)$ is closed since $E'(p)$ consists of finitely many points of $\mathbb{R}^s$. For each $\hat{p} \in P$ by the proof of Lemma 3.2, there is a $\delta > 0$ such that $E'(p) \subseteq E'(\hat{p})$ for $p \in B(\hat{p},\delta)$. Therefore $F(p) \subseteq F(\hat{p})$ for $p \in B(\hat{p},\delta)$. This relation and the closedness of $F(\hat{p})$ prove the upper semi-continuity of F.

□

Lemma 3.4. There exist a price vector $\tilde{p} \in P$ and an $(x^1,\ldots,x^n) \in D_1'(\tilde{p})\times\ldots\times D_n'(\tilde{p})$ such that

$$\sum_{i\in N} x_j^i \leqq \kappa_j \quad \text{if } \tilde{p}_j = 0$$
$$= \kappa_j \quad \text{if } 0 < \tilde{p}_j < \bar{m} \tag{3.5}$$
$$\geqq \kappa_j \quad \text{if } \tilde{p}_j = \bar{m}.$$

Proof. By the definitions of $D_i'(p)$ and $E'(p)$, $F(p)$ is included in some compact subset of $\mathbb{R}^s$ for all $p \in P$. Hence by the Lemmas 3.1 and 3.3 there is a price vector $\tilde{p} \in P$ such that $F(\tilde{p})$ has a vector z satisfying

$$z_j \leqq 0 \quad \text{if } \tilde{p}_j = 0$$
$$= 0 \quad \text{if } 0 < \tilde{p}_j < \bar{m}$$
$$\geqq 0 \quad \text{if } \tilde{p}_j = \bar{m},$$

namely, there is a $(y^1,\ldots,y^n) \in \text{co.}D_1'(\tilde{p})\times\ldots\times\text{co.}D_n'(\tilde{p})$ such that

$$\sum_{i\in N} y_j^i \leqq \kappa_j \quad \text{if } \tilde{p}_j = 0$$
$$= \kappa_j \quad \text{if } 0 < \tilde{p}_j < \bar{m} \tag{3.6.a}$$
$$\geqq \kappa_j \quad \text{if } \tilde{p}_j = \bar{m},$$

where co. means convex hull. Now for $i \in N$ let c^i be a vector of $\mathbb{R}^s$ whose j-th component is defined by

$$c^i_j = 1 \qquad \text{if } e^j \in D'_i(\tilde{p})$$
$$= 0 \qquad \text{otherwise.}$$

Then $(y^1,\ldots,y^n)$ satisfies

$$\sum_{j\in M} y^i_j \leqq 1 \qquad \text{if } 0 \in D'_i(\tilde{p}) \qquad (3.6.b)$$
$$= 1 \qquad \text{otherwise,}$$

$$0 \leqq y^i_j \leqq c^i_j \text{ for all } i \in N \text{ and all } j \in M. \qquad (3.6.c)$$

Since the linear system (3.6) has the integrality property (see for example Hoffman and Kruskal [3]), there is an integer solution $(x^1,\ldots,x^n)$ of the system. Let us show that $x^i \in D'_i(\tilde{p})$ for each $i \in N$. If $x^i = 0$, then $\Sigma_{j\in M} x^i_j < 1$, and hence by (3.6.b) $x^i = 0 \in D'_i(\tilde{p})$. If $x^i \neq 0$, then $x^i = e^j$ for some $j \in M$ because x^i is an integer vector satisfying (3.6.b). Therefore by (3.6.c) $x^i_j = 1 \leqq c^i_j$. This and the definition of c^i_j imply that $x^i = e^j \in D'_i(\tilde{p})$. Thus we have an $(x^1,\ldots,x^n) \in D'_1(\tilde{p})\times\ldots\times D'_n(\tilde{p})$ satisfying (3.5).

□

To show that $\tilde{p}$ is an equilibrium price vector we introduce several graph theoretic terminologies. Let $G = (V,A)$ be a directed graph with node-set V and arc-set A. For each node $i \in V$ let $d^+(i) = \{(i,j)|(i,j) \in A\}$ and $d^-(i) = \{(j,i)|(j,i) \in A\}$. A path is an alternate sequence of nodes and arcs $(v_0,a_1,v_1,\ldots,v_{h-1},a_h,v_h,\ldots,v_k)$ such that a_h joins v_{h-1} and v_h for $1 \leqq h \leqq k$. When $v_0 = v_k$, it is called a cycle. When a_h is directed from v_{h-1} to v_h, i.e., $a_h = (v_{h-1},v_h)$, a path (or cycle) is called a directed path (or cycle). We do not exclude a path consisting of a single node, which is said to be degenerate. For a subset A' of A, a subgraph $G' = (V',A')$ is said to be generated by A' if V' is the set of all nodes incident to some arc of A'. A connected directed graph is called an arborescence if it has no cycles and it has exactly one node, say t, called root such that $d^-(t) = \emptyset$.

Now let $A = \{(j,i) | x_j^i = 1\}$ for $(x^1,\ldots,x^n) \in D_1'(\tilde{p})\times\ldots\times D_n'(\tilde{p})$ of Lemma 3.4 and define a directed graph $G = (N,A)$. Then it has the following properties:

i) $|d^-(i)| \leqq 1$ for all $i \in N$

ii) if $j \in M$ and $|d^+(j)| < \kappa_j$, then $\tilde{p}_j = 0$.

Lemma 3.5. Let t be a node of G with $d^+(t) \neq \emptyset$. For each arc $(t,j) \in d^+(t)$, let $A(t,j)$ be the set of all arcs (h,k) such that there is a directed path of the form $(t,(t,j),j,\ldots,h,(h,k),k,\ldots)$ in which node t appears at most twice as the first and the last term and let $G(t,j) = (N(t,j), A(t,j))$ be the subgraph generated by $A(t,j)$. If $|d^+(t)| > 1$, then there is an arc $(t,j^*) \in d^+(t)$ such that $G(t,j^*)$ is an arborescence with root t.

Proof. We first consider the case where node t has no self-loop $(t,(t,t),t)$. Let (t,j) and (t,j') be distinct arcs of $d^+(t)$. Note that $A(t,j) \cap A(t,j') = \emptyset$ by property i). Suppose $G(t,j)$ is not an arborescence then $G(t,j)$ has a cycle. By i) the cycle is a directed cycle having t. Therefore since $A(t,j) \cap A(t,j') = \emptyset$, if further $G(t,j')$ is not an arborescence either, we have $|d^-(t)| > 1$. This contradicts property i).

When a node t has a self-loop, it is seen in the same way that $G(t,j)$ is an arborescence for all non self-loop arcs of $d^+(t)$.

□

Lemma 3.6. For $(x^1,\ldots,x^n) \in D_1'(\tilde{p})\times\ldots\times D_n'(\tilde{p})$ of Lemma 3.4 it holds that $\Sigma_{i\in N}\, x_j^i = \kappa_j$ if $\tilde{p}_j > 0$.

Proof. Suppose there is a $t \in M$ such that $\Sigma_{i\in N}\, x_t^i > \kappa_t$ and $\tilde{p}_t = \bar{m}$. By the definition of G, $|d^+(t)| > \kappa_t \geqq 1$. Then by Lemma 3.5 there is an arc $(t,j^*) \in d^+(t)$ such that $G(t,j^*)$ is an arborescence with root t. For each node i of $G(t,j^*)$ let $\gamma(i) = \{k | k \in N(t,j^*)$ and (i,k) is an arc of $G(t,j^*)\}$, $\Gamma(i) = \{k | k \in N(t,j^*)$ and there is a nondegenerate directed path of $G(t,j^*)$ from i to $k\}$. We will show by induction that

$$\tilde{p}w^i \leqq \sum_{k\in\Gamma(i)} I_k \qquad \text{for } i \in N(t,j^*)\backslash\{t\}. \tag{3.7}$$

If $\Gamma(i) = \emptyset$, then $|d^+(i)| = 0$ and hence $i \notin M$ or $\tilde{p}_i = 0$ by property ii). Therefore (3.7) holds by equality. Consider a node i with $\gamma(i) = \Gamma(i) \neq \emptyset$. Note that $\tilde{p}_i \leqq I_j$ for each $j \in \Gamma(i)$ because $\Gamma(j) = \emptyset$ and $e^i = x^j \in D_j'(\tilde{p})$.

If $|\gamma(i)| = |d^+(i)| < \kappa_i$, then $\tilde{p}_i = 0$ by ii) and (3.7) holds. If $|\gamma(i)| \geqq \kappa_i$, $\tilde{p}w^i = \kappa_i\tilde{p}_i \leqq \Sigma_{j\in\Gamma(i)} I_j$ and (3.7) holds. Consider an arbitrary node i with nonempty $\Gamma(i)$. Since (3.7) trivially holds when $|\gamma(i)| < \kappa_i$, we suppose $|\gamma(i)| \geqq \kappa_i$. For each $j \in \gamma(i)$, $\tilde{p}_i \leqq I_j + \Sigma_{k\in\Gamma(j)} I_k$ by the definition of G and by the induction hypothesis. Therefore

$$\tilde{p}w^i = \kappa_i\tilde{p}_i \leqq \sum_{j\in\gamma(i)} \tilde{p}_i \leqq \sum_{j\in\gamma(i)} (I_j + \sum_{k\in\Gamma(j)} I_k) = \sum_{k\in\Gamma(i)} I_k.$$

Thus we have (3.7) and especially

$$\tilde{p}w^{j^*} \leqq \sum_{k\in\Gamma(j^*)} I_k.$$

Since $j^* \in \gamma(t)$, i.e., $e^t = x^{j^*}$,

$$\bar{m} = \tilde{p}_t \leqq I_{j^*} + \tilde{p}w^{j^*} \leqq I_{j^*} + \sum_{k\in\Gamma(j^*)} I_k \leqq \sum_{k\in N} I_k.$$

This contradicts the choice of $\bar{m}$.

□

Now we are ready to prove that $0 \in E(\tilde{p})$, i.e., $\tilde{p}$ is an equilibrium price vector.

Proof of the theorem and Corollary 2.1. We show that there is an $(\tilde{x}^1,\ldots,\tilde{x}^n) \in D_1(\tilde{p})\times\ldots\times D_n(\tilde{p})$ such that $\Sigma_{i\in N} \tilde{x}^i = \kappa = \Sigma_{i\in N} w^i$.

Since we have seen in Lemma 3.6 that $\Sigma_{i\in N} x_j^i = \kappa_j$ whenever $\tilde{p}_j > 0$, there is nothing to prove if $\Sigma_{i\in N} x_j^i = \kappa_j$ for all $j \in M$ with $\tilde{p}_j = 0$. Then suppose $M' = \{j | j \in M, \Sigma_{i\in N} x_j^i < \kappa_j, \tilde{p}_j = 0\}$ is not empty. Let y^i's be nonnegative integer vectors such that $\Sigma_{i\in N} y^i = \kappa - \Sigma_{i\in N} x^i$ and let $\tilde{x}^i = x^i + y^i$ for $i \in N$. Since $\tilde{p}_j = 0$ for $j \in M'$ and $y_j^i = 0$ for $j \in M\backslash M'$, $\tilde{p}\tilde{x}^i = \tilde{p}x^i$ for all $i \in N$. Therefore $u_i(\tilde{x}^i,\tilde{p}w^i+I_i-\tilde{p}\tilde{x}^i) = u_i(\tilde{x}^i,\tilde{p}w^i+I_i-\tilde{p}x^i) \geqq u_i(x^i,\tilde{p}w^i+I_i-\tilde{p}x^i)$ by Assumption C, and hence $\tilde{x}^i \in D_i(\tilde{p})$ for all $i \in N$. Since it is clear by the definition of the y^i's that $\Sigma_{i\in N} \tilde{x}^i = \kappa = \Sigma_{i\in N} w^i$, we have proved the theorem.

Suppose that $\Sigma_{j\in M} \kappa_j \leqq n$. Then there are at least $\Sigma_{j\in M} \kappa_j - \Sigma_{i\in N}\Sigma_{j\in M} x^i_j$ number of agents with $x^i = 0$. Therefore we can choose y^i's from $\{0,e^1,\ldots, e^s\}$ for these agents and $y^i = 0$ for the other agents. This completes the proof of Corollary 2.1.

□

Proof of Corollary 2.2. Let $(x^1,\ldots,x^n)$ be the allocation of Lemma 3.6. Suppose $x^i = e^j$ for some $i \in N$ and some $j \in M_i$. Then since $x^i \in D_i(\tilde{p})$ we have by the definition of M_i that $u_i(e^j,\tilde{p}w^i+I_i) \leqq u_i(0,\tilde{p}w^i+I_i) \leqq u_i(e^j,\tilde{p}w^i+I_i-\tilde{p}e^j)$. This relation and Assumption Dii) imply $\tilde{p}_j = 0$ and $0 \in D_i(\tilde{p})$. Therefore $\bar{x}^i$ defined below belongs to $D_i(\tilde{p})$ for each $i \in N$:

$$\bar{x}^i = 0 \text{ if } x^i = e^j \text{ for some } j \in M_i,$$

$$= x^i \text{ otherwise.}$$

Let $\lambda_j = \kappa_j - \Sigma_{i\in N} \bar{x}^i_j$ for $j \in M$. By Assumption Di) for each $j \in M$ there is an $i \in N$ with $j \notin M_i$. Let $i(j)$ be one of such agents for each j and let

$$\tilde{x}^i = \bar{x}^i + \sum_{i(j)=i} \lambda_j e^j.$$

Suppose $\lambda_j > 0$, then $\kappa_j - \Sigma_{i\in N} x^i_j > 0$ or $\Sigma_{i\in N} x^i_j > \Sigma_{i\in N} \bar{x}^i_j$. We have seen that $\tilde{p}_j = 0$ in either case. Therefore, by Assumption C, $u_i(\tilde{x}^i,\tilde{p}w^i+I_i-\tilde{p}\tilde{x}^i) \geqq u_i(\bar{x}^i,\tilde{p}w^i+I_i-\tilde{p}\bar{x}^i)$, and $\tilde{x}^i \in D_i(\tilde{p})$ for each $i \in N$. Since $\Sigma_{i\in N} \tilde{x}^i_j = \kappa_j$ by the definition of the λ_j's, we have proved that $(\tilde{p},\tilde{x}^1,\ldots,\tilde{x}^n)$ is a competitive equilibrium with the desired property.

□

REFERENCES

[1] D. Gale, "Equilibrium in a discrete exchange economy with money", *International Journal of Game Theory* 13 (1984) 61-64.

[2] D. Gale and L.S. Shapley, "College admissions and the stability of marriage", *American Mathematical Monthly* 69 (1962) 9-15.

[3] A.J. Hoffman and J.B. Kruskal, "Integral boundary points of convex polyhedra", in: *Annals of Mathematical Studies* 38, H.W. Kuhn and A.W. Tucker, eds., 1956.

[4] M. Kaneko, "The central assignment game and the assignment markets", *Journal of Mathematical Economics* 10 (1982) 205-232.

[5] M. Kaneko, "Housing markets with indivisibilities", *Journal of Urban Economics* 13 (1983) 22-50.

[6] M. Kaneko and M. Wooders, "Cores of partitioning games", *Mathematical Social Sciences* 3 (1982) 313-327.

[7] M. Kaneko and Y. Yamamoto, "The existence and computation of competitive equilibria in markets with an indivisible commodity", *Journal of Economic Theory* 38 (1986) 118-136.

[8] M. Kojima and R. Saigal, "On the number of solutions to a class of complementarity problems", *Mathematical Programming* 21 (1981) 190-203.

[9] M. Quinzii, "Core and competitive equilibria with indivisibilities", *International Journal of Game Theory* 13 (1984) 41-60.

[10] L.S. Shapley and H. Scarf, "On cores and indivisibilities", *Journal of Mathematical Economics* 1 (1974) 23-37.

[11] L.S. Shapley and M. Shubik, "The assignment game I: the core", *International Journal of Game Theory* 1 (1972) 111-130.

[12] L.-G. Svensson, "Competitive equilibria with indivisible goods", *Journal of Economics* 44 (1984) 373-386.

The Computation and Modelling of Economic Equilibria
A.J.J. Talman, G. van der Laan (Editors)

COMPUTATION OF AN INDUSTRIAL EQUILIBRIUM*

Pieter H.M. RUYS

Department of Econometrics, Tilburg University, P.O. Box 90153, 5000 LE Tilburg, The Netherlands

Gerard van der LAAN

Department of Economics and Econometrics, Free University, De Boelelaan 1105, 1081 HV Amsterdam, The Netherlands

In this paper we develop and use the concept of a semi-public good. A semi-public good is defined as an ordered pair of commodities, the first one being a private commodity and the second one a public good, which are related to each other by an inequality constraint for each individual agent. This approach allows us to design economic institutions which carry out price discrimination among users of a semi-public good. People who are seriously hampered by too small a provision of a public good, because it constrains their use of the private commodity, are willing to pay a mark-up on the price for the latter one if this mark-up is spent for expanding the provision of the public good. In the model the availability of a public good is planned and organized by a central planner. The consumer's willingness to pay an individual mark-up on the price of a private commodity reflects his preferences for the availability of the public good. These mark-ups are collected by the private goods industry and transferred to the central planner in order to cover the costs of the public good infrastucture. This framework of a private industry and a central planner providing semi-public goods is called an industrial economy. The model will be illustrated by some numerical examples.

1. INTRODUCTION

General equilibrium models in economic theory are isomorphic to fixed point theorems. This insight is due to Von Neumann [18], who applied Brouwer's fixed point theorem to prove the existence of a process of pro-

* This research is part of the VF-program "Equilibrium and disequilibrium in demand and supply", which has been approved by the Netherlands Ministry of Education and Sciences.

portional growth in a competitive economy. McKenzie [11], Arrow and Debreu [1] and other authors used this tool in the fifties to prove existence of an equilibrium for the model designed by Walras [19]. Thus they have put the general equilibrium model for an economy with private goods only and with private ownership, on a solid axiomatic foundation.

The mathematical tools were strong enough to extend the economy with public goods, a concept introduced by Samuelson [15]. The concept of public goods has been studied intensively, for example see Cornes and Sandler [3]. The problems raised since Samuelson in public good models are more related to economic behaviour and institutions than to mathematical limitations. One of the fundamental issues in the theory of public goods is the individual's revelation of preferences about the provision of public goods. It is individually rational to behave as a free rider, but it is socially harmful. Many solutions for this problem have been proposed and rejected. It is still an unresolved issue in economic theory. For a recent survey we refer to Blümel, Pethig and Von dem Hagen [2].

In this paper we develop and use the concept of a semi-public good, introduced by Ruys [14]. A semi-public good is defined as an ordered pair of commodities, the first one being a private good and the second one a public good. The amount y^i of consumption of agent i of the private good and the amount z of availability of the public good are related to each other by an individual inequality constraint $y^i \leq c^i(z)$ for each agent i. This constraint might be implicitly expressed in the consumer's utility function or the producer's production function. But the explicit formulation makes it possible to distinguish between whether an individual constraint is binding or not. If for some agent, say consumer i, the constraint is binding, then an increase of z has a direct effect on his demand because of the fact that z appears in the consumer's utility function, but it also has an indirect effect through the weakening of the constraint. The price for raising z offered by a truth-telling consumer will reflect the impact of both effects on his utility. The part reflecting the constraint will show up as a mark-up on the market price the consumer is willing to pay for the private commodity. If no agent in the economy feels himself constrained, the semi-public good reduces to a private good having a uniform market price, and a pure public good with, if desired, Lindahl prices. In general, the definition of a semi-public good is relevant only if the constraints are binding for a considerable number of agents.

The main advantage of this approach is that economic institutions can be designed which make price discrimination possible among users of a semi-public good. People who are seriously hampered by too small a provision of a public good, because it constrains their use of the private commodity, are thought of forming (political) pressure groups to expand its provision, or are informing the industry otherwise. They are also willing to pay a mark-up on the price of the private commodity if this mark-up is spent on expanding the provision of the public good. In the context of an industrial economy the enterprises in an industry discriminate between consumers by setting different prices, and not the public authority or the planner. These differentiated prices inform the planner and partially finance the public good.

We will explore a model in which there is just one industry producing private goods, which form semi-public goods with a public good. The infrastructure of this public good is planned and organized by a central planner. The consumer's willingness to pay an individual mark-up on each of the prices of these private commodities reflects his preferences for the infrastructure of the public good. These mark-ups are collected by the private goods industry and transferred to the central planner in order to cover the costs of the public good infrastructure. As an alternative the private goods industry may levy a uniform mark-up on the prices of the private commodities to provide an infrastructure necessary for using their products. We call this framework of a central planner and private firms providing together semi-public goods an industrial economy.

It is evident that there are many spill-over effects resulting from any decision about the provision of a semi-public good. This calls for a general equilibrium approach, with an associated fixed point or zero point formulation. In order to calculate a fixed point, simplicial algorithms first have been designed by Scarf [16,17] and Kuhn [6,7] for fixed point problems on the unit price simplex. Van der Laan and Talman [9] developed a variable dimension algorithm for problems on the unit simplex. Similar algorithms for fixed or zero point problems on $\mathbb{R}^n$ have been introduced by van der Laan and Talman [10], Wright [20], Kojima and Yamamoto [5], and others. These algorithms allow for fast movements in lower dimensional spaces and are therefore very efficient. A code for these algorithms has been implemented on the computer by Seelen, see [8]. We will use this code for solving some numerical examples to illustrate the framework of an industrial economy.

This paper is organized as follows. In the next section we discuss the framework of an industrial economy by giving some examples. The mathematical model is given in Section 3. In this section we also state the first order conditions for a Pareto efficient allocation. The institutional framework to reach a Pareto efficient allocation is given in Section 4. In Section 5 we give some numerical examples to illustrate the concept of an industrial economy. Finally, in Section 6 we make some concluding remarks and we discuss the possibilities for further research.

2. AN INDUSTRIAL ECONOMY

An industrial economy consists of a number of (small) enterprises which produce private commodities that are close substitutes or complements and which have a common interest in maintaining the availability of a public good, called the infrastructure. The presence of an infrastructure increases the utility of the private goods or may even be a necessary complement to them. Examples are:

a) *airline transportation:* several carrier companies provide substitutable transport services; they have a common interest in for example airports, a reservation network, safety measures,
b) *tourist industry:* there are many enterprises providing services that are close substitutes and complements (hotels, restaurants, entertainment, travel agencies); these enterprises have a common interest in for example a clean and attractive environment, promotion activities and a reputation for good quality of services,
c) *surface transport:* there are several modes of transportation which are close substitutes and complements (bicycle, car, taxi, tramway, bus, railroad); for each mode there are one or more enterprises providing transportation services; producers of a mode have a common interest, such as a road system or a railroad system and time and working schedules.

Of course, there are much more examples, but the three given here are specific in some aspects. In example a) the private goods are close substitutes. The enterprises compete and they are comparable. Moreover, there is only one public good for all, called the infrastructure. In example b) the private goods are both substitutes and complements. The enterprises can be clustered in various branches each having a completely different production technology (hotels, attractions, souvenir shops), and most of these branches are competitive. The common infrastructure is induced rather than planned and organized. In example c) the private goods are again close substitutes and complements (trains have connections with buses). Some modes of transportation are competitive (taxis), but others are monopolistic and regulated. Again there is a common infrastructure from which some of the modes may benefit and some others may not. This infrastructure is planned.

The central problem in all examples is the way in which the infrastructure is provided and financed. In the air industry example it seems to be obvious that the enterprises organize and finance the infrastructure and pass on the costs in the prices the consumers have to pay. However, the consumers also benefit directly from the infrastructure. It enlarges their possibilities to travel and therefore they should also show a willingness to pay for having an airport. On the other hand, people living close to the airport may suffer from its noise. We have similar characteristics in the other examples. For organizing and financing the infrastructure we distinguish the following cases:

i) the infrastructure is not planned or decided upon, but it results from unorganized individual actions of the agents (e.g. it is attractive to do shopping in a city with a wide variety of supplies),

ii) there is an agent (a government or a private enterprise), who provides the infrastructure and who determines tariffs or prices for making use of it (e.g. shopping center or airport); an agent can decide to take or leave the offer,

iii) the infrastructure is planned and organized by a specific agent who has been established by the enterprises and by others who have interest in the production of the industry.

Case i) is not relevant for our problem. Case ii) gives a way out of our problem if the agent providing the infrastructure is economically self-supporting or can make profits. It remains interesting to analyse the rules of price setting with the theory developed here. Our approach is mainly relevant for case iii). In this case either the infrastructure is not apt for private (or profitable) exploitation, or there are political, juridical and other non-economic elements involved that influence the productivity of an industry and its chances of survival. In the next section we present a model for this case. From this model we derive conditions for an efficient allocation. These conditions show that the prices the agents are willing to pay for the private commodities reveal their preferences for the infrastructure.

3. THE MATHEMATICAL MODEL

We consider a model of an industrial economy with two semi-public goods, composed from private goods a and b and a public good. For example, the public good is a road system that is used both by private cars, a, and by public buses, b. There are two other commodities, private goods 1 and 2. There is a (possibly private) producer who plans and organizes the level of the public infrastructure, z, taking into account the wishes of the (transportation) industry. This industry has two branches, Y^a and Y^b, each consisting of a representative private firm producing commodity a and b respectively. For instance, the first firm leases private cars to consumers and the second firm exploits the public bus system.

There are h consumers, indexed by i = 1,...,h. Each consumer i has a utility function $u^i(x_1^i,x_2^i,y_a^i,y_b^i,z)$ on $X^i = \mathbb{R}_+^5$. Furthermore, each consumer i faces individual semi-public (quantity) constraints on the consumption y_a^i and y_b^i of the private goods a and b. That means, each consumer is constrained in his' or her's car driving and public transportation because of the limitations of the road system. So, we assume that there are constraints $c_a^i(z)$ and $c_b^i(z)$ for i = 1,...,h, such that the consumption of consumer i is restricted by

$$y_a^i \leq c_a^i(z) \tag{3.1}$$

$$y_b^i \leq c_b^i(z). \tag{3.2}$$

The industry is aware of these (subjective) constraints because it observes rationing in the demand functions. Separate from these subjective feasibility constraints, the respective technical production constraints of the firms Y^a and Y^b are given by

$$F^a(y_a;x_1^a,x_2^a) \leq 0 \tag{3.3}$$

and

$$F^b(y_b;x_1^b,x_2^b) \leq 0, \qquad (3.4)$$

where x_1^a, x_2^a and x_1^b, x_2^b are the amounts of input of commodity 1 and 2 in the production of a and b respectively, whereas y_a and y_b are the amounts of output of commodity a and b respectively. Moreover, we assume that firm Y^b faces a constraint

$$y_b \leq c_b(z). \qquad (3.5)$$

This constraint reflects the fact that the system of public transportation is restricted by the limitations of the road system.

The enterprise producing the (public) infrastructure is given by the technical constraint

$$F^z(z;x_1^z,x_2^z) \leq 0, \qquad (3.6)$$

with x_1^z and x_2^z the amounts of input. Finally, there is a firm which produces the commodities 1 and 2 from a production factor. Initially there is a total endowment w of this production factor available. The technical constraint of this firm is given by

$$F^o(x_1^o,x_2^o;w) \leq 0, \qquad (3.7)$$

where x_1^o and x_2^o are the output amounts of commodities 1 and 2 respectively.

We assume that this economy, denoted by $E = \{(u^i,c_a^i,c_b^i)$, $i = 1,\ldots,h$, F^a, (F^b,c_b), F^z, F^o, $w\}$, is *regular*, i.e., the utility and production functions and the constraint functions are continuously differentiable, the utility functions u^i are quasi-concave, the production functions are concave, and w is positive. Furthermore, we assume that in all technical constraints both the inputs and the outputs are measured positively. From this it follows that for $r \in \{a,b,z,o\}$, and for the variables $v = x_1^o$, x_2^o, x_1^a, x_2^a, x_1^b, x_2^b, x_1^z, x_2^z. y_a, y_b and z, holds

$$\partial F^r/\partial v < 0 \text{ if v is an input,}$$

and

$$\partial F^r/\partial v > 0 \text{ if } v \text{ is an output.}$$

We are now ready to give some definitions.

Definition 3.1. An allocation $e = \{(x_1^i, x_2^i, y_a^i, y_b^i),\ i = 1,\ldots,h,\ (y_a, x_1^a, x_2^a), (y_b, x_1^b, x_2^b),\ (z, x_1^z, z_2^z),\ (x_1^o, x_2^o)\}$ is in the set A of *feasible* allocations if the constraints (3.1) - (3.7) hold, and if

$$\Sigma_i\ x_j^i + x_j^a + x_j^b + x_j^z \leq x_j^o \qquad j = 1,2 \tag{3.8}$$

$$\Sigma_i\ y_a^i \leq y_a \tag{3.9}$$

$$\Sigma_i\ y_b^i \leq y_b. \tag{3.10}$$

Observe that this definition includes the subjective constraints (3.1) and (3.2). The quantity constraints (3.8) - (3.10) require that total demand is less than or equal to total supply.

Definition 3.2. A feasible allocation e is *efficient* if there is a distribution of strictly positive individual weights ϑ_i, $i = 1,\ldots,h$, for which e maximizes the social welfare function

$$\Sigma_i\ \vartheta_i u^i(x_1^i, x_2^i, y_a^i, y_b^i, z)$$

over the set A of feasible allocations.

According to Definition 3.2 the necessary conditions for an allocation of a regular economy to be efficient follow from the maximization problem,

$$\max\ \Sigma_i\ \vartheta_i u^i(x_1^i, x_2^i, y_a^i, y_b^i, z), \tag{3.11}$$

such that, with the shadow prices of the constraints between brackets,

(α^i) $\quad y_a^i - c_a^i(z) \leq 0 \qquad i = 1,\dots,h$

(β^i) $\quad y_b^i - c_b^i(z) \leq 0 \qquad i = 1,\dots,h$

(γ) $\quad y_b - c_b(z) \leq 0$

(λ^a) $\quad F^a(y_a;x_1^a,x_2^a) \leq 0$

(λ^b) $\quad F^b(y_b;x_1^b,x_2^b) \leq 0$

(λ^z) $\quad F^z(z;x_1^z,x_2^z) \leq 0$

(λ^o) $\quad F^o(x_1^o,x_2^o;w) \leq 0$

(μ^j) $\quad \Sigma_i\, x_j^i + x_j^a + x_j^b + x_j^z \leq x_j^o \qquad j = 1,2$

(μ^a) $\quad \Sigma_i\, y_a^i \leq y_a$

(μ^b) $\quad \Sigma_i\, y_b^i \leq y_b.$

Differentiating the corresponding Lagrange function with respect to the variables between brackets, with j = 1,2 and i = 1,...,h, gives,

(x_j^i) $\quad \vartheta_i\, \partial u^i/\partial x_j^i - \mu^j = 0$

(y_a^i) $\quad \vartheta_i\, \partial u^i/\partial y_a^i - \alpha^i - \mu^a = 0$

(y_b^i) $\quad \vartheta_i\, \partial u^i/\partial y_b^i - \beta^i - \mu^b = 0$

(y_a) $\quad -\lambda^a\, \partial F^a/\partial y_a + \mu^a = 0$

(y_b) $\quad -\gamma - \lambda^b\, \partial F^b/\partial y_b + \mu^b = 0$

(z) $\quad \Sigma_i\, \vartheta_i\, \partial u^i/\partial z + \Sigma_i\, \alpha^i\, \partial c_a^i/\partial z + \Sigma_i\, \beta^i\, \partial c_b^i/\partial z +$

$$+ \gamma\, \partial c_b/\partial z - \lambda^z\, \partial F^z/\partial z = 0$$

$$(x_j^a) \qquad \lambda^a\, \partial F^a/\partial x_j^a + \mu^j = 0$$

$$(x_j^b) \qquad \lambda^b\, \partial F^b/\partial x_j^b + \mu^j = 0$$

$$(x_j^z) \qquad \lambda^z\, \partial F^z/\partial x_j^z + \mu^j = 0$$

$$(x_j^o) \qquad \lambda^o\, \partial F^o/\partial x_j^o - \mu^j = 0,$$

with all shadow prices nonnegative. With commodity 1 taken as the numeraire, we obtain from these equations the next first order conditions for an efficient allocation. For all i,

$$\frac{\partial u^i/\partial x_2^i}{\partial u^i/\partial x_1^i} = \frac{\partial F^r/\partial x_2^r}{\partial F^r/\partial x_1^r} \qquad r \in \{a,b,z,o\}, \tag{3.12}$$

$$\frac{\partial u^i/\partial y_a^i}{\partial u^i/\partial x_1^i} = \frac{\partial F^a/\partial y_a}{-\partial F^a/\partial x_1^a} + \frac{\alpha^i}{-\lambda^z \partial F^z/\partial x_1^z} \tag{3.13}$$

$$\frac{\partial u^i/\partial y_b^i}{\partial u^i/\partial x_1^i} = \frac{\partial F^b/\partial y_b}{-\partial F^b/\partial x_1^b} + \frac{\gamma}{-\lambda^z \partial F^z/\partial x_1^z} + \frac{\beta^i}{-\lambda^z \partial F^z/\partial x_1^z}, \tag{3.14}$$

and

$$\Sigma_k \frac{\partial u^k/\partial z}{\partial u^k/\partial x_1^k} + \frac{\Sigma_k\, \alpha^k \partial c_a^k/\partial z}{-\lambda^z \partial F^z/\partial x_1^z} + \frac{\Sigma_k\, \beta^k \partial c_b^k/\partial z}{-\lambda^z \partial F^z/\partial x_1^z} + \frac{\gamma \partial c_b/\partial z}{-\lambda^z \partial F^z/\partial x_1^z}$$
$$= \frac{\partial F^z/\partial z}{-\partial F^z/\partial x_1^z}\,. \tag{3.15}$$

Condition (3.12) is the usual condition for private goods, saying that the marginal rate of substitution (MRS) equals the marginal rate of transformation (MRT). Notice that for each firm the two private commodities are either both an output with positive derivative, or both an input with negative derivative. The latter fact explains the minus signs in (3.13) - (3.15). If $\alpha^i = 0$ for all i, then no consumer feels himself constrained in the use of commodity a. This commodity is then a private good, having a uniform MRS equal to the MRT between a and the numeraire commodity. However, if $\alpha^i > 0$ for some i, then consumer i is willing to pay a mark-up on the MRT of commodity a in order to subsidize an expansion of the infrastructure. In the condition (3.14) for commodity b an extra term appears in the equation. This term reflects the constraint of producer Y^b with respect to the availability z of the public good. If $\gamma = 0$ then the producer is not constrained and we have the same situation as for commodity a. If $\gamma > 0$, the second term on the right hand side of equation (3.14) reflects the additional costs the producer is willing to make for an expansion of the infrastructure, in order to enlarge his production possibilities. If $\beta^i > 0$, then consumer i is willing to pay a mark-up on the costs of commodity b, including the costs the producer has to pay for the expansion. All the mark-ups and the producer's costs for expanding the public good reappear in (3.15). Notice that the mark-ups in (3.13) and (3.14) reveal the willingness to pay for weakening of the constraints c_a^i, c_b^i and c_b, whereas the terms in (3.15) reveal the willingness to pay for an expansion of the infrastructure. We see that the sum of the MRS's plus the sum of the mark-ups of the consumers plus the mark-up of the producer is equal to the MRT of the public good. If all mark-ups are equal to zero, then the public good behaves as a pure public good.

The main advantage of introducing semi-public goods in this way is that an industrial economy can discriminate between agents who are and who are not constrained by the infrastructure, because it can observe demand-behaviour. This information can partially (and sometimes completely) solve the difficult problem of determining the individual contributions to the provision of a public good.

4. THE INSTITUTIONAL FRAMEWORK

In this section we describe the institutional framework under which an industrial equilibrium can be formulated satisfying the first order conditions for efficiency. This institutional framework is the private ownership industrial economy. In the economy E there are four private good markets in operation: one for each good 1, 2, a and b. The demands and supplies on these markets depend on the prices p_1, p_2, p_a, and p_b, respectively, with the price of the numeraire commodity, p_1, equal to one. In an efficient allocation these prices are equal to the respective MRT's. For the fifth commodity, the public good, the situation is much more complicated. Later on we will make some simplifying assumptions. For the moment we deal with the general model given in the previous section.

We assume that the industry is able to discriminate among consumers who are constrained and who are not. At some allocation e, let, for i = 1,...,h,

$$t_a^i(e) = -\alpha^i(\lambda^z \partial F^z/\partial x_1^z)^{-1}$$

and

$$t_b^i(e) = -\beta^i(\lambda^z \partial F^z/\partial x_1^z)^{-1}$$

be the willingness of consumer i to pay for the weakening of the constraints $c_a^i(z)$ and $c_b^i(z)$ respectively. Then the sum of $T_a^i(e) = t_a^i(e)\partial c_a^i/\partial z$ and $T_b^i(e) = t_b^i(e)\partial c_b^i/\partial z$ is his willingness to pay for the expansion of the infrastructure. Suppose that this willingness to pay is known to the industry. Of course this is not an innocuous assumption, but it can be approached in reality under the simplifications we will make later on. Furthermore, let $t_b(e) = -\gamma(\lambda^z \partial F^z/\partial x_1^z)^{-1}$ and $T_b(e) = t_b(e)\partial c_b/\partial z$ be the willingness of firm Y^b to pay for weakening $c_b(z)$ and expanding z respectively. This information is of course known to the industry. Finally, at some allocation e, denote the marginal rate of substitution of consumer i between z and x_1 by $p_z^i(e)$, i = 1,...,h. Now, the planner's task is to find the desired level of infrastructure, i.e., to plan and to organize an amount z such that the sum of the MRS's plus the total willingness to pay is equal to the marginal rate of transformation, denoted by $p_z(e)$.

Planner's problem: Find z such that

$$\Sigma_i\ [p_z^i(e) + T_a^i(e) + T_b^i(e)] + T_b(e) = p_z(e). \tag{4.1}$$

The price p_z is the price to be paid by the planner to the producer for each unit of the public good and equals the MRT. On the other hand, the revenues of the planner consists of the consumers' contributions p_z^i per unit, and the mark-ups t_a^i, t_b^i and t_b, per unit of consumption y_a^i, y_b^i and per unit of production y_b, respectively. Since $y_b = \Sigma_i y_b^i$ if $t_b > 0$, the planner's profit $\pi^q(p,z)$, where $p = (p_1,p_2,p_a,p_b)^T$, equals

$$\pi^q(p,z) = \Sigma_i p_z^i z + \Sigma_i [t_a^i y_a^i + (t_b^i + t_b)y_b^i] - p_z z =$$

$$\Sigma_i (t_a^i y_a^i + t_b^i y_b^i) + t_b y_b - \Sigma_i (T_a^i + T_b^i)z - T_b z.$$

To complete the description of the economy, we assume that the private firms are profit maximizing producers. We denote the respective profits by $\pi^o(p,z)$, $\pi^a(p,z)$, $\pi^b(p,z)$ and $\pi^z(p,z)$. Since we assume that only the firm producing the private commodities 1 and 2 is endowed with a production factor, all individual labour and wealth in the economy is put in the production function F^o. Wages are paid as profits. All profits are distributed among the consumers, with, for $i = 1,\ldots,h$ and $r \in \{o,a,b,z,q\}$, φ^{ir} the share of consumer i in the profit of firm (or planner) r. All shares are nonnegative and $\Sigma_i \varphi^{ir} = 1$ for all r. The income of consumer i at (p,z) is given by $w^i(p,z) = \Sigma_r \varphi^{ir}\pi^r(p,z)$.

We are now able to define an <u>industrial equilibrium</u> for the economy E. Recall that a feasible allocation satisfies (3.1) - (3.10).

<u>Definition 4.1</u>. An industrial equilibrium for the economy E is a feasible allocation $e = \{(x_1^i,x_2^i,y_a^i,y_b^i),\ i = 1,\ldots,h,\ (y_a,x_1^a,x_2^a),\ (y_b,x_1^b,x_2^b),\ (z,x_1^z,x_2^z),\ (x_1^o,x_2^o)\}$, a set of prices p_1, p_2, p_a, p_b for the private commodities and a price p_z for the public good, a set of individual prices p_z^i, $i = 1,\ldots,h$, and a set of mark-ups t_a^i, t_b^i, $i = 1,\ldots,h$, and t_b, such that

1) for all i, $(x_1^i,x_2^i,y_a^i,y_b^i,z)$ maximizes $u^i(\tilde{x}_1^i,\tilde{x}_2^i,\tilde{y}_a^i,\tilde{y}_b^i,\tilde{z})$ under the budget constraint

$$p_1\tilde{x}_1^i + p_2\tilde{x}_2^i + (p_a+t_a^i)\tilde{y}_a^i + (p_b+t_b+t_b^i)\tilde{y}_b^i + p_z^i\tilde{z} = w^i(p,z),$$

2) each producer maximizes profit subject to his technical constraint, i.e.,

$$\pi^o(p,z) = p_1x_1^o + p_2x_2^o = \max\{p_1\tilde{x}_1^o + p_2\tilde{x}_2^o | F^o(\tilde{x}_1^o,\tilde{x}_2^o;w) \le 0\}$$

$$\pi^z(p,z) = p_z z - p_1x_1^z - p_2x_2^z = \max\{p_z\tilde{z} - p_1\tilde{x}_1^z - p_2\tilde{x}_2^z | F^z(\tilde{z};\tilde{x}_1^z,\tilde{x}_2^z) \le 0\}$$

$$\pi^a(p,z) = p_a y_a - p_1 x_1^a - p_2 x_2^a = \max\{p_a \tilde{y}_a - p_1 \tilde{x}_1^a - p_2 \tilde{x}_2^a | F^a(\tilde{y}_a; \tilde{x}_1^a, \tilde{x}_2^a) \le 0\}$$

$$\pi^b(p,z) = p_b y_b - p_1 x_1^b - p_2 x_2^b = \max\{p_b \tilde{y}_b - p_1 \tilde{x}_1^b - p_2 \tilde{x}_2^b | F^b(\tilde{y}_b; \tilde{x}_1^b, \tilde{x}_2^b) \le 0\},$$

3) for all i, $t_a^i > 0$ implies $y_a^i = c_a^i(z)$ and $t_b^i > 0$ implies $y_b^i = c_b^i(z)$,

4) $t_b > 0$ implies $y_b = c_b(z)$,

5) (4.1) is satisfied, i.e., the planner equates marginal social costs with marginal social benefits of z,

6) (3.8) - (3.10) are satisfied with equalities, i.e., the markets clear demand and supply.

Notice that the availability of the public good is completely determined by the planner. So, actually the consumers do not maximize their utility over z. Instead the prices p_z^i are determined such that for all i, z is optimal under p_z^i. The same reasoning holds for the public good producer, who determines p_z given the amount z. The third condition has analogies in fixed price theory, from which it is well-known that quantity-constrained allocations can be sustained by virtual prices (see e.g. Neary and Roberts [12], Ruys [13], and Cornielje and van der Laan [4]). Here condition 3) says that a consumer is not willing to pay a mark-up on the cost price of a commodity if he or she is not constrained in the use of that commodity. Analogously, condition 4) says that the producer is willing to levy a mark-up on his output price p_b if he is constrained by the infrastructure level z. In this paper we assume that an equilibrium exists. We will address the existence problem in a subsequent paper, see also Section 6.

We now make some simplifying assumptions. Firstly, we assume without loss of generality that the public good does not appear in the utility function of the consumers, i.e., $p_z^i = 0$ for all i. In this case the consumers are only interested in the infrastructure if they are constrained. Now, the planner's problem becomes: find z such that

$$\Sigma_i \, [T_a^i(e) + T_b^i(e)] + T_b(e) = p_z(e). \tag{4.2}$$

Secondly, we assume that the consumers' constraint functions are linear with constant term equal to zero, i.e. for all i,

$$c_a^i(z) = a^i z$$

$$c_b^i(z) = b^i z.$$

In general, we are not able to say anything about the concavity or convexity of the constraint functions. Both cases may occur. Therefore the assumption of linear functions is very simplifying, but not too bad. For simplicity we also assume that $c_b(z) = b^p z$. Now (4.2) becomes

$$\Sigma_i \, [a^i t_a^i(e) + b^i t_b^i(e)] + b^p t_b(e) = p_z(e).$$

From this it follows that the planner's profit becomes equal to zero. Moreover, the coefficients a^i and b^i follow from the consumption level of the goods a and b of the constrained consumers. The willingness to pay can be approached in reality if the consumers are partitioned in classes with different needs to expand the infrastructure. These needs can be inferred from the unconstrained demands for the goods a and b.

Under these simplifying assumptions the planner can obtain enough information to decide upon the infrastructure level z, given the mark-ups on the cost-prices p_a and p_b. In this linear case, the infrastructure is completely financed by the returns on the mark-ups on the prices of the private goods.

5. EXAMPLES

For all firms we take constant returns to scale production functions, implying that the firm with production function F^a, F^b and F^z respectively is cost minimizing with, in equilibrium, zero profit. The income of consumer i equals $\varphi^i \pi^o$, with φ^i the share of i in the profit of the firm with production function F^o. For the consumers we take Cobb-Douglas utility functions. Recall that we assume that z does not appear in these functions. Furthermore we assume that the consumers are not constrained in the use of commodity b, i.e., $b^i = \infty$ for all i. This gives the next example. For i = 1,...,h, the utility of consumer i is given by

$$u^i = \rho_1^i \ln x_1^i + \rho_2^i \ln x_2^i + \rho_a^i \ln y_a^i + \rho_b^i \ln y_b^i$$

under $y_a^i \le a^i z$, where $\rho_1^i + \rho_2^i + \rho_a^i + \rho_b^i$ is normalized to one. The production constraints are given by

$$F^o = \varphi_1^o (x_1^o)^2 + \varphi_2^o (x_2^o)^2 - w^2 \le 0$$

$$F^z = \ln z - \varphi_1^z \ln x_1^z - \varphi_2^z \ln x_2^z \le 0 \quad \text{with } \varphi_1^z + \varphi_2^z = 1,$$

and for $r \in \{a,b\}$

$$F^r = \ln y_r - \varphi_1^r \ln x_1^r - \varphi_2^r \ln x_2^r \le 0 \quad \text{with } \varphi_1^r + \varphi_2^r = 1.$$

For firm Y^b we have the quantity constraint $y_b \le b^p z$.
Given prices p_1 and p_2 we obtain from cost minimizing that for $r \in \{a,b,z\}$ the conditional factor demand per unit of output is given by

$$x_1^r = (\varphi_1^r p_2 / \varphi_2^r p_1)^{\varphi_2^r} \tag{5.1}$$

$$x_2^r = (\varphi_2^r p_1 / \varphi_1^r p_2)^{\varphi_1^r}. \tag{5.2}$$

The zero profit condition gives

$$p_r = p_1 x_1^r + p_2 x_2^r. \tag{5.3}$$

Maximizing profit under $F^o \le 0$ gives the private goods supply functions

$$x_j^o = p_j w / \varphi_j^o c \qquad j = 1,2, \tag{5.4}$$

while the profit is given by

$$\pi^o = cw, \tag{5.5}$$

with $c^2 = p_1^2/\varphi_1^o + p_2^2/\varphi_2^o$.
Utility maximizing of consumer i under the budget constraint

$$p_1x_1^i + p_2x_2^i + (p_a+t_a^i)y_a^i + (p_b+t_b)y_b^i = \varphi^i cw$$

gives for the consumer's demand

$$x_j^i = \rho_j^i\varphi^i cw/p_j \qquad j = 1,2 \tag{5.6}$$

$$y_a^i = \rho_a^i\varphi^i cw/(p_a+t_a^i) \tag{5.7}$$

$$y_b^i = \rho_b^i\varphi^i cw/(p_b+t_b). \tag{5.8}$$

For given z and demand y_a^i, the mark-up t_a^i is determined by firm Y^a by setting

$$t_a^i = \max\{0, (\rho_a^i\varphi^i cw/a^i z) - p_a\}. \tag{5.9}$$

So, the mark-ups are determined by the industry such that the individual demands do not exceed the individual constraints $a^i z$. From (5.7) and (5.9) we obtain that

$$y_a^i = \rho_a^i\varphi^i cw/p_a \text{ and } t_a^i = 0 \qquad \text{if } \rho_a^i\varphi^i cw/p_a \leq a^i z \tag{5.10}$$

and

$$y_a^i = a^i z \text{ and } t_a^i = (\rho_a^i\varphi^i cw/a^i z) - p_a \text{ if } \rho_a^i\varphi^i cw/p_a > a^i z. \tag{5.11}$$

Observe that the discrimination among consumers is determined by the parameters ρ_a^i, φ^i and a^i. In fact, the willingness to pay increases with ρ_a^i and φ^i and decreases with a^i. Firm Y^b determines the mark-up t_b on his output price p_b such that the total demand y_b does not exceed the constraint $b^p z$. We obtain from (5.8) that

$$t_b = \max\{0, (\Sigma_i\ \rho_b^i\varphi^i cw/b^p z) - p_b\}. \tag{5.12}$$

Hence

$$y_b^i = \rho_b^i\varphi^i cw/p_b \text{ and } t_b = 0 \qquad \text{if } \Sigma_i\ \rho_b^i\varphi^i cw/p_b \leq b^p z \tag{5.13}$$

and

$$y_b^i = \rho_b^i \varphi^i cw/(p_b + t_b) \text{ and } t_b = (\Sigma_i \rho_b^i \varphi^i cw/b^p z) - p_b$$

$$\text{if } \Sigma_i \rho_b^i \varphi^i cw/p_b > b^p z. \quad (5.14)$$

Finally the production levels y_a and y_b are set by the producers such that they are equal to the total consumption, i.e.,

$$y_a = \Sigma_i y_a^i \text{ and } y_b = \Sigma_i y_b^i. \quad (5.15)$$

Notice that $y_b = b^p z$ if $\Sigma_i \rho_b^i \varphi^i cw/p_b > b^p z$. Consequently, given the prices p_1 and p_2 and the infrastructure level z, the values of all other variables, prices, quantities and mark-ups, can be calculated through (5.1) - (5.15). So, the equilibrium problem is to find market prices p_1 and p_2 and a level z of the infrastructure such that the markets for the private commodities 1 and 2 clear and the mark-up revenues are equal to the costs of the infrastructure, i.e.,

$$\Sigma_i x_j^i + x_j^a + x_j^b = x_j^o - x_j^z, \; j = 1,2 \quad \text{(market-condition)}$$

and

$$\Sigma_i a^i t_a^i + b^p t_b = p_z. \quad \text{(planner-condition)}$$

In the next section we discuss this problem both from a numerical and an economic viewpoint. Here we concentrate ourselves on the numerical results. Using the computer code described in van der Laan and Seelen [8] we have calculated the equilibrium with the following data.

Example 1. Number of consumers: 4. Input: w = 100. Constraint coefficient producer Y^b : $b^p = 4$. The data of the other coefficients are given in the Tables 1 and 2.

Table 1. Coefficients of the producers

Producer r	o	a	b	z
φ_1^r	1	.5	.5	.5
φ_2^r	1	.5	.5	.5

Table 2. Coefficients of the consumers

Consumer i	1	2	3	4
ρ_1^i	.4	.3	.2	.1
ρ_2^i	.1	.1	.1	.1
ρ_a^i	.5	.6	.7	.8
ρ_b^i	0	0	0	0
φ^i	.1	.2	.3	.4
a^i	1	1	1	1

Observe that the budget shares for commodity b are zero for all consumers. So, the demands for commodity b are zero, implying that firm Y^b is not active and $t_b = 0$. The equilibrium values are given in Table 3 with the unconstrained demands (i.e., with $t_a^i = 0$) between brackets.

Example 2. Same data as in Example 1 except that the budget shares for a and b are equal to $\rho_a^i = 0.1, 0.2, 0.3, 0.4$, for $i = 1,\ldots,4$, respectively, and $\rho_b^i = 0.4$ for all i. The equilibrium values are given in Table 4 with again the unconstrained demands between brackets.

Table 3. Equilibrium values Example 1.

	x_1	x_2	y_a	y_b	z	t_a^i	$\varphi^i\pi^0$
price	1	0.905	1.902	1.902	1.902		
mark-up t_b				0			
Producers:							
output	74.2	67.1	37.1	0	12.5		
input a	35.3	39.0					
b	0	0					
z	11.9	13.2					
Consumers:							
1	5.4	1.5	3.5	0		0	13.5
2	8.1	3.0	8.5	0		0	27.0
3	8.1	4.5	12.5 (14.9)	0		0.36	40.5
4	5.4	6.0	12.5 (22.7)	0		1.54	53.9

In the two examples the expenditures for the private commodities 1 and 2 are equal to each other. The only difference comes from the budget shares for a and b. So, the total budget share for the "public" sector is the same. This budget spent on the public sector finances the costs of the total output of the three firms. Since the three firms have identical cost structure and have constant returns to scale, the total output of the three firms is equal for the two examples. However, in Example 1 all income spent on the public sector is spent on commodity a. Because of the constraints on the use of this commodity it results in a higher need for the public good than in Example 2.

The results show that in Example 1 the consumers 3 and 4, being the consumers with the highest profit shares and the highest budget shares for a, are constrained in the use of the private commodity a. Notice that the sum of the mark-ups these consumers are willing to pay for an expansion of the infrastructure equals the price of one unit of the public good.

Table 4. Equilibrium values Example 2.

	x_1	x_2	y_a	y_b	z	t_a^i	$\varphi^i\pi^0$
price	1	0.905	1.902	1.902	1.902		
mark-up t_b				0.136			
Producers:							
output	74.2	67.1	16.5	26.5 (28.3)	6.617		
input a	15.8	17.3					
b	25.2	27.8					
z	6.3	7.0					
Consumers:							
1	5.4	1.5	0.71	2.65 (2.84)		0	13.5
2	8.1	3.0	2.84	5.30 (5.67)		0	27.0
3	8.1	4.5	6.38	7.94 (8.50)		0	40.5
4	5.4	6.0	6.617 (11.3)	10.59 (11.3)		1.36	53.9

For each consumer the sum of the unconstrained demands for a and b in Example 2 is equal to the unconstrained demand for a in Example 1. Observe that in Example 2 both the individual unconstrained demand for a and the total unconstrained demand for b are less than the corresponding constraint function values given the level of infrastructure found in Example 1. So, for this level neither an individual nor the firm Y^b is willing to pay. Consequently, the infrastructure has been cut down to the level at which the mark-ups are again high enough to cover the costs. In equilibrium, only consumer 4 is constrained in the use of commodity a. Moreover, the production of firm Y^b is constrained by the infrastructure, which results in a mark-up t_b on the price of commodity b, so that $t_a^4 + 4t_b = p_z$ (planner-condition).

It is not difficult to gain some more insight from these examples. Decreasing the coefficients a^i will result in a higher willingness of the consumers to pay (see formula (5.11)). To remain in equilibrium this induces a higher value of z, so that the producer would become unconstrained for low enough values of the consumers' constraint coefficients. In this case the infrastructure is financed by the consumers' mark-ups only. For example, taking $a^i = 0.75$ for all i, the equilibrium values of t_a^i, t_b and z become

$$t_a^i = 0 \text{ for } i=1,2,\ t_a^3 = 0.380,\ t_a^4 = 2.155,\ t_b = 0, \text{ and } z = 7.09.$$

On the other hand, increasing the coefficients a^i and/or decreasing the producer's constraint coefficient b^p results in a lower willingness of the consumers to pay and/or a higher mark-up t_b on the producer's price p_b. For $a^i = 0.75i$ for $i = 1,\dots,4$, and $b^p = 2$ we obtain that in equilibrium

$$t_a^i = 0 \text{ for all } i,\ t_b = 0.95, \text{ and } z = 9.452.$$

In this case the infrastructure is completely financed through the mark-up the producer is willing to levy on his price p_b. Because the consumers are willing to spend 40% of their income on commodity b, the low constraint coefficient b^p enforces a (relatively) high level of z. In the first case the infrastructure can be seen as a public good for which the willingness to pay expresses the marginal utilities. In the latter case the infrastructure can be seen as an investment of producer Y^b, without which the producer is not able to produce anything. For both alternatives the prices are equal to those given in the examples.

6. CONCLUDING REMARKS AND FURTHER RESEARCH

This paper has been concerned with the problem of financing an infrastructure needed for operating and utilizing private services and commodities. The paper has to be seen as a first attempt to give a solid framework for the idea that the industry plays a central role in financing the infrastructure. In fact, the infrastructure is financed through mark-ups on the private services and commodities that make use of it. These mark-ups come from the constraints experienced by the agents. With respect to the consumers, the level of the infrastructure yields a (subjective) constraint on their private consumption. In case of producers the level of the infrastructure puts a constraint on their production possibilities.

The mark-ups reveal these constraints and therefore the need for the infrastructure. Given the mark-ups the agents are willing to pay, the planner determines the optimal level of the infrastructure. In subsequent papers we will develop this idea.

A first question concerns the existence of an industrial equilibrium and the way in which the optimal level is determined. We want to make some remarks on this subject. Therefore we return to the previous section, in which we formulated the market-condition and the planner-condition. To solve these equilibrium conditions we used a computer code based on simplicial approximation. We remark that the computational procedure adjusts prices and quantities until an approximate equilibrium has been found. It should be observed that all quantities are homogeneous of degree zero in prices and mark-ups. So, by setting $p_1 = 1$, we can take commodity 1 as the numeraire commodity. Then, for the examples considered in the previous section, the problem reduces to finding a price p_2 and a quantity z such that the market-condition holds for $j = 2$ and the planner-condition is satisfied. Then there is also equilibrium on the numeraire market (Walras' property), since all consumers spend all their income. The algorithm adjusts p_2 and z simultaneously until (approximate) equilibrium values have been reached. So, numerically the price p_2 and the quantity z are determined simultaneously. However, from an economic viewpoint we may consider the following procedure. Suppose that, given p_2, the industry (or planner) solves the planner-condition, i.e., given p_2 the planner searches for a quantity z for which the planner-condition holds. Let $z(p_2)$ be this quantity as a function of p_2. On the other hand, let the market solve the market-condition for $j = 2$ given a quantity z. So, the market determines a price $p_2(z)$ for which the market for commodity 2 is in equilibrium. Starting with either some p_2 or some z, the quantity z and price p_2 are adjusted subsequently and alternately until a price p_2^* and a quantity z^* are found such that

$$z^* = z(p_2^*) \text{ and } p_2^* = p_2(z^*).$$

Such a pair (p_2^*, z^*) solves the equilibrium problem. Using this "Nash formulation" we will investigate the conditions for the existence of an industrial equilibrium in a subsequent paper. One of the issues showing up is whether the constraint functions have to satisfy certain conditions.

A second question concerns the problem of determining the mark-ups. We want to elaborate the idea that the individual mark-ups are determined by the industry and are corporated in the prices the producers set for their products. We may think of a partitioning of the consumers into a number of groups. Then for each group the industry sets the mark-ups by considering a representative agent. So, in this way we get different prices for different types of agents.

A third topic concerns the characterization of public goods by classifying the agents who pay for it. The examples have shown that within the same model the equilibrium may result in a situation in which either the consumers, or the producers, or both types of agents finance the infrastructure. This result urges us to be careful in making recommendations for the way in which the costs of public goods should be shared. In the near future we plan to do "cost-sharing" analysis for some (Dutch) "public sector" industries.

REFERENCES

[1] K.J. Arrow and G. Debreu, "Existence of an equilibrium for a competitive economy", *Econometrica* 26 (1954) 522-552.

[2] W. Blümel, R. Pethig and O. Von dem Hagen, "The theory of public goods: a survey of recent issues", *Journal of Institutional and Theoretical Economics* 142 (1986) 241-309.

[3] R. Cornes and T. Sandler, *The theory of externalities, public goods, and club goods*, Cambridge University Press, Cambridge, 1986.

[4] O.J.C. Cornielje and G. van der Laan, "The computation of quantity-constrained equilibria by virtual taxes", *Economic Letters* 22 (1986) 1-6.

[5] M. Kojima and Y. Yamamoto, "A unified approach to the implementation of several restart fixed point algorithms and a new variable dimension algorithm", *Mathematical Programming* 28 (1984) 288-328.

[6] H.W. Kuhn, "Simplicial approximation of fixed points", *Proc. Nat. Acad. Sci. U.S.A.* 61 (1968) 1238-1242.

[7] H.W. Kuhn, "Approximate search for fixed points", *Computing Methods in Optimization Problems* 2 (1969) 199-211.

[8] G. van der Laan and L.P. Seelen, "Efficiency and implementation of simplicial zero point algorithms", *Mathematical Programming* 30 (1984) 196-217.

[9] G. van der Laan and A.J.J. Talman, "A restart algorithm for computing fixed points without an extra dimension", *Mathematical Programming* 17 (1979) 74-84.

[10] G. van der Laan and A.J.J. Talman, "A class of simplicial restart fixed point algorithms without an extra dimension", *Mathematical Programming* 20 (1981) 33-48.

[11] L.W. McKenzie, "On the existence of general equilibrium for a competitive market", *Econometrica* 27 (1959) 54-71.

[12] J.P. Neary and K.W.S. Roberts, "The theory of household behaviour under rationing", *European Economic Review* 13 (1980) 25-42.

[13] P.H.M. Ruys, "Disequilibrium characterized by implicit prices in terms of effort", in: *Econometric modelling in theory and practice*, J.E.J. Plasmans, ed., Sijthoff and Noordhoff, 1982, pp. 1-29.
[14] P.H.M. Ruys, "Algemeen evenwicht met semi-publieke goederen", in: *De praktijk van de econometrie*, P.A. Verheyen et al., eds., Stenfert Kroese, Leiden, 1984, pp. 85-95.
[15] P.A. Samuelson, "The pure theory of public expenditure", *Review of Economics and Statistics* 37 (1954) 350-356.
[16] H. Scarf, "The approximation of fixed points of a continuous mapping", *SIAM Journal of Applied Mathematics* 15 (1967) 1328-1343.
[17] H. Scarf, *The computation of economic equilibria*, Yale University Press, New Haven, 1973.
[18] J. Von Neumann, "Uber ein ökonomisches Gleichungssystem und eine Verallgemeinerung des Brouwerschen Fixpunktsatzes", *Ergebnisse eines Mathematischen Kolloquiums* 8 (1937) 73-83.
[19] L. Walras, *Eléments d'économie politique pure*, Corbaz, Lausanne, 1874.
[20] A.H. Wright, "The octahedral algorithm, a new simplicial fixed point algorithm", *Mathematical Programming* 21 (1981) 47-69.